CLYMER®

YAMAHA

650cc TWINS • 1970-1982

The world's finest publisher of mechanical how-to manuals

PRIMEDIA
Business Directories & Books

P.O. Box 12901, Overland Park, Kansas 66282-2901

Copyright ©1987 PRIMEDIA Business Magazines & Media Inc.

FIRST EDITION
First Printing February, 1973

SECOND EDITION
First Printing July, 1974

THIRD EDITION
First Printing October, 1976

FOURTH EDITION
First Printing July, 1978

FIFTH EDITION
First Printing November, 1980

SIXTH EDITION
First Printing February, 1981

SEVENTH EDITION
Revised by Ron Wright to include 1981 models
First Printing November, 1982
Second Printing June, 1983
Third Printing December, 1983
Fourth Printing February, 1985
Fifth Printing December, 1985

EIGHTH EDITION
Updated by Ron Wright to include 1982 models
First Printing March, 1987
Second Printing November, 1987
Third Printing October, 1988
Fourth Printing July, 1989
Fifth Printing May, 1990
Sixth Printing August, 1991
Seventh Printing August, 1992
Eighth Printing July, 1993
Ninth Printing December, 1994
Tenth Printing July, 1996
Eleventh Printing September, 1997
Twelfth Printing May, 1999
Thirteenth Printing November, 2000
Fourteenth Printing June, 2002

Printed in U.S.A.

CLYMER and colophon are registered trademarks of PRIMEDIA Business Magazines & Media Inc.

ISBN: 0-89287-233-0

MEMBER
MOTORCYCLE INDUSTRY COUNCIL, INC.

EDITOR: Eric Jorgenson

TECHNICAL ASSISTANCE: Thousand Oaks Yamaha

COVER: Photography by Bob Eckles, XS 2 courtesy of Bob Eckles.

TOOLS AND EQUIPMENT: K & L Supply Co. at www.klsupply.com.

CONTENTS

QUICK REFERENCE DATA

CONTACT POINT IGNITION

A = Top dead center
B¹ and B² = Ignition fire marks
C = Mark for "fully advanced"
     ignition timing

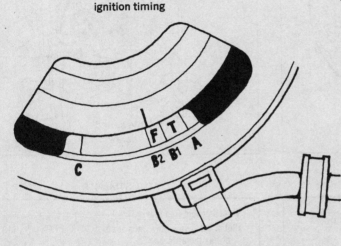

TRANSISTORIZED IGNITION 1981

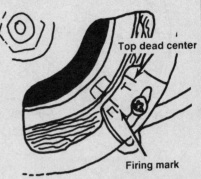

Top dead center

Firing mark

TUNE-UP SPECIFICATIONS

Spark plug type		
XS1, XS2, TX650, XS650B	B8ES (NGK)	W24ES (ND)
TX650A	B7ES (NGK)	W22ES (ND)
1976 and later	BP7ES (NGK)	N7Y (Champion)
Spark plug gap		
1970-1977	0.024-0.028 in. (0.6-0.7 mm)	
1978 and later	0.028-0.032 in. (0.7-0.8 mm)	
Valve clearance	**Intake**	**Exhaust**
XS1, XS1B, XS2, TX650	0.003 in. (0.074 mm)	0.006 in. (0.15 mm)
TX650A, XS650B	0.002 in. (0.05 mm)	0.004 in. (0.10 mm)
XS650C, XS650D	0.002 in. (0.05 mm)	0.006 in. (0.15 mm)
1978	0.004 in. (0.10 mm)	0.006 in. (0.15 mm)
1979 and later	0.0024 in. (0.06 mm)	0.006 in. (0.15 mm)
Breaker point gap	0.012-0.016 in. (0.3-0.4 mm)	
Carburetor air screw	**Turns out from seated**	
XS1, XS1B	½	
XS2, TX650, XS650B	¾	
XS650C, XS650D	1½	
1978 (early)	2¼	
1978 (late) — 1979	Preset	
1980 and later	Not equipped	
Idle speed		
1970-1978 (early)	1,100-1,200 rpm	
1978 (late) and later	1,200 rpm	

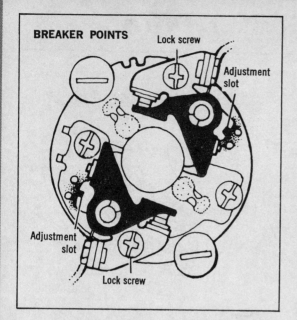

BREAKER POINTS

Lock screw

Adjustment slot

Adjustment slot

Lock screw

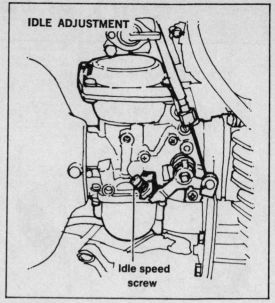

IDLE ADJUSTMENT

Idle speed screw

RECOMMENDED FUEL AND LUBRICANTS

Fuel	Regular, low-lead, or unleaded
Engine oil	SAE 30W or SAE 20W/40 (SE rating)
Fork oil	10, 20, or 30W motor oil or special fork oil

ADJUSTMENTS

Throttle cable free play	6mm (1/4 in.)
Clutch cable free play (measured at handlebar lever)	2-3mm (1/16-1/8 in.)
Front drum brake cable free play	6mm (1/4 in.)
Rear brake pedal free play	25mm (1 in.)
Drive chain free play (measured in middle of lower chain run with rider on seat)	20mm (3/4 in.)

CAPACITIES

Model	Front Forks (Each Leg) cc (oz.)	Engine/Transmission Oil Liters (Quarts)	
XS1	240 (7.5)	3.0 (3.2)	
XS1B	223 (7.0)	3.0 (3.2)	
XS2; TX650	135 (4.25)	2.5 (2.6)	
TX650A	160 (5.4)	*2.5 (2.6)	(see note)
XS650B	160 (5.4)	*2.5 (2.6)	(see note)
XS650C	155 (5.2)	2.5 (2.6)	
XS650D	168 (5.7)	*2.5 (2.6)	
1978 and later	169 (5.7)	*2.5 (2.6)	

*Quantity is for engine overhaul. Capacity for periodic oil change is 2.0 liters (2.1 qt.).

NOTE: Oil capacity stated represents revised Yamaha specifications to prevent oil misting from the breather pipes. XS650B models after engine No. 103747 are equipped with a modified dipstick to measure lowered oil level. Earlier XS650B and TX650A models should have dipstick modified by a dealer to correspond with lower recommended oil level.

CHAPTER ONE

GENERAL INFORMATION

This manual is designed to help owners service and repair the Yamaha 650cc motorcycle. Specific service procedures are given for the most commonly imported models.

For ease in identifying correct repair procedures, the service has been broken down by models and/or year. It is important to determine year and model so the proper procedure and specifications can be used. Procedures common to several years are consolidated in one section to avoid duplication.

The main body of this book (Chapters One through Nine) contains service information for 1970 through early 1978 non-emission controlled motorcycles. The supplement at the end of the book contains information for late 1978 and later emission controlled bikes. If you have a 1978 bike, you can use the appendix (Chapter Ten) and your bike's frame number to determine whether or not it is an early or late 1978 model. If a procedure does not appear in the supplement, then it remains the same as for earlier models.

MANUAL ORGANIZATION

This manual provides service information and procedures for all models since 1970. All dimensions and capacities are expressed in inch units familiar to U.S. mechanics as well as in metric units. When working with critical dimensions (cylinder bore, crankshaft journal diameter, etc.), the metric figures should be used.

This chapter provides general information and discusses equipment and tools useful both for preventive maintenance and troubleshooting.

Chapter Two explains all periodic lubrication and routine maintenance necessary to keep your motorcycle running well. Chapter Two also includes recommended tune-up procedures, eliminating the need to constantly consult chapters on the various subassemblies.

Chapter Three provides methods and suggestions for quick and accurate diagnosis or repair of problems. Troubleshooting procedures discuss typical symptoms and logical methods to pinpoint trouble.

Subsequent chapters describe specific systems such as the engine, transmission, and electrical system. Each chapter provides disassembly, repair, and assembly procedures in simple step-by-step form. If a repair is impractical for home mechanics, it is so indicated. It is usually faster and cheaper to take such repairs to a dealer or competent repair shop. Specifications concerning a particular system are included.

Some of the procedures in this manual specify special tools. In all such cases, the tool is illustrated either in actual use or alone. A well-equipped mechanic may find he can substitute simiar tools already on hand or can fabricate his own.

The terms NOTE, CAUTION, and WARNING have specific meanings in this manual. A NOTE provides additional information to make a step or procedure easier or clearer. Disregarding a NOTE could cause inconvenience, but would not likely cause damage or personal injury.

A CAUTION emphasizes areas where equipment damage could result. Disregarding a CAUTION could cause permanent mechanical damage, however, personal injury is unlikely.

A WARNING emphasizes areas where personal injury or even death could result from negligence. Mechanical damage may also occur. WARNINGS are to be taken seriously.

Throughout this manual keep in mind 2 conventions, "Front" refers to the front of motorcycle. The front of any component such as the engine is that end which faces toward the front of the bike. The left and right side refer to a person on the bike facing forward. For example, the shift lever is on the left side. These rules are simple, but even experienced mechanics occasionally become disoriented.

SERVICE HINTS

Most of the service procedures covered are straightforward and can be performed by anyone reasonably handy with tools. It is suggested, however, that you consider your own capabilities carefully before attempting any operation involving major disassembly of the engine.

Some operations, for example, require the use of a press. It would be wiser to refer such work to a shop equipped for such work, rather than to try to do the job yourself with makeshift equipment. Other procedures require precision measurements. Unless you have the skills and equipment required, it would be better to have a qualified repair shop make the measurements for you.

Repairs go much faster and easier if your machine is clean before you begin work. There are special cleaners for washing the engine and replated parts. Just brush or spray on the cleaning solution, let it stand, then rinse it away with a garden hose. Clean all oily or greasy parts with cleaning solvent as you remove them.

WARNING
Never use gasoline as a cleaning agent. It presents an extreme fire hazard. Be sure to work in a well-ventilated area when using cleaning solvents. Keep a fire extinguisher, rated for gasoline fires, handy.

Special tools are required for some repair procedures. These may be purchased at a dealer (or borrowed if you're on good terms with the service department) or may be fabricated by a mechanic or machinist, often at considerable savings.

Much of the labor charge for repairs made by dealers are for the removal and disassembly of various parts to reach a defective unit. It is frequently possible to perform the preliminary operations yourself and then take the defective unit to a dealer for repair at considerable savings.

Once you have decided to tackle a job yourself, read the entire section in this manual which pertains to it, making sure you have identified the correct one. Study the illustrations and text until you have a good idea of what is involved in completing the job satisfactorily. If special tools are required, make arrangements to get them before starting. It is frustrating and time-consuming to get partly into a job and then be unable to complete it.

Simple wiring checks are easily made at home; but knowledge of electronics is almost a necessity for performing tests with complicated electronic testing gear.

During disassembly of parts keep a few general cautions in mind. Force is rarely needed to get components apart. If parts are a tight fit, there is usually a tool designed to separate them. Never use a screwdriver to pry apart parts with machined-surfaces such as crankcase halves. You could mar the surfaces and end up with leaks.

Make diagrams wherever similar-appearing parts are found. For instance, case cover screws are often not the same length. You may think you can remember where everything came from —but mistakes are costly. There is also the possibility you may be sidetracked and not return to work for days or even weeks—during which interval, carefully laid out parts may have become disturbed.

Tag all similar internal parts for location and mark all mating parts for position. Record number and thickness of any shims as they are removed. Small parts such as bolts can be identified by placing them in plastic sandwich bags. Seal and label the bags with masking tape.

Wiring should be tagged with masking tape and marked as each wire is removed. Again, don't rely on memory alone.

Disconnect the battery ground cable before working near electrical connections and before disconnecting wires. Never run the engine with the battery disconnected; the electrical system could be seriously damaged.

Protect finished surfaces from physical damage or corrosion. Keep gasoline and brake fluid off painted surfaces.

Frozen or very tight bolts and screws can often be loosened by soaking with penetrating oil, then sharply striking the bolt head a few times with a hammer and punch (or screwdriver for screws). Avoid heat unless absolutely necessary, since it may melt, warp, or remove the temper from many parts.

No parts, except those assembled with a press fit, require force during assembly. If a part is hard to remove or install, find out why before proceeding.

Avoid flames or sparks when working near a charging battery or a flammable liquid such as gasoline.

Cover all openings after removing parts to keep dirt, small tools, etc., from falling in.

When assembling 2 parts, start all fasteners, then tighten evenly.

Clutch plates, wiring connections, and brake shoes and drums should be kept clean and free of grease and oil.

When assembling parts, be sure all shims and washers are replaced exactly as they came out.

Whenever a rotating part butts against a stationary part, look for a shim or washer. Use new gaskets if there is any doubt about the condition of old ones. Generally you should apply gasket cement to one mating surface only so the parts may be easily disassembled in the future. A thin coat of oil on gaskets help them seal effectively.

Heavy, chilled grease can be used to hold small parts in place if they tend to fall out during assembly. However, keep grease and oil away from electrical components and brake shoes and drums.

High spots may be sanded off a piston with sandpaper, but emery cloth and oil do a much more professional job.

Carburetors are best cleaned by disassembling them and soaking the parts in a commercial carburetor cleaner. Never soak gaskets or rubber or plastic parts in these cleaners. Never use wire to clean jets and air passages; they are easily damaged. Use compressed air to blow out the carburetor only if the float has been removed first.

A baby bottle makes a good measuring device for adding oil to the forks and transmission. Get one that is graduated in ounces and cubic centimeters.

Take your time and do the job right. Do not forget that a newly rebuilt motorcycle engine must be broken in the same as a new one. Keep rpm within the limits given in your owner's manual when you get back on the road.

SAFETY FIRST

Professional motorcycle mechanics can work for years and never sustain a serious injury. If you observe a few rules of common sense and safety, you can enjoy many safe hours servicing your own machine. You could hurt yourself or damage the bike if you ignore the following tips:

1. Never use gasoline as a cleaning solvent.

2. Never smoke or use a torch in the vicinity of flammable liquids such as cleaning solvent in open containers or in an area where batteries are being charged. Highly explosive hydrogen gas is formed during the charging process.

3. If welding or brazing is required on the machine, remove the fuel tank to a safe distance, at least 50 feet away. Welding on gas tanks requires special safety procedures and must be performed only by someone skilled in the process.

4. Use the proper size wrenches to avoid damage to nuts and bolts and injury to yourself.

5. When loosening a tight or stuck nut, be guided by what would happen if the wrench should slip. Protect yourself accordingly.

6. Keep your work area clean and uncluttered.

7. Wear safety goggles during operations involving drilling, grinding, use of an air hose, or use of a cold chisel.

8. Never use worn tools.

9. Keep a fire extinguisher handy and be sure it is rated for gasoline and electrical fires.

PARTS REPLACEMENT

When you order parts from a dealer or parts distributor, always order by engine and chassis number. Write the numbers down and carry them in your wallet. Compare new parts to old before purchasing them. If they are not alike, have the parts person explain the difference.

TOOLS

Tool Kit

The Yamaha 650 comes equipped with a fairly complete tool kit. These tools are satisfactory for most small jobs and emergency roadside repairs. After using tools from the tool kit, the tools should be returned to the tool bag and stored in the proper compartment on the motorcycle.

Shop Tools

Top quality tools are essential and more economical than less expensive ones. Poor grade tools are made of inferior material and are usually thick, heavy and clumsy. Their rough finish makes them difficult to clean and they usually do not last as long as quality tools.

Quality tools are made of alloy steel and are heat-treated for greater strength. The initial cost of quality tools may be relatively high, but longer life and ease of use make them less expensive in the long run.

Before purchasing tools, question the salesman on the tools' guarantee. Generally, you will find that the higher the quality of the tool, the better the guarantee.

It is aggravating to search for a certain tool in the middle of a repair, only to find it covered with grime. Keep your tools clean and in a tool box. Keep wrench sets, socket sets, etc., together. After using a tool, wipe off dirt and grease with a clean cloth and return it to its proper place.

To properly service your motorcycle, you will need an assortment of basic tools. As a minimum, these include:
   a. Combination wrench
   b. Socket wrenches
   c. Plastic mallet
   d. Small hammer
   e. Snap ring pliers
   f. Phillips screwdrivers

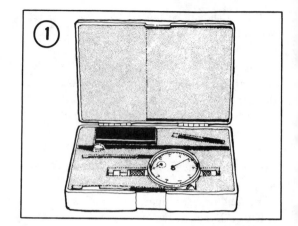

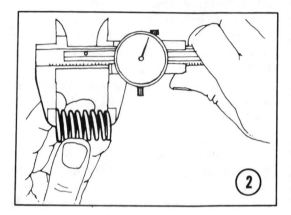

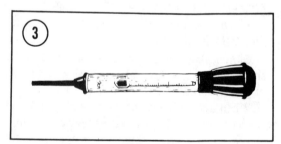

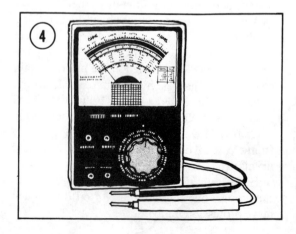

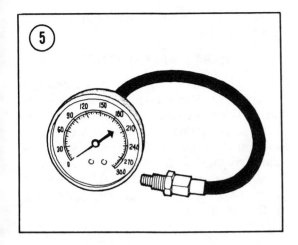

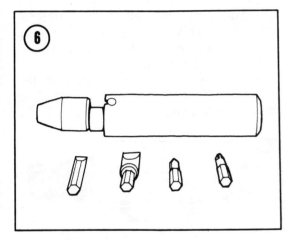

g. Slot screwdrivers
h. Impact driver and bits
i. Assorted pliers
j. Feeler gauges
k. Spark plug gauge
l. Spark plug wrench
m. Drift
n. Torque wrench
o. Allen wrenches
p. Safety glasses

A few special tools, described in the following sections, are required for specific jobs.

Dial Indicator

A dial indicator can be used to determine piston position and to check dimension variations on parts during engine or chassis inspection and assembly. The dial indicator, when positioned by any number of available holding devices, can perform these and other jobs when accurate measurement is required. The tool is available from motorcycle dealers and mail order houses. See **Figure 1**.

Vernier Caliper

This tool is invaluable when reading inside or outside measurements to close precision. The vernier caliper can be purchased from large dealers or mail order houses. See **Figure 2**.

Hydrometer

This instrument measures state of charge of the battery and tells much about battery condition. Such an instrument is available at any auto parts store and through most larger mail order outlets. See **Figure 3**.

Multimeter or VOM

This instrument is invaluable for electrical system troubleshooting and service (**Figure 4**). A few of its functions may be duplicated by cheaper substitutes, but for the serious mechanic, it is a must. Its uses are described in the applicable sections of this manual. Multimeters are available at electronics hobbyist's stores and mail order outlets.

Compression Gauge

An engine with low compression cannot be properly tuned and will not develop full power. A compression gauge measures engine compression. The one shown in **Figure 5** has a flexible stem, which enables it to reach cylinders where there is little clearance between the cylinder head and frame. Gauges are available at auto accessory stores or by mail order from large catalog firms.

Impact Driver

This tool makes removal of engine components easy and eliminates damage to bolt and screw heads. Good ones are available at larger hardware stores. When purchasing an impact driver, choose one that has the same size drive head as that of your socket set. For example, if your ratchet and socket set is mainly 3/8 in., select an impact driver with a 3/8 in. drive head. **Figure 6** shows the impact driver with a number of useful bits.

Ignition Gauge

This tool has round wire gauges for measuring spark plug gap. See **Figure 7**.

Strobe Timing Light

This instrument is necessary for ignition timing. By flashing a light at the precise instant the spark plug fires, the position of the flywheel at that instant can be seen. Marks on the ignition governor plate and the stationary scale on the crankcase must align.

Suitable lights range from inexpensive neon bulb types to powerful xenon strobe lights. See **Figure 8**. Neon timing lights are difficult to see and must be used in dimly lit areas. Xenon strobe timing lights can be used outside in bright sunlight. Both types work on this motorcycle; use according to the manufacturer's instructions.

Vacuum Gauges

A vacuum gauge is essential for accurately synchronizing the carburetors. Several types are available, including needle gauges and mercury filled manometers. Manometers come with detailed instructions on use. See **Figure 9**.

Other Special Tools

A few other special tools may be required for major service. These are described in the appropriate chapters and are available from Yamaha dealers.

EXPENDABLE SUPPLIES

Expendable supplies are required which include grease, oil, gasket cement, rags, cleaning solvent and distilled water. Ask your dealer for the special locking compounds, silicone lubricants and commercial chain lube products which make maintenance simpler. Solvent is available at most service stations and distilled water for the battery is available at most supermarkets.

PARTS REPLACEMENT

Yamaha makes frequent changes during a model year—some minor, some relatively major. When you order parts from the dealer or other parts distributor, always order by engine and frame number. Write the numbers down and carry them with you. Compare new parts to old before purchasing them. If they are not alike, have the parts manager explain the difference to you.

SERIAL NUMBERS

You must know the model serial number for registration and when ordering special parts. These identification numbers are located in the same general area on all models.

The engine number is located on the crankcase. The frame number is stamped on the steering head down-tube.

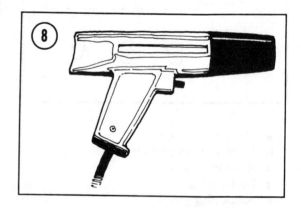

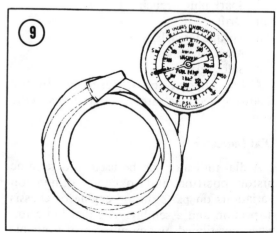

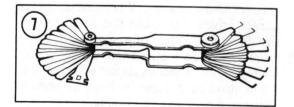

NOTE: If you own a 1978 or later model, first check the Supplement at the back of the book for any new service information.

2

CHAPTER TWO

PERIODIC SERVICE AND GENERAL MAINTENANCE

This manual covers both emission-controlled motorcycles manufactured after January 1, 1978, and non-controlled motorcycles built before that date. Refer to the supplement at the end of this book for scheduled maintenance on emission-controlled models. If a procedure does not appear in the supplement, then it remains the same as described in this chapter.

Be sure to perform general or preventive maintenance at regular intervals as recommended. To ignore this is an expensive mistake. The difference can mean thousands of trouble-free miles and hundreds of dollars saved in repair bills. **Table 1** and **Table 2** list required maintenance.

LUBRICATION

Frequency

Change the oil as indicated in the charts or 30-60 days, whichever comes first. See **Table 2**. Every 30 days may seem like a waste of time and oil, but the interval is as important as elapsed mileage. Acids formed by gasoline vapor blown by the piston rings will contaminate the oil even if the cycle is not run for several weeks.

If your motorcycle is run under dusty conditions the oil will get dirty faster. Change the oil more frequently under such conditions.

ENGINE OIL CHANGING

The engine oil should be drained while the engine is warm. Change the oil according to the maintenance schedule. Riding in dusty areas, or riding short trips when the oil doesn't get fully warmed up requires more frequent changing.

1. Remove both drain plugs from the bottom of the crankcase (**Figure 1**). Allow the oil to drain for about 10 minutes. Tilting the engine may help the oil drain completely.

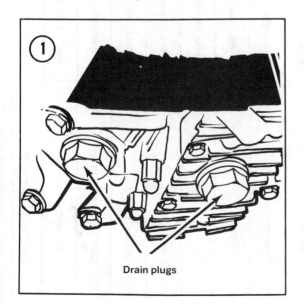
Drain plugs

Table 1 SERVICE INTERVALS—1970 TO EARLY 1978

Item	Remarks	Initial Service				Normal Maint.		
		250	500	1,000	2,000	1,000	2,000	8,000
Brakes	Check, adjust or repair as needed		X	X			X	
Clutch	Check, adjust or repair as needed		X	X			X	
Battery	Check fluid level	X	X	X		X		
Spark plugs	Check, clean or replace as needed	X	X	X		X		
Wheels and tires	Check tire pressure, spokes	X	X	X		X		
Nuts, bolts and screws	Check before each trip	X	X	X		X		
Drive chain	Check chain tension and alignment	X	X	X		X		
Engine oil	Check level	X	X	X		X		
Air filter	Clean element or replace as needed	X	X	X		X		
Fuel system	Clean petcock filters and flush tank	X		X			X	
Ignition timing	Adjust, replace points as needed		X	X			X	
Carburetor adjustment	Adjust idle, synchronization as needed		X	X			X	
Carburetor overhaul	Major adjustments and float level				X			X
Cylinder compression	Check with compression gauge	X	X				X	

Table 2   LUBRICATION INTERVALS—1970 TO EARLY 1978

Item	Remarks	(see below)	Period							
			Initial				Thereafter Every			
			250	500	1,000	2,000	1,000	2,000	4,000	8,000
Transmission oil	Warm engine before draining	1				X		X		
Drive chain	Lube/adjust as required	2			See below					
Drive chain	Remove/clean/lube/adjust	2				X		X		
Control and meter cables	Apply thoroughly	3		X				X		
Throttle grip and housing	Light application	4		X		X		X		
Tach and speedo gear housings	Light application	4			X				X	
Rear arm pivot shaft	Apply until shows	5			X			X		
Brake pedal shaft	Light application	4			X	X		X		
Gearshift shaft	Light application	4			X			X		
Stand shaft pivot	Light application	4			X			X		
Front forks	Drain completely—check specs.	8				X			X	
Steering ball races	Inspect thoroughly/med. pack	6				X			X	
Point cam lubrication wick	Very light application	7			X				X	
Wheel bearings	Do not over-pack	6				X			X	

1. At ambient temperatures of 45-90°F, use 10W-30 "SD"
2. Use special chain lube every 200-250 miles; more often if hard or dirty riding is done.
3. Use graphite base type (specialty types available—use name-brand, quality manufacturer).
4. Light duty: smooth, light-weight, "white" grease. Heavy duty: Standard 90 wt. lube grease (do not use lube grease on throttle/housing).
5. Use standard 90 wt. lube grease—smooth, not coarse.
6. Medium-weight wheel bearing grease of quality mfr.— preferably waterproof.
7. Light-weight machine oil.
8. Use 10-30W motor oil or special fork oil.

2. Check the drain plug and gasket for wear or damage. Reinstall the plug.

3. Refer to **Table 3** and **Table 4** and fill the crankcase with the specified quantity and type of engine oil.

4. If oil is just being added, set the machine on its centerstand on a level surface and add oil as necessary to bring level up to the mark on the dipstick.

5. Let the engine run for a few minutes, shut it off, and let stand for approximately one minute. Check the oil level again and add more oil if necessary. See **Figure 2**.

> *NOTE*
> *Never dispose of motor oil in the trash, on the ground, or down a storm drain. Many service stations accept used motor oil and waste haulers provide curbside used motor oil collection. Do not combine other fluids with motor oil to be recycled. To locate a recycler, contact the American Petroleum Institute (API) at www.recycleoil.org.*

OIL FILTER

Replacement

Operation of the bypass mechanism located in the oil filter is shown in **Figure 3.**

1. Remove the cover on the right case cover. Take off the cavity plate and remove the oil filter securing bolt. Refer to **Figure 4.**

2. Check the filter for trapped particles or foreign matter and clean the filter and filter cavity with solvent. Blow dry with compressed air if available.

3. Replace the filter in the cavity and install the filter securing bolt, taking care not to overtighten it. Replace the cover O-ring if it is damaged or deteriorated.

CONTROL CABLES

Every 2,000 miles (3,200 km) the control cables should be lubricated. Also, they should be inspected at this time for fraying and the cable sheath should be checked for chafing.

The cables are relatively inexpensive and should be replaced when found to be faulty.

The control cables can be lubricated either with oil or any of the popular cable lubricants

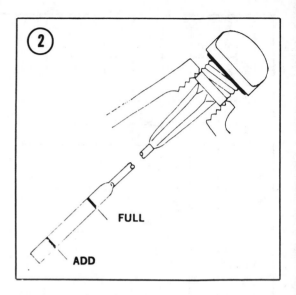

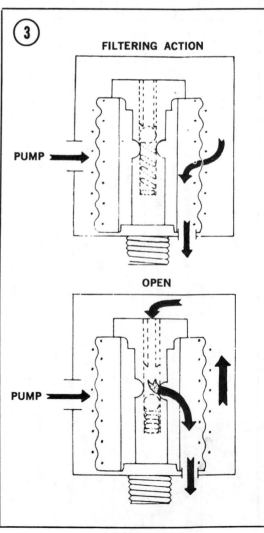

2

Table 3   CAPACITIES

Model	Front Forks (Each Leg) cc (oz.)	Engine/Transmission Oil Liters (Quarts)	
XS1	240 (7.5)	3.0 (3.2)	
XS1B	223 (7.0)	3.0 (3.2)	
XS2; TX650	135 (4.25)	2.5 (2.6)	
TX650A	160 (5.4)	*2.5 (2.6)	(see note)
XS650B	160 (5.4)	*2.5 (2.6)	(see note)
XS650C	155 (5.2)	2.5 (2.6)	
XS650D	168 (5.7)	*2.5 (2.6)	
XS650E; XS650F; XS650SF	169 (5.7)	*2.5 (2.6)	

*Quantity is for engine overhaul. Capacity for periodic oil change is 2.0 liters (2.1 qt.).

NOTE: Oil capacity stated represents revised Yamaha specifications to prevent oil misting from the breather pipes. XS650B models after engine No. 103747 are equipped with a modified dipstick to measure lowered oil level. Earlier XS650B and TX650A models should have dipstick modified by a dealer to correspond with lower recommended oil level.

Table 4   RECOMMENDED FUEL AND LUBRICANTS

Fuel	Regular, low-lead, or unleaded
Engine oil	SAE 30W or SAE 20-40W (SE rating)
Fork oil	10, 20, or 30W motor oil or special fork oil

and a cable lubricator. The first method requires more time and the complete lubrication of the entire cable is less certain.

NOTE
When control cables are not properly maintained, they stiffen considerably and force the rider to work harder when operating the throttle or clutch. Furthermore, more tension is applied to the balls on the ends of the cable. Consequently this will weaken the cable and cause it to break.

Oil method

1. Disconnect the cable from the clutch lever (**Figure 5**) and the throttle grip assembly. On the throttle cable, it is necessary to remove the

2 screws that clamp the housing together to gain access to the cable end.

2. Make a cone of stiff paper and tape it to the end of the cable sheath (**Figure 6**).

3. Hold the cable upright and pour a small amount of light oil (SAE 10W/30) into the cone. Work the cable in and out of the sheath for several minutes to help the oil work its way down to the end of the cable.

4. Remove the cone, reconnect the cable and adjust the cable(s) as described in this chapter.

NOTE
While the throttle housing is separated, apply a light coat of grease to the metal surfaces of the grip assembly.

Lubricator method

This method of lubricating control cables is preferable because it forces the lubricant through the entire cable. In addition, the lubricator can be carried in a tool bag, together with chain and cable lube, and used to lube cables on long trips.

1. Disconnect the cables as previously described.

2. Attach the lubricator following the manufacturer's instructions.

3. Insert the nozzle of the lubricant can in the lubricator, press the button on the can and hold it down until the lubricant begins to flow out the other end of the cable.

4. Remove the lubricator, reconnect the cable(s) and adjust as described in this chapter.

SPEEDOMETER CABLE

A jumping or vibrating speedometer needle usually means that lubrication is needed. Lubricate the speedometer cable by disconnecting it from the speedometer and removing the inner cable. Clean and grease it lightly along its entire length except for the top 6 inches. Replace the inner cable, turning it to ensure that its end is inserted in the drive mechanism and reconnect the outer cable at the speedometer.

CHANGING FORK OIL

The fork oil should be changed according to the maintenance schedule. Change more frequently if riding off-road or racing.

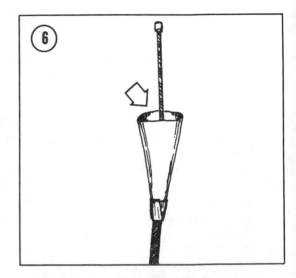

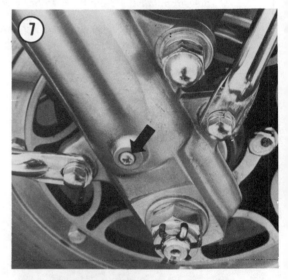

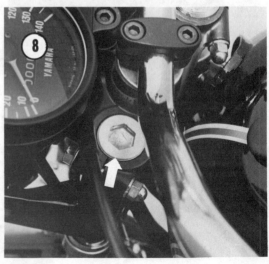

Table 5   TUNE-UP SPECIFICATIONS

Spark plug type		
XS1, XS2, TX650, XS650B	B8ES (NGK)	W24ES (ND)
TX650A	B7ES (NGK)	W22ES (ND)
1976 and later	BP7ES (NGK)	N7Y (Champion)

Spark plug gap	
1970-1977	0.024-0.028 in. (0.6-0.7 mm)
1978 and later	0.028-0.032 in. (0.7-0.8 mm)

Valve clearance	Intake	Exhaust
XS1, XS1B, XS2, TX650	0.003 in. (0.074 mm)	0.006 in. (0.15 mm)
TX650A, XS650B	0.002 in. (0.05 mm)	0.004 in. (0.10 mm)
XS650C, XS650D	0.002 in. (0.05 mm)	0.006 in. (0.15 mm)
1978	0.004 in. (0.10 mm)	0.006 in. (0.15 mm)
1979 and later	0.0024 in. (0.06 mm)	0.006 in. (0.15 mm)

Breaker point gap	0.012-0.016 in. (0.3-0.4 mm)

Carburetor air screw	Turns out from seated
XS1, XS1B	½
XS2, TX650, XS650B	¾
XS650C, XS650D	1½
1978 (early)	2¼
1978 (late) — 1979	Preset
1980 and later	Not equipped

Idle speed	
1970-1978 (early)	1,100-1,200 rpm
1978 (late) and later	1,200 rpm

The front fork must have the same amount of oil in each fork leg to operate correctly. Leakage may mean that the fork seals and O-rings need to be replaced. If the forks begin to malfunction, check first to see that each has the proper amount of oil.

1. Remove the drain plug and fiber washer from the bottom rear of each fork leg (**Figure 7**).

2. Apply the front brake and pump repeatedly on the handlebars to force oil out of the forks.

3. Check the drain plugs and fiber washers for wear or damage. Replace if necessary and install them in the fork legs.

4. Prop up the motorcycle with the front wheel off the ground. Remove the cap nuts from the top of the fork tubes (**Figure 8**).

5. Refer to **Table 3** and **Table 4** and fill each fork tube with oil.

ENGINE TUNE-UP

This tune-up section covers non-emission controlled motorcycles. If you have an emission controlled bike, refer to the supplement at the end of this book for additional tune-up information.

Check the engine carefully, and proceed systematically. Consult Chapter Three for troubleshooting procedures when you suspect more serious trouble. Refer to **Table 5** for tune-up specifications.

1. Inspect the air filter; clean it or install a new one.

2. Clean the fuel strainer, if equipped, and the fuel petcocks. Inspect the fuel lines for cracks or leakage.

3. Check cam chain tension, and adjust if necessary as described under *Cam Chain Tensioner* in Chapter Four.

4. Inspect valve clearance, and adjust if necessary.

5. Check and record cylinder compression.

6. Inspect the spark plugs, clean them, adjust the gap, or replace them if necessary.

7. Inspect the contact breaker points, adjust the gap, or replace the points if necessary. Lubricate the point cam wick very lightly.

8. Inspect the ignition timing and adjust if necessary.

9. Adjust the carburetors if required.

10. Inspect the alternator brushes as described in Chapter Three under *Charging Circuit Troubleshooting*, and replace them if required.

VALVES

Adjustment

On all 650's, exhaust valves are located at the front of the engine; intake valves are at the rear. See **Figure 9**.

1. Valve adjustment must be made only on a cold engine.

2. Remove the tappet covers and the alternator cover.

3. Refer to **Figure 10** and line up the "T" mark on the stator with the timing mark on the rotor to put one piston at top dead center.

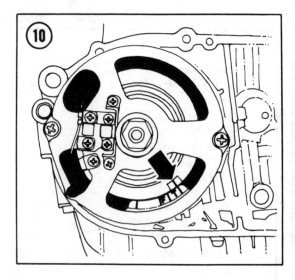

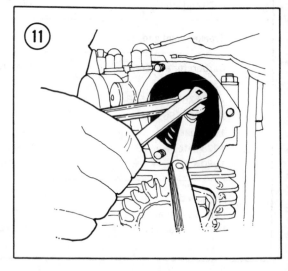

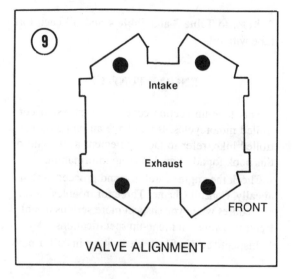

VALVE ALIGNMENT

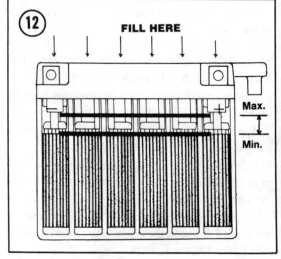

FILL HERE

Max.

Min.

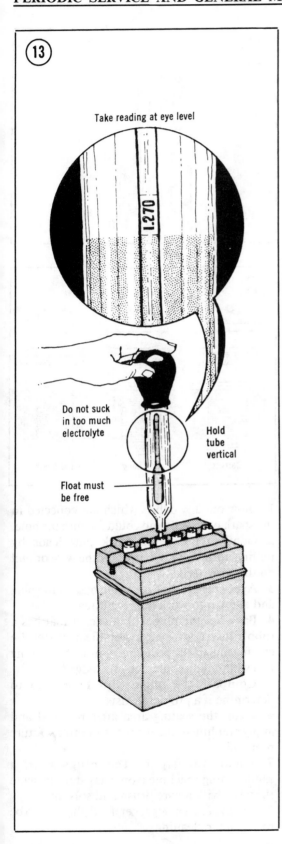

(13)

Take reading at eye level

1.270

Do not suck
in too much
electrolyte

Hold
tube
vertical

Float must
be free

2

4. Check which cylinder has clearance at both intake and exhaust valve adjusters and adjust the valves on that one. Refer to **Figure 11** and use the valve adjusting tool found in the motorcycle's tool kit to adjust clearance. The locknut on the adjuster has to be loosened and the adjuster turned in or out to obtain proper clearance. Measure with a feeler gauge as shown. Set valve clearances as specified in **Table 5**. Tighten the locknut while holding the adjuster in place and check the clearance again to make sure it has not changed.

5. Turn the engine over one complete revolution and set the valves on the other cylinder in the same manner.

BATTERY

Inspection

1. Use distilled water only to keep the battery liquid level up to the line shown in **Figure 12**. Check once a month; more often in hot weather or when battery is discharged or charged often.

High rate of evaporation from cells necessitating frequent refilling could be a sign of overcharging. Check the alternator output.

Consistent low level in one cell only indicates a shorted cell. The battery will eventually have to be replaced.

2. Check the specific gravity of the electrolyte solution with a hydrometer (**Figure 13**). A fully charged battery will show a reading of between 1.260 and 1.280. The battery should be charged if it reads less than 1.230.

If the battery will not hold a charge, check for loose terminal connections.

3. Be sure the battery terminals are hooked up properly. The red wire goes to the positive terminal and the black wire goes to the negative terminal.

FUSES

1. A fuse can be checked visually to determine if it is burned out (blown).

2. Always replace a blown fuse with one having the same capacity.

3. Chronically blown fuses indicate a short circuit in the wiring or a defective component. Correct the problem before replacing the fuse. Never replace a blown fuse with one of a higher rating.

SPARK PLUGS

Spark plugs are available in various heat ranges hotter or colder than the plugs originally installed at the factory.

Select plugs of a heat range designed for the loads and temperature conditions under which the bike will run. Use of incorrect heat ranges can cause seized pistons, scored cylinder walls, or damaged piston crowns.

In areas where seasonal temperature variations are great, use a colder plug for hard summer riding and a hotter plug for slower winter operation.

The reach (length) of a plug is also important. A longer than normal plug could interfere with the piston causing permanent and severe damage. Refer to **Figure 14** and **Figure 15**.

Testing

A quick and simple test can be made to determine if the plug is correct for your type of riding. Accelerate hard through the gears and maintain a high, steady speed. Shut the throttle off, and kill the engine at the same time, allowing the bike to slow, out of gear. Do not allow the engine to slow the bike. Remove the plug and check the condition of the electrode area. A spark plug of the correct heat range, with the engine in a proper state of tune, will appear light tan. See **Figure 16**.

If the insulator is white or burned, the plug is too hot and should be replaced with a colder one. Also check the setting of the carburetor for it may be too lean.

A too cold plug will have sooty deposits ranging in color from dark brown to black. Replace with a hotter plug and check for too rich carburetion or evidence of oil blow-by at the piston rings.

Removal/Installation

Remove and clean the spark plugs according to the maintenance schedule. Measure the electrode gap (**Figure 17**) with a round feeler gauge and set it as specified in **Table 5**. Refer to **Table 5** for the recommended plugs.

Often, heat and corrosion can cause the plug to bind in the head making removal difficult. Do not use force; the head is easily damaged.

The proper way to replace a plug is:

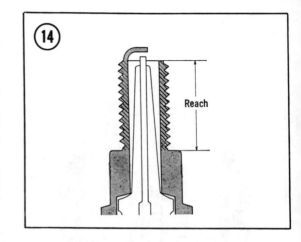

Reach

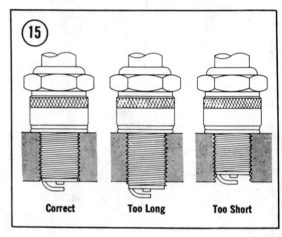

Correct   Too Long   Too Short

1. Blow out any debris which has collected in the spark plug wells and could fall into the hole.
2. Gently remove the spark plug leads by pulling up and out. Do not jerk the wire or pull on the wire itself.
3. Apply penetrating oil to the base of the plug and allow it to work into the threads.
4. Back out the plug with a socket that has a rubber insert designed to grip the insulator. Be careful not to drop the plugs into the cooling fins where they could become lodged.
5. Compare the plugs with **Figure 16** to determine if a problem exists.
6. Clean the seating area after removal and apply graphite to the threads to simplify future removal.
7. Clean the tip of the plugs with a sandblasting machine (some gas stations have them) or with a wire brush and solvent.
8. Always use a new gasket if old plugs are to be reused after cleaning.

SPARK PLUG CONDITION   ⑯

NORMAL

- Identified by light tan or gray deposits on the firing tip.
- Can be cleaned.

GAP BRIDGED

- Identified by deposit buildup closing gap between electrodes.
- Caused by oil or carbon fouling. If deposits are not excessive, the plug can be cleaned.

OIL FOULED

- Identified by wet black deposits on the insulator shell bore and electrodes.
- Caused by excessive oil entering combustion chamber through worn rings and pistons, excessive clearance between valve guides and stems, or worn or loose bearings. Can be cleaned. If engine is not repaired, use a hotter plug.

CARBON FOULED

- Identified by black, dry fluffy carbon deposits on insulator tips, exposed shell surfaces and electrodes.
- Caused by too cold a plug, weak ignition, dirty air cleaner, too rich a fuel mixture, or excessive idling. Can be cleaned.

LEAD FOULED

- Identified by dark gray, black, yellow, or tan deposits or a fused glazed coating on the insulator tip.
- Caused by highly leaded gasoline. Can be cleaned.

WORN

- Identified by severely eroded or worn electrodes.
- Caused by normal wear. Should be replaced.

FUSED SPOT DEPOSIT

- Identified by melted or spotty deposits resembling bubbles or blisters.
- Caused by sudden acceleration. Can be cleaned.

OVERHEATING

- Identified by a white or light gray insulator with small black or gray brown spots and with bluish-burnt appearance of electrodes.
- Caused by engine overheating, wrong type of fuel, loose spark plugs, too hot a plug, or incorrect ignition timing. Replace the plug.

PREIGNITION

- Identified by melted electrodes and possibly blistered insulator. Metallic deposits on insulator indicate engine damage.
- Caused by wrong type of fuel, incorrect ignition timing or advance, too hot a plug, burned valves, or engine overheating. Replace the plug.

9. Run the plug in finger-tight, then torque to 14 ft.-lb. (2.0 mkg). Further tightening will flatten the gasket and cause binding.

NOTE
A short piece of fuel line can be used to install the plug initially in areas where space is a problem.

CONDENSERS (CAPACITORS)

Condensers (capacitors) are sealed units and require no maintenance. Be sure the connections are clean and tight.

The only possible proper test is to measure the resistance of the insulation with an ohmmeter. The valve should be 5,000 ohms.

A make-do test is to charge the capacitor by hooking the leads, or case and lead, to a 12V battery. After a few seconds, touch the leads together, or lead to case, and check for a spark as shown in **Figure 18**. A damaged capacitor will not store electricity or spark.

The 2 condensers are mounted as a single unit and must be replaced in tandem if one fails.

No spark or severe arcing at the points could be indications of condenser failure.

Most mechanics prefer to dicard the condensers and replace them with new ones during engine tune-up. See *Breaker Point Replacement* in this chapter for removal/installation.

IGNITION COIL

The ignition coil is a step-up transformer which increases the low voltage produced by the alternator to the high voltage required to jump the spark plug gap. The only service required is periodic inspection of the electrical leads to make sure they are clean and tight, and checking to see that the coil is mounted securely.

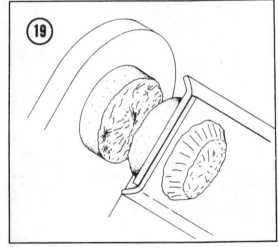

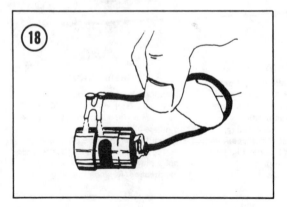

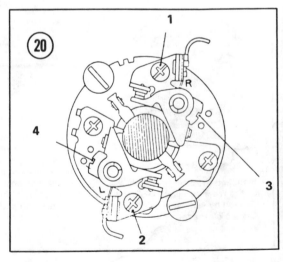

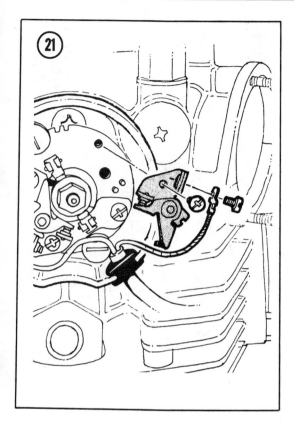

BREAKER POINTS

Inspection/Adjustment

1. Check the points for metal build-up as shown in **Figure 19**. If they cannot be filed clean with a few strokes of a point file, replace the points.

2. With prolonged use, the fiber cam follower wears against the point cam. This can alter point gap and timing on that particular cylinder. Reset the point gap and check timing periodically as detailed in the following steps.

3. Occasionally check the point return spring. Use a scale and buzz box. The points should open with approximately 700 to 800 grams pressure.

4. The points should be cleaned and regapped, and the timing checked according to the maintenance schedule.

5. Check for burned oil film on the points from time to time and clean as necessary. Clean the points with a point file and electrical contact cleaner. Run a business card or other clean card between the points until the card comes out clean.

6. To set the point gap, rotate the engine until one set of points is open to its widest position. Insert the proper feeler gauge and adjust for a tight slip fit by loosening the appropriate point lock screw (1 or 2, **Figure 20**) and using a screwdriver in the adjustment slots (3 or 4) to open or close the gap. Set points to 0.012-0.016 in. (0.3-0.4 mm). Tighten the lock screw and check the gap. Rotate the engine to open the other set of points and repeat the procedure. Lightly oil the felt rubbing pad against the point cam surface each time the points are adjusted. Too much oil at this point will foul the points later.

2. Remove the entire point assembly as shown in **Figure 21**. When reassembling, note the locating pin on the point assembly which fits into a guide hole in the baseplate. See **Figure 22**.

3. Replace and tighten the point lock screw and attach the point wire to the stationary point.

4. Gap the new point assembly as described previously.

IGNITION TIMING

1. Before setting ignition timing, adjust the cam chain as detailed in Chapter Four.

2. Both sets of points must be correctly gapped prior to timing.

3. Refer to **Figure 23** for identification of the timing marks found on the stator. The engine should fire when the rotor mark is between the 2 stator marks identified as B1 and B2. Letter "A" indicates top dead center (TDC) and the "C" mark shows the firing point at the fully advanced position.

4. Refer to Chapter Four if necessary and remove the alternator inspection plate, ignition point cover, and ignition advance unit cover.

5. Anchor the advance weight securely as shown in **Figure 24**.

6. Use a buzz box or ohmmeter hooked to the points to determine the exact time of point opening. Connect one lead to a good ground (**Figure 25**) and the other lead to the gray point wire to time the right cylinder.

7. The letters "L" and "R" are stamped next to the appropriate set of points. The right cylinder must be timed first.

8. Begin timing the right cylinder by rotating the engine in a counterclockwise (CCW) direction as viewed from the left side, until the points just open. Check the rotor timing mark. It should be exactly midway between the 2 marks shown in **Figure 26**. If an adjustment is needed, loosen both baseplate lock screws (**Figure 27**) and turn the baseplate until the points just start to open. Be sure the rotor and stator are still lined up correctly. Tighten the lock screws and check the adjustment. Connect the buzz box or ohmmeter to the left set of points (orange wire) and rotate the engine until the left set just begins to open. If the rotor and stator marks do not line up, loosen the lock screws securing the left set of points and move the point set until the points just start to open with the rotor and stator marks aligned.

9. The ignition timing is now set correctly at the retarded position. It must also be checked at the fully advanced position. Wedge the advance mechanism weight in a fully open position. Connect a buzz box or ohmmeter as

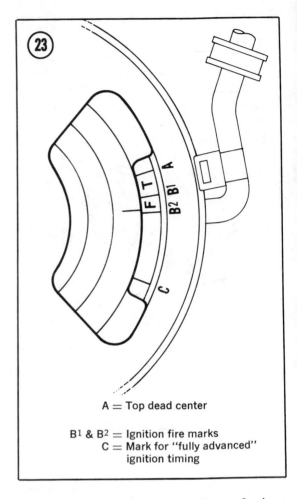

A = Top dead center

B1 & B2 = Ignition fire marks

C = Mark for "fully advanced" ignition timing

before to the orange wire. The left set of points should open when the rotor mark lines up with the stator mark shown in **Figure 28**. Switch the test lead to the gray wire and check the right cylinder. A tolerance of 0.12 in. (3 mm) is allowed in either direction from the mark. With the cylinders timed correctly at the retarded position the marks should line up at the advanced position. Do not bend the advance weight stops to change the amount of advance. These stops will snap off. Change the advance unit instead.

Check all timing settings again before replacing the ignition advance unit cover, point cover, and alternator inspection plate.

CARBURETOR

Adjustments

Refer to **Figure 29** to adjust idle mixture and idle speed.

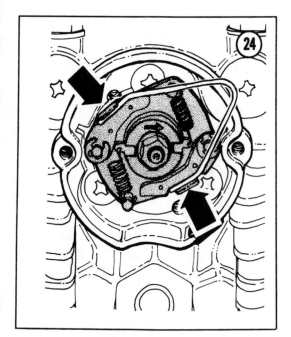

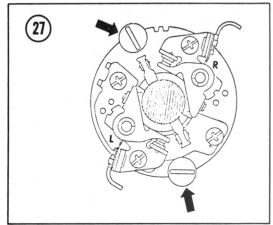

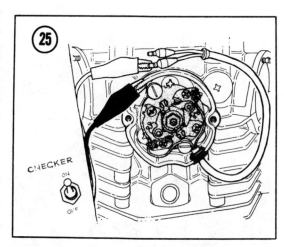

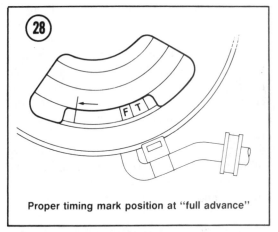

Proper timing mark position at "full advance"

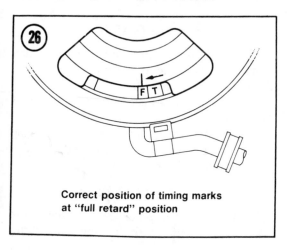

Correct position of timing marks
at "full retard" position

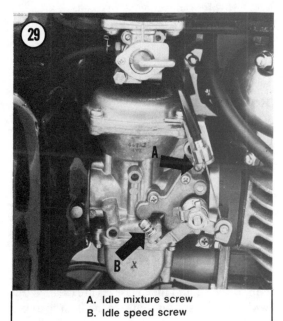

A. Idle mixture screw
B. Idle speed screw

1. Turn idle mixture screw in until it seats lightly and back it out 1/2 turn on XS1 and XS1B models; 3/4 turn on XS2, TX650, TX650A, and XS650B models; 1 1/2 +/- 1/2 turn on XS650C and XS650D models; and 2 1/4 turns on the XS650E.

2. Turn both idle speed screws equal amounts to obtain a fast idle. Remove either of the spark plug leads. Back out the idle speed screw on the firing cylinder until the engine dies. Reconnect the spark plug lead and restart the engine. Remove the other lead and adjust the idle speed screw on the firing cylinder until the engine dies again. Reconnect spark plug leads and start engine. Both cylinders should be idling at the same speed. Adjust idle speed screws in tandem until idle speed is between 1,000-1,200 rpm.

3. Mid-range mixture adjustment is shown in **Figure 30**. The needle clip is normally in the fourth groove from the top. Move the clip one groove higher to lean out the mixture and move it one groove lower to enrich the mixture.

4. High-speed mixture is governed by the size of the main jet. The 650 comes standard with a No. 130 jet. Install a No. 140 jet to enrich the mixture and a No. 120 jet to lean it out.

CAUTION
Mixture changes should be considered carefully. Too lean a mixture can cause overheating and severe engine damage.

5. Use the cable adjusters to adjust the butterfly valves so they open simultaneously. Refer to **Figure 31**. There should also be 1/4 in. (6 mm) free play in the throttle before the butterflies start to move.

6. Fuel around the outside of the carburetor may be an indication of dirt in the float valve or a punctured float. Clean the float valve or replace the damaged float. If the vacuum slide lifts slowly or not at all, check the vacuum slide diaphragm.

If gas is getting to the carburetor but not to the engine, check for water blocking the main jet, improper float level, or a loose jet needle clip. If the air and fuel passages are cleaned out with compressed air, remove the float to avoid damaging it.

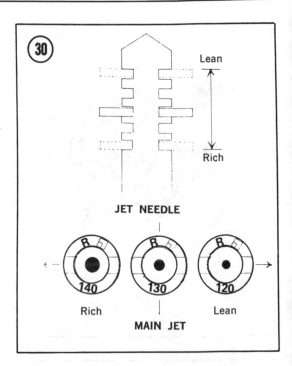

JET NEEDLE

MAIN JET

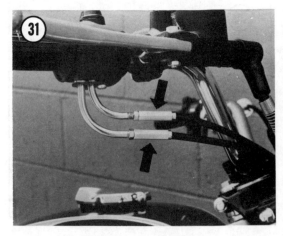

FUEL STRAINER

The fuel strainer filters out particles which might otherwise enter the carburetor and cause the float needle valve to remain open. Such particles also tend to get into the engine and cause damage.

Remove the fuel strainer and clean during each tune-up. Clean with solvent and blow dry with compressed air.

AIR CLEANER

A clogged air cleaner can decrease the efficiency and life of the engine. Never run

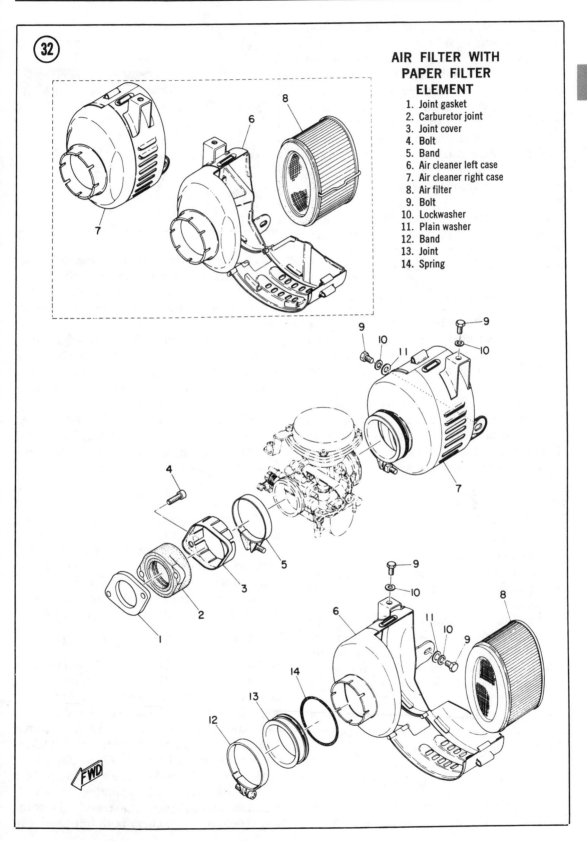

AIR FILTER WITH PAPER FILTER ELEMENT

1. Joint gasket
2. Carburetor joint
3. Joint cover
4. Bolt
5. Band
6. Air cleaner left case
7. Air cleaner right case
8. Air filter
9. Bolt
10. Lockwasher
11. Plain washer
12. Band
13. Joint
14. Spring

without a filter; even minute particles of dust can cause severe wear.

Check the air filter according to the maintenance schedule. Riding in dusty or sandy areas will require more frequent checks.

Replace the element if it is clogged with dirt, caked with oil, or if it shows deterioration.

Light dust can be shaken off the element by tapping it while using a soft brush on the outside. If necessary, carefully blow compressed air through the element from the inside.

If the bike has a wet foam filter, clean it in kerosene. Allow the foam filter to air dry, dip it in lightweight oil, squeeze out the excess oil, and insert it in the stock housing.

Models with Paper Filter Element

1. To remove the air filters for servicing, take off both frame side covers and press down on the spring clip on top of the filter containers so air cleaners can be removed (**Figure 32** and **Figure 33**).
2. Do not use any kind of solvent on the paper elements. Blow them clean with compressed air or use a brush to clean away accumulation of dirt. **Figure 34** shows the 2 types of cleaner housings used.

Models with Washable Foam Filter Element

Refer to **Figure 34**.
1. Remove the chassis side covers.
2. Remove the single filter case cap bolt to expose the filter case cap. Lift this off. Pull the filter out.
3. The filter is reusable foam. Soak and squeeze the foam in kerosene until all dirt is washed away. Let dry, then completely impregnate the foam with oil, then squeeze out the surplus. It should be impregnated but not dripping.
4. Grease the front filter end, the rubber part that butts up against the intake portion of the filter case. This ensures proper sealing.

CLUTCH ADJUSTMENT

Refer to **Figure 35** for adjustment procedure.
1. After the engine is reassembled and anytime

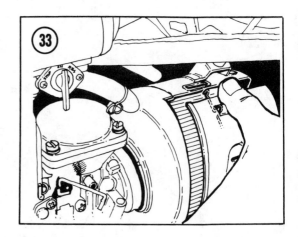

the clutch slips or will not disengage fully, the main clutch adjustment must be performed.
2. Remove the large threaded plug in the center of the left engine case cover. See **Figure 36**.
3. Loosen the locknut. Turn the adjustment screw until it bottoms slightly. Turn it back out 1/4 turn. Tighten the locknut, holding the adjustment screw so it does not turn. Replace and tighten the case plug.
4. Adjust cable free play at the handlebar lever by loosening the adjuster locknut and turning the adjuster so there is 1/16-1/8 in. (2-3 mm) free play. Tighten the locknut. See **Figure 37**.

DISC BRAKE

The front disc brake is self-adjusting once set at installation.

Check brake fluid level in the handlebar mounted reservoir once a week. Top up as required with DOT 3 disc brake fluid.

If fluid level drops too low, you may have to bleed the system as described in Chapter Eight.

DRUM BRAKE ADJUSTMENT

1. The front drum brake must be adjusted so both shoes contact the drum simultaneously. Disconnect the brake cable at the handlebar lever. Loosen the interconnecting rod locknut and turn the rod so both brake arms move away from each other until all free play is taken up. Tighten the locknut. See **Figure 38**.
2. Reconnect the brake cable and turn out on the cable adjuster while spinning the wheel. When the brake shoes start to contact the drum you should be able to hear both front and rear

2

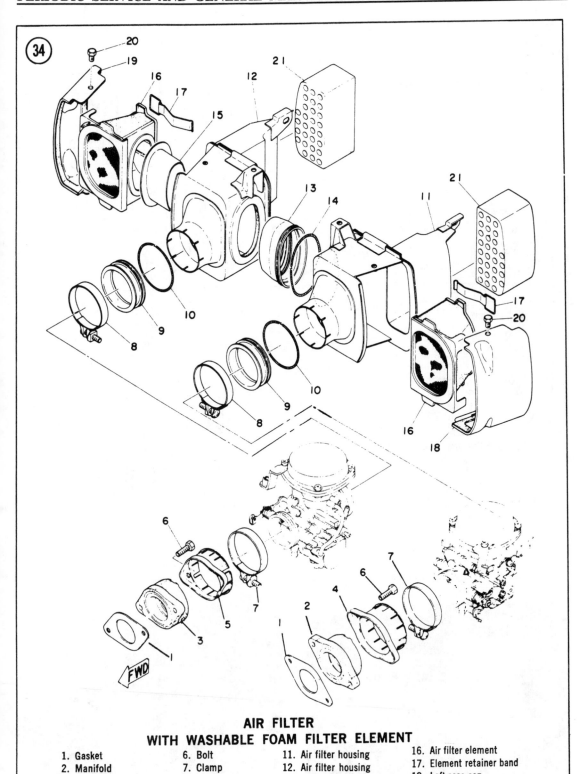

AIR FILTER
WITH WASHABLE FOAM FILTER ELEMENT

1. Gasket
2. Manifold
3. Manifold
4. Manifold bracket
5. Manifold bracket
6. Bolt
7. Clamp
8. Clamp
9. Connector
10. Band
11. Air filter housing
12. Air filter housing
13. Cross-over tube
14. Band
15. Connector
16. Air filter element
17. Element retainer band
18. Left case cap
19. Right case cap
20. Bolt
21. Silencer

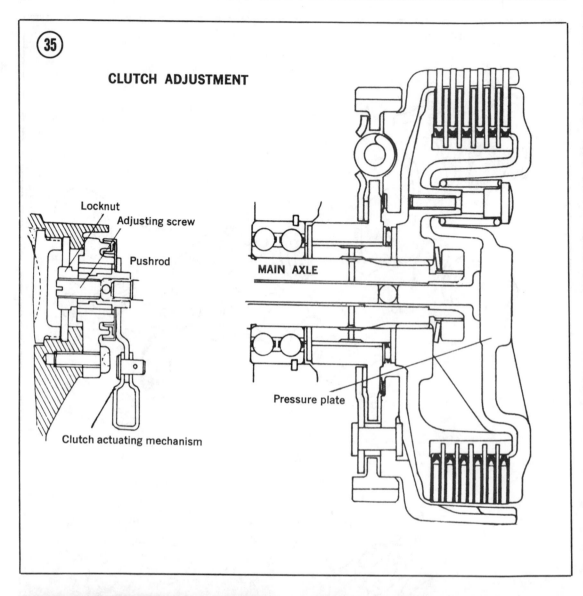

35

CLUTCH ADJUSTMENT

Locknut

Adjusting screw

Pushrod

MAIN AXLE

Clutch actuating mechanism

Pressure plate

36

37

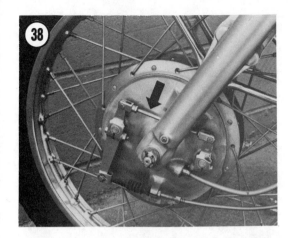

shoes at the same time. If you cannot, the interconnecting rod is not properly adjusted. Loosen the locknut and turn the brake cable adjuster until the front shoe can be heard scraping against the drum as the wheel is turned. Turn the interconnecting rod until the rear shoe can be heard against the drum. Tighten the locknut and adjust the cable adjuster as described below.

3. Loosen the brake cable adjuster locknut at the wheel and turn the adjuster in or out until there is about 1/4 in. (6mm) cable slack at the adjuster. To measure slack, grasp the cable where it exits from the adjuster (**Figure 39**) and push it in and out. Measure cable movement. Then adjust the brake lever adjuster at the handlebar so that there is 3/32-1/8 in. (2-3mm) slack at the point where the brake lever is pulled at rest until cable resistance is felt.

4. Rear brake adjustment should be checked each time the rear wheel is removed or the chain is adjusted.

5. Turn the brake rod adjuster as required to obtain about 1 inch (25 mm) free play at the brake pedal. See **Figure 40**.

BRAKE LIGHT ADJUSTMENT

1. To adjust the rear brake light switch, loosen one locknut and turn the other. Adjust the switch so the brake light comes on when the brake pedal is touched. See **Figure 41**.

2. Adjusting the rear brake or moving the rear wheel may change the brake switch adjustment.

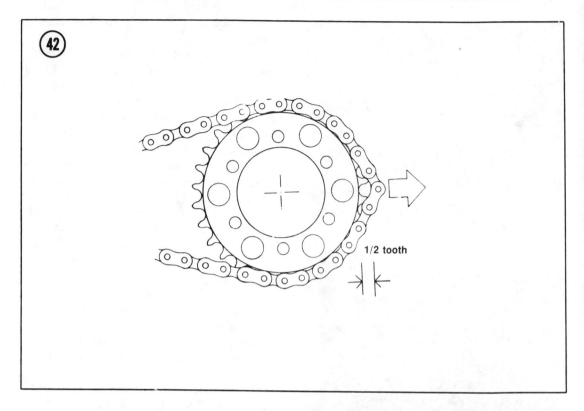

1/2 tooth

3. Adjust the front brake lever so it moves far enough to activate the front brake light switch.

DRIVE CHAIN

Inspection/Removal/Installation

1. Place the motorcycle on its centerstand.

2. Check the drive chain for wear while the chain is still installed on the machine by lifting the chain away from the sprocket as shown in **Figure 42**. The chain is worn out if it can be lifted away from the sprocket more than 1/2 the length of a link. If chain is in good condition, check for proper free play and adjust if necessary as described in this chapter. If the chain is worn, replace it by performing Steps 3-6. Chain lubrication is described in Step 7.

3. On XS1, XS1B and XS2 models, rotate the rear wheel until the master link is on the rear sprocket. On all other models, turn the rear wheel and position the master link so that it stops just before the rear sprocket.

4A. *XS1, XS1B, XS2*: Remove the master link clip with pliers as shown in **Figure 43**.

4B. *All other models*: The chain is connected and held together with a press fitted master

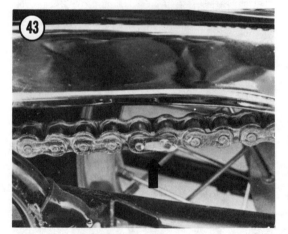

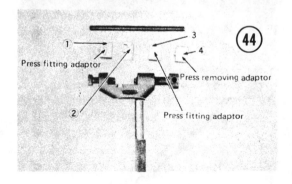

Press fitting adaptor
Press removing adaptor
Press fitting adaptor

link. To disconnect the chain, remove the master link clip as in Step 3. Then, using the Yamaha drive chain cutter (part No. 90890-01081) shown in **Figure 44**, push out the press-fit master link. See **Figure 45**.

5. After removing the chain, soak it thoroughly in solvent and hold as shown in **Figure 46** to check for kinks or binding. Replace the chain if necessary.

6A. *XS1, XS1B, XS2*: To install the chain, run the chain on both sprockets and connect the chain with the master link. Install the outer link plate and master link clip. Make sure the clip is secured in place with its closed end facing the direction of chain rotation, as shown in **Figure 47**.

6B. *All other models*: Run the chain over both sprockets and bring the ends to meet just before the rear sprocket. Slide a new master link through both loose chain ends. Place a new link plate onto the master link. Then select the proper chain press adapters shown in **Figure 44**. Press the link plate onto the master link, alternating between the left and right side master link pins, as shown in **Figure 45**. Install a new master link clip with its closed end facing the direction of chain rotation (**Figure 47**).

7. The chain should be lubricated every 200 miles. Use Yamaha chain and cable lube or 10W/30 motor oil or one of the many commercial chain lubes on the market. Clean the chain by soaking in solvent.

Adjustment

1. Periodically check the rear chain for proper adjustment. It should have 3/4 in. (20 mm) free play as shown in **Figure 48** with both wheels on the ground and the rider sitting on the seat. Make the measurement at the middle of the lower chain run.

2. Remove the cotter pin and loosen the rear axle nut. See **Figure 49**.

3. Loosen each chain adjuster locknut and turn the chain adjuster bolts to obtain proper chain tension. Be sure the axle remains perpendicular to the machine by using the guide marks stamped into the swing arm just above and to the rear of the axle nut. Tighten the locknuts. Tighten the rear axle nut to 108.5 ft.-lb. (15.0 mkg), then install a new cotter pin. Check the chain free play again to be sure it is still correct and adjust the rear brake pedal and stoplight switch if necessary as described previously.

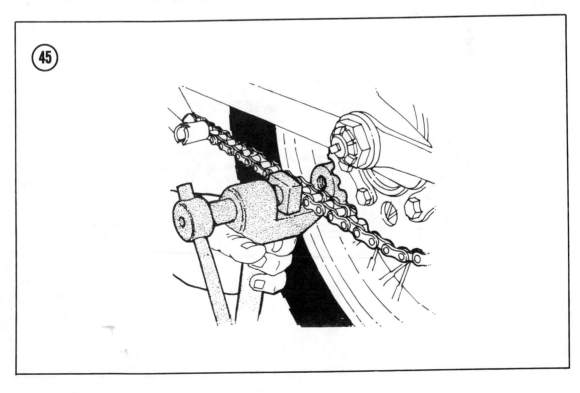

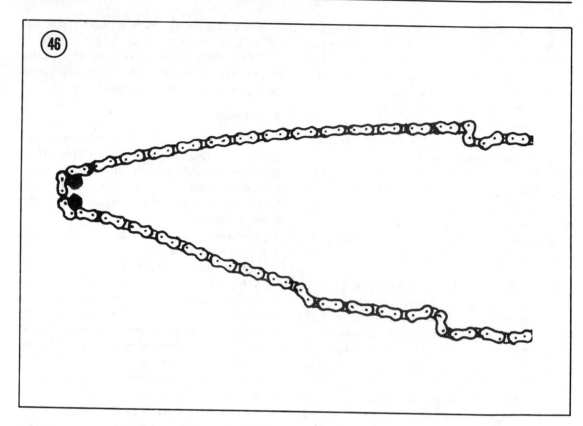

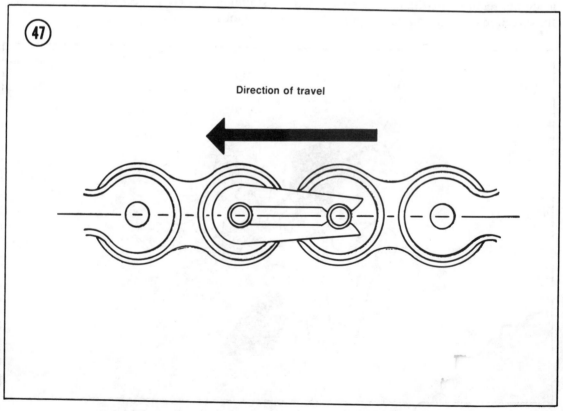

Direction of travel

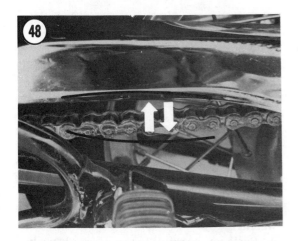

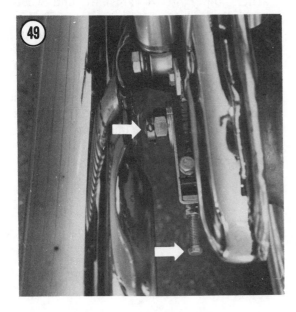

STORAGE

Several months of inactivity can cause serious problems and a general deterioration of motorcycle condition. This is especially true in areas of extreme cold weather. During winter months it is advisable to specially prepare a bike for "hibernation."

Selecting a Storage Area

Most cyclists store their motorcycles in their home garages. If you do not have a home garage, facilities suitable for long-term motorcycle storage are readily available for rent or lease in most areas. In selecting a building, consider the following points.

1. The storage area must be dry, free from dampness and excessive humidity. Heating is not necessary, but building should be well-insulated to minimize extreme temperature variations.
2. Buildings with large window areas should be avoided, or such windows should be masked (a good security measure) if direct sunlight can fall on the motorcycle.
3. Buildings in industrial areas, where factories are liable to emit corrosive fumes, are not desirable, nor are facilities near bodies of salt water.
4. The area should be selected to minimize the possibility of loss by fire, theft, or vandalism. It is strongly recommended that the areas be fully insured, perhaps with a package covering fire, theft, vandalism, weather and liability. The advice of your insurance agent should be solicited on these matters. The building should be fireproof and items such as the security of the doors and windows, alarm facilities, and proximity of the police should be considered.

Preparing for Storage

Careful pre-storage preparation will minimize deterioration and will ease restoring the motorcycle to service in the spring. The following procedure is recommended.
1. Wash the motorcycle completely, making sure to remove any accumulated road salt that may have collected during the first weeks of winter. Wax all painted and polished surfaces.
2. Run the engine for 20-30 minutes to stabilize oil temperature. Drain oil regardless of mileage since last oil change and replace with a normal quantity of fresh oil.
3. Remove battery and coat cable terminals with petroleum jelly. If there is evidence of acid spillage in the battery box, neutralize with baking soda, wash clean, and repaint. Batteries should be kept in an area where they will not freeze, and where they can be recharged every 2 weeks.
4. Drain all gasoline from the fuel tank, settling bowl, and carburetor float bowls. Leave petcock on the RESERVE position.
5. Remove the spark plugs and add a small quantity of oil to the cylinders. Turn the engine a few revolutions by hand. Install spark plugs.

6. Run a paper card, lightly saturated with silicone oil, between the points.

7. Check tire pressures. Move the motorcycle to storage area and store on center stand. If preparation is performed in an area far from the storage facility, the motorcycle should be trucked, not ridden, into storage.

Inspection During Storage

Try to inspect the motorcycle weekly while in storage. Any deterioration should be corrected as soon as possible. For example, if corrosion of bright metal parts is observed, cover them with a light film of grease or silicone spray.

Restoring to Service

A motorcycle that has been properly prepared, and stored in a suitable area, requires only light maintenance to restore it to service. It is advisable, however, to perform a spring tune-up.

1. Before removing the motorcycle from the storage area, re-inflate the tires to the correct pressures. Air loss during storage period may have nearly flattened the tires, and moving the motorcycle can cause damage to tires, tubes and rims.

2. When the motorcycle is brought to the work area, immediately install the battery (fully charged) and fill the fuel tank. The petcock should still be on the RESERVE position; do not move yet.

3. Check the fuel system for leaks. Remove carburetor float bowls or open the float bowl drain cocks and allow several cups of fuel to pass through the system. Move the fuel cock slowly to the CLOSE position, remove the settling bowl and empty any accumulated water.

4. Perform normal tune-up, as described earlier, apply oil to camshaft, and when checking spark plugs add a few drops of oil in the cylinders. Be especially certain to de-grease ignition points if an oily card was used to inhibit oxidation during storage; use a non-petroleum solvent.

5. Check safety items, i.e., lights, horn, etc., as oxidation on switch contacts and/or sockets during storage may make one or more of these critical devices inoperative.

6. Test ride and clean the motorcycle.

NOTE: If you own a 1978 or later model, first check the Supplement at the back of the book for any new service information.

CHAPTER THREE

TROUBLESHOOTING

Diagnosing mechanical problems is relatively simple if you use orderly procedures and keep a few basic principles in mind.

The troubleshooting procedures in this chapter analyze typical symptoms, and show logical methods of isolating causes. These are not the only methods. There may be several ways to solve a problem, but only a systematic, methodical approach can guarantee success.

Never assume anything. Do not overlook the obvious. If you are riding along and the motorcycle suddenly quits, check the easiest, most accessible problem spots first. Is there gasoline in the tank? Is the gas petcock in the ON or RESERVE position? Has a spark plug wire fallen off? Check ignition switch. Sometimes the weight of keys on a key ring may turn the ignition off suddenly.

If nothing obvious turns up in a cursory check, look a little further. Learning to recognize and describe symptoms will make repairs easier for you or a mechanic at the shop. Describe problems accurately and fully. Saying that "it won't run" isn't the same as saying "it quit on the highway at high speed and wouldn't start," or that "it sat in my garage for 3 months and then wouldn't start."

Gather as many symptoms together as possible to aid in diagnosis. Note whether the engine lost power gradually or all at once, what color smoke (if any) came from the exhaust, and so on. Remember that the more complicated a machine is, the easier it is to troubleshoot because symptoms point to specific problems.

After the symptoms are defined, areas which could cause problems are tested and analyzed. Guessing at the cause of a problem may provide the solution, but it can easily lead to frustration, wasted time, and a series of expensive, unnecessary parts replacements.

You don't need fancy equipment or complicated test gear to determine whether repairs can be attempted at home. A few simple checks could save a large repair bill and time lost while the motorcycle sits in a dealer's service department. On the other hand, be realistic and don't attempt repairs beyond your abilities. Service departments tend to charge heavily for putting together a disassembled engine that may have been abused. Some won't even take on such a job—so use common sense; don't get in over your head.

OPERATING REQUIREMENTS

An engine needs 3 basics to run properly: correct gas/air mixture, compression, and a spark at the right time. If one or more are missing, the engine won't run. The electrical system is the weakest link of the 3 basics. More problems result from electrical breakdowns than from any other source. Keep that in mind before you begin tampering with carburetor adjustments and the like.

If a motorcycle has been sitting for any length of time and refuses to start, check the battery for a charged condition first, and then look to the gasoline delivery system. This includes the tank, fuel petcocks, lines, and the carburetors. Rust may have formed in the tank, obstructing fuel flow. Gasoline deposits may have gummed up carburetor jets and air passages. Gasoline tends to lose its potency after standing for long periods. Condensation may contaminate it with water. Drain the old gas and try starting with a fresh tankful.

TROUBLESHOOTING INSTRUMENTS

Chapter One lists many of the instruments needed and detailed instructions on their use.

STARTING DIFFICULTIES

Check gas flow first. Remove the gas cap and look into the tank. If gas is present, pull off a fuel line at the carburetor and see if gas flows freely. If none comes out, the fuel tap may be shut off, blocked by rust or other foreign matter, or the fuel line may be stopped up or kinked. If the carburetor is getting usable fuel, inspect the electrical system next.

Check that the battery is charged by turning on the lights or by beeping the horn (this does not apply to competition models). Refer to your owner's manual for starting procedures with a dead battery. Have the battery recharged if necessary.

Pull off a spark plug cap, remove the spark plug, and reconnect the cap. Lay the plug against the cylinder head so its base makes a good connection, and turn the engine over with the kickstarter (engine rotation of at least 500 rpm). A fat, blue spark should jump across the electrodes. If there is no spark, or only a weak one, there is electrical system trouble. Check for a defective plug by replacing it with a known good

one. Do not assume a plug is good just because it is new.

Once the plug has been cleared of guilt, but there is still no spark, start backtracking through the system. If the contact at the end of the spark plug wire can be exposed, it can be held about ⅛ in. from the head while the engine is turned over to check for a spark. Remember to hold the wire only by its insulation to avoid a nasty shock. If the plug wires are dirty, greasy, or wet, wrap a rag around them so you do not get shocked. If you do feel a shock or see sparks along the wire, clean or replace the wire and/or its connections.

If there is no spark at the plug wire, look for loose connections at the coil and battery. If all seems in order there, check next for oily or dirty contact points. Clean points with electrical contact cleaner, or a strip of paper. With the ignition switch turned on, open and close the points manually with a screwdriver.

No spark at the points with this test indicates a failure in the ignition system. Refer to this chapter for checkout procedures for the entire system and individual components. Refer to this chapter also for ignition timing.

Note that spark plugs of the incorrect heat range (too cold) may cause hard starting. Set gaps to specifications. If you have just ridden through a puddle or washed the motorcycle and it will not start, dry off plugs and plug wires. Water may have entered the carburetor and fouled the fuel under these conditions, but wet plugs and wires are the more likely problem.

If a healthy spark occurs at the right time, and there is adequate gas flow to the carburetor, check the carburetor itself at this time. Make sure all jets and air passages are clean, check float level, and adjust if necessary. Shake the float to check for gasoline inside it, and replace or repair as indicated. Check that the carburetors are mounted snugly, and no air is leaking past the manifold. Check for a clogged air filter.

Compression, or the lack of it, usually enters the picture only in the case of older motorcycles. Worn or broken pistons, rings, and cylinder bores could prevent starting. Generally a gradual power loss and harder starting will be readily apparent in this case.

Compression may be checked in the field by turning the kickstarter by hand and noting that an adequate resistance is felt.

An accurate compression check gives a good idea of the condition of the basic working parts of the engine. To perform this test, you need a compression gauge. The motor should be warm.

1. Remove the plug on the cylinder to be tested and clean out any dirt or grease.

2. Insert the tip of the gauge into the hole, making sure it is seated correctly.

3. Open the throttle all the way and make sure the chokes on the carburetors are open.

4. Crank the engine several times and record the highest pressure reading on the gauge. Run the test on both cylinders.

5. If the readings vary more than 15 psi between cylinders, proceed to the next step.

6. Pour a tablespoon of motor oil into the suspect cylinder and record the compression.

If oil raises the compression significantly—10 psi in an old engine the rings are worn and should be replaced.

If the compression does not rise, one or both valves are probably not seating correctly.

Valve adjustments should be checked next. See Chapter Two. Sticking, burned, or broken valves may hamper starting. As a last resort, check valve timing. See Chapter Four.

STARTER

Starter system troubles are relatively easy to isolate. The following are common symptoms and causes.

1. *Engine cranks very slowly or not at all.* Turn on the headlight. If the light is very dim, the battery or connecting wires are probably at fault. Check the battery. Check the wiring for breaks, shorts, or dirty connections.

If the battery or connecting wires are not at fault, turn the headlight on and try to crank the engine. If the light dims drastically, the starter is probably shorted to ground. Remove it and test as described.

If the light remains bright, or dims only slightly when trying to start the engine, the trouble may be in the starter, relay, or wiring. Perform the following steps to isolate the cause.

WARNING
Disconnect the coil wire to prevent accidental starting. Keep away from moving parts when working near the engine.

a. If the starter does not respond at all, connect a 12-volt test lamp between the starter terminal and ground. Turn the ignition key to START. If the lamp lights, the starter is probably at fault. Remove it and test the unit. If the lamp does not light, the problem is somewhere in the starting circuit. Perform the next steps.

b. Connect a jumper wire between the battery and starter terminals on the starter relay. If the starter does not respond at all, the relay is probably defective. If the starter cranks normally, perform the next step.

c. Connect a test lamp between the starter terminal on the starter relay and ground. Turn the ignition key to START. If the lamp does not light, check the ignition switch and associated wiring. Turn the key to START and work it around in the switch. If the lamp lights erratically, the ignition switch is probably defective.

d. If the problem still has not been isolated, check all wiring in the starting circuit with an ohmmeter or other continuity tester. See wiring diagrams in Chapter Seven.

2. *Starter turns, but does not engage.* This problem may be caused by a defective starter drive mechanism, or broken gear teeth. Remove and inspect starter as described in Chapter Seven.

3. *Loud grinding noises when starter runs.* This may mean the teeth are not meshing properly, or it may mean the starter drive mechanism is damaged. In the first case, remove the starter and examine the gear teeth. In the latter case, remove the starter and replace the starter drive mechanism.

POOR IDLING

Poor idling may be caused by incorrect carburetor adjustment, incorrect timing, or ignition system defects. Check the gas cap vent for an obstruction.

MISFIRING

Misfiring can be caused by a weak spark or dirty plugs. Check for fuel contamination. Run the machine at night to check for spark leaks along plug wires and under the spark plug cap.

WARNING
Do not run engine in dark garage to check for spark leaks. There is considerable danger of carbon monoxide poisoning.

If misfiring occurs only at certain throttle settings, refer to Chapter Seven for specific carburetor problem involved. Misfiring under heavy load, as when climbing hills or accelerating, is usually caused by bad spark plugs.

FLAT SPOTS

If the engine seems to die momentarily when the throttle is opened and then recovers, check for a dirty main jet in the carburetor, water in the fuel, or an excessively lean mixture.

POWER LOSS

Poor condition of rings, pistons, or cylinders will cause a lack of power and speed. Ignition timing should be checked.

OVERHEATING

If the engine seems to run too hot all the time, be sure you are not idling it for long periods. Air-cooled engines are not designed to operate at a standstill for any length of time. Heavy stop-and-go traffic or slow hill climbing is hard on a motorcycle engine. A spark plug of the wrong heat range can burn the piston. An excessively lean gas mixture may cause overheating. Check ignition timing. Do not ride in too high a gear. Broken or worn rings may permit compression gases to leak past them, heating the head and cylinder excessively. Check oil level and use the proper grade of lubricants.

ENGINE NOISES

Experience is needed to diagnose accurately in this area. Noises are hard to differentiate and harder yet to describe. Deep knocking noises usually mean main bearing failure. A slapping noise generally comes from loose pistons. A light knocking noise during acceleration may be a bad connecting rod bearing. Pinging should be corrected immediately or damage to pistons will result. Compression leaks at the head/cylinder joint will sound like a rapid on-and-off squeal.

PISTON SEIZURE

Piston seizure is caused by incorrect piston clearances when fitted, fitting rings with improper end gap, too thin an oil being used, incorrect spark plug heat range, or incorrect ignition timing. Overheating from any cause may result in seizure.

EXCESSIVE VIBRATION

Excessive vibration may be caused by loose motor mounts, worn engine or transmission bearings, loose wheels, worn swing arm bushings, a generally poor running engine, broken or cracked frame, or one that has been damaged in a collision. See also *Poor Handling*.

CLUTCH SLIP OR DRAG

Clutch slip may be due to worn or glazed plates or improper adjustment. A dragging clutch could result from damaged or bent plates, improper adjustment, or uneven clutch spring pressure.

All clutch problems, except adjustments or cable replacement, require removal to identify the cause and make repairs.

1. *Slippage*—This condition is most noticeable when accelerating in high gear at relatively low speed. To check slippage, drive at a steady speed in fourth or fifth gear. Without easing up on the throttle, push in the clutch long enough to let engine speed increase (one or two seconds). Then let the clutch out rapidly. If the clutch is good, engine speed will drop quickly or the bike will jump forward. If the clutch is slipping, engine speed will drop slowly and the bike will not jump forward.

Slippage results from insufficient clutch lever free play, worn friction plates, or weak springs.

Riding the clutch can cause the disc surfaces to become glazed, resulting in slippage.

2. *Drag or failure to release*—This trouble usually causes difficult shifting and gear clash especially when downshifting. The cause may be excessive clutch lever free play, warped or bent plates, stretched clutch cable, or broken or loose disc linings.

3. *Chatter or grabbing*—Check for worn or misaligned steel plate and clutch friction plates.

TRANSMISSION

Transmission problems are usually indicated by one or more of the following symptoms:

a. Difficulty in shifting gears

b. Gear clash when downshifting

c. Slipping out of gear

d. Excessive noise in neutral

e. Excessive noise in gear

Transmission symptoms are sometimes hard to distinguish from clutch symptoms. Be sure the clutch is not causing the trouble before working on the transmission.

POOR HANDLING

Poor handling may be caused by improper tire pressure, a damaged frame or swing arm, worn shocks or front forks, weak fork springs, a bent or broken steering stem, misaligned wheels, loose or missing spokes, worn tires, bent handlebars, worn wheel bearings, or dragging brakes.

BRAKE PROBLEMS

Sticking brakes may be caused by broken or weak return springs, improper cable or rod adjustment, or dry pivot and cam bushings. Grabbing brakes may be caused by greasy linings which must be replaced. Brake grab may also be due to out-of-round drums or linings which have broken loose from the brake shoes. Glazed linings or glazed brake pads will cause loss of stopping power.

ELECTRICAL PROBLEMS

Bulbs which continuously burn out may be caused by excessive vibration, loose connections that permit sudden current surges, poor battery connections, installation of the wrong type light bulb, or a faulty voltage regulator.

A dead battery, or one which discharges quickly, may be caused by a faulty alternator or rectifier. Check for loose or corroded terminals. Shorted battery cells or broken terminals will keep a battery from charging. Low water level will decrease a battery's capacity. A battery left uncharged after installation will sulphate, rendering it useless.

A majority of light and horn or other electrical accessory problems are caused by loose or corroded ground connections. Check those first, and then substitute known good units for easier troubleshooting.

IGNITION SWITCH TROUBLESHOOTING

The ignition switch can be reached for trouble shooting tests without removing it from the machine.

1. Disconnect the main switch connector as shown in **Figure 1**.

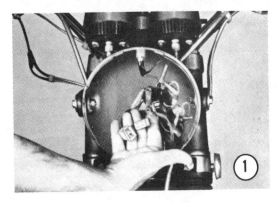

2. Check that voltage is getting to the switch at the red wire and proceed to isolate the trouble.

3. Use a continuity tester or ohmmeter to check for continuity between the red wire and the switch housing. There should be none.

4. Turn the switch to the DAY-NIGHT position and with one probe on the red wire, touch the brown wire end and then the red/yellow wire

end. There should be continuity at both these points. Turn the switch to the PARKING position and check for continuity between the red wire and the blue wire. There should be continuity.

5. If all of these tests check out, look for breaks in the main switch wires. If the wires are not broken or shorted, the main switch should be replaced.

CHARGING CIRCUIT TROUBLESHOOTING

Most charging system problems are caused by worn brushes (see Step 6), or by inadequate battery maintenance. Refer to the schematic (**Figure 2**) of the charging circuit for the following procedure.

1. Charging voltage output can be adjusted at the regulator as shown in **Figure 3**.

2. Start the engine and remove the housing and disconnect the fuse box wire leading to the battery. Hook up a voltmeter from the fuse box to ground. Rev the engine up to 2,500 rpm. The voltmeter should read 14.5-15 volts DC. Rotate the adjusting screw in to raise voltage or out to lower voltage. See **Figure 4** for schematic diagram of the hookup.

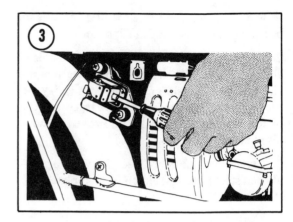

3. If the voltage cannot be brought within specified limits with the adjusting screw, troubleshoot the system in the order given below:

a. Check all connectors and wires for breaks or shorts. Engine vibration can loosen the connectors.

b. Check the voltage regulator. Look for dirty or pitted point surfaces. The central contact point occasionally fuses together. Look for broken wires. Clean the points if possible and solder any broken wires. Replace the regulator if any of the above conditions exist and cannot be corrected.

c. Connect an ohmmeter in the system after the regulator multiple connector is sepa-

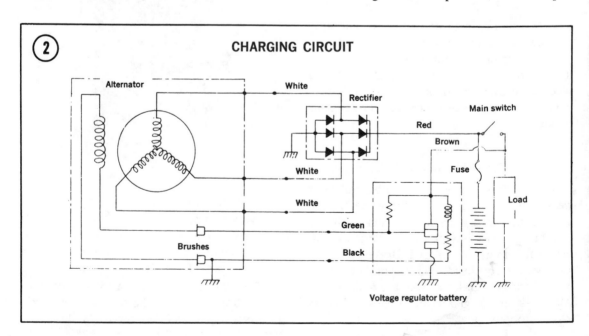

CHARGING CIRCUIT

Alternator — White — Rectifier — Main switch — Red — Brown — White — Fuse — White — Load — Green — Brushes — Black

Voltage regulator battery

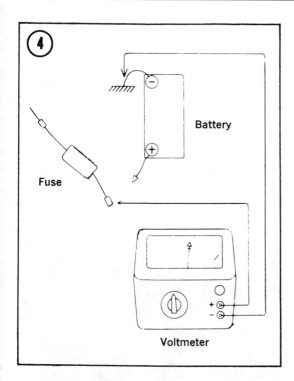

as 2 ohms resistance indicates a broken wire, cold-soldered joint, or burned points. Leave the connections as they are and push the central point arm midway between the top and bottom points. The reading should be around 9-10 ohms. If not, the 10-ohm regulator resistor or its connections are at fault.

e. With the same connections as in Step 3d, push the central point down until it contacts the bottom point. There should be a 7-8 ohm reading. Burned points can cause an incorrect reading, so be sure they are clean.

f. Connect the ohmmeter to the black and brown wires. Let the central point come up against the top point. Resistance now should read 36-38 ohms. Any incorrect reading not remedied by fixing a broken wire or cleaning points indicates a faulty regulator. If all tests check out, proceed to the rectifier.

rated. Connect one probe to the black wire and the other probe to the regulator base. It should read zero ohm resistance. Several ohms resistance means a frayed or broken black wire. Be sure the needle has been set to zero for all ohmmeter tests. Hook one meter probe to the brown wire and one 'o the green wire. See **Figure 5**.

4. Disconnect the rectifier wiring connector. See **Figure 6**. Check all rectifier wiring for breaks. If none are found, use an ohmmeter indexed on the 0-1,000-ohm scale for the following tests:

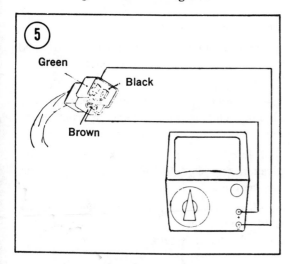

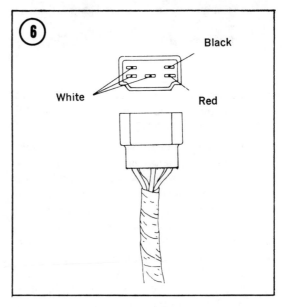

d. Remove the regulator cover and hold the central contact point against the top point. There should be no resistance. As little

a. Connect the black ohmmeter probe to the black wire. Touch the red probe to each white wire in turn. Reverse the probes and repeat the test. There should be a resistance of 75-150 ohms (1970-1973 models) or 9-10 ohms (1974-on models) one way and almost infinite resistance the other way.

b. Repeat the entire test, this time hooking up one probe to the red wire and touching each of the white wires and then reversing the probes. The results must be the same as above. Replace the rectifier if current flows both ways in either test above or if it does not flow at all. The rectifier must also be replaced if any wires are broken off at the diodes.

5. Check the alternator circuits as follows:

a. Disconnect the alternator multiple connector as shown in **Figure 7**.

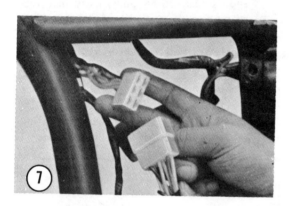

b. Check resistance between each white wire and any of the other white wires. All measurements should read 0.8-1.0 ohm.

c. With the ohmmeter set to read on the kilo ohms scale, clamp one probe to the stator housing and touch the other to each white wire. The meter should read infinity. Any readings other than described here indicate a faulty stator. It should be replaced.

6. Refer to the engine service chapter for brush service and perform the following checks:

a. Look for obvious wear or broken components. Wear limit for the brushes is 0.276 in. (7.0 mm).

b. Brush wiring shares the stator connector which was disconnected in the previous test. Check resistance between the green wire and the brush and between the black wire and the brush. There must be zero resistance or the wiring is frayed or broken.

7. Check the rotor windings with an ohmmeter as shown in **Figure 8**. Reading from one clean slip ring to the other should be 5-7 ohms. Set the ohmmeter to the kilo ohms scale and measure resistance between each slip ring and the core. The meter should read infinity. Any deviation from readings described indicates a faulty rotor.

TROUBLESHOOTING GUIDE

The following guide summarizes part of the troubleshooting process. Use it to outline possible problem areas, then refer to the specific chapter or section involved.

Loss of Power

1. *Poor compression*—Check piston rings and cylinder, head gasket, and for crankcase leak.

2. *Overheated engine*—Check lubricating oil supply, clogging of cooling fins, ignition timing, slipping clutch, and carbon in combustion chamber.

3. *Improper mixture*—Check for dirty air cleaner, restricted fuel flow, and clogged gas cap vent hole.

4. *Miscellaneous*—Check for dragging brakes, tight wheel bearings, defective chain, and clogged exhaust system.

Gearshifting Difficulties

1. *Clutch*—Check adjustment, springs, friction plates, steel plates, and oil quantity.

2. *Transmission*—Check oil quantity, oil grade, return spring or pin, change lever or spring, drum position plate, change drum, and change forks.

Brake Troubles

1. *Poor brakes* — Check brake adjustment, brake drum out-of-round or excessive disc run-out, oil or water on brake linings, and loose brake linkage or cables.

2. *Noisy brakes*—Check for worn or scratched linings, scratched drums or disc, and dirt in brakes.

3. *Unadjustable brakes*—Check for worn linings, drums, disc, and brake cams.

4. *Miscellaneous*—Check for dragging brakes, tight wheel bearings, defective chain, and clogged exhaust system.

Steering Problems

1. *Hard steering*—Check steering head bearings, steering stem head, and correct tire pressures.

2. *Pulls to one side*—Check for worn swing arm bushings, bent swing arm, bent steering head, bent frame, and front and rear wheel alignment.

3. *Shimmy*—Check for improper drive chain adjustment, loose or missing spokes, deformed wheel rims, worn wheel bearings, and improper wheel balance.

3

NOTE: If you own a 1978 or later model, first check the Supplement at the back of the book for any new service information.

CHAPTER FOUR

CYLINDER, CYLINDER HEAD, AND LUBRICATION SYSTEM

This chapter and Chapter Five provide information and procedures for removal, disassembly, repair, replacement, reassembly, and installation of the engine. If major work is to be done, it will be easier if the engine is on a bench or work stand rather than in the frame.

It is easier to work on a clean engine than a dirty one, and you will do a better job. Before starting, have engine and chassis steamed cleaned or clean them with a good commercial degreaser, following manufacturer's instructions.

Make certain you have the necessary tools available and a clean place in which to work.

It is a good idea to identify and mark parts as they are removed so that errors will be avoided during assembly and installation. Make certain all parts related to a particular cylinder, piston, connecting rod, and/or valve assembly are identified for installation in the proper place. Do not rely too heavily on memory; it may be days or weeks before you complete the job.

ENGINE

Removal

Figure 1 shows a sectional view of the 650 engine.

1. Drain the oil from the engine and transmission. See Chapter Two. Refer to **Figure 2**.
2. Turn vacuum (automatic) petcocks ON.

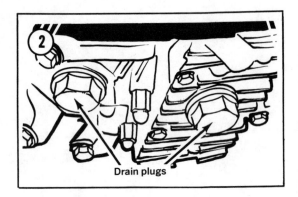
Drain plugs

Turn manual petcocks OFF. Disconnect the fuel crossover tube, if so equipped.

3. Raise the seat and lift the rear of the gas tank as shown (**Figure 3**) until the mounting bushing is clear of the anchor pin. The tank can then be slid toward the rear until it is free of the front mounts.

4. Remove the bolts holding both side covers as shown in **Figure 4**. Note that there is a flat washer, spring washer, and another flat washer under the bolt.

5. Disconnect the alternator wire loom found behind the air filter housing. See **Figure 5**.

6. Disconnect both throttle cables from their respective carburetors. See **Figure 6**.

7. On models equipped with foam air filters enclosed in a single housing, disconnect the

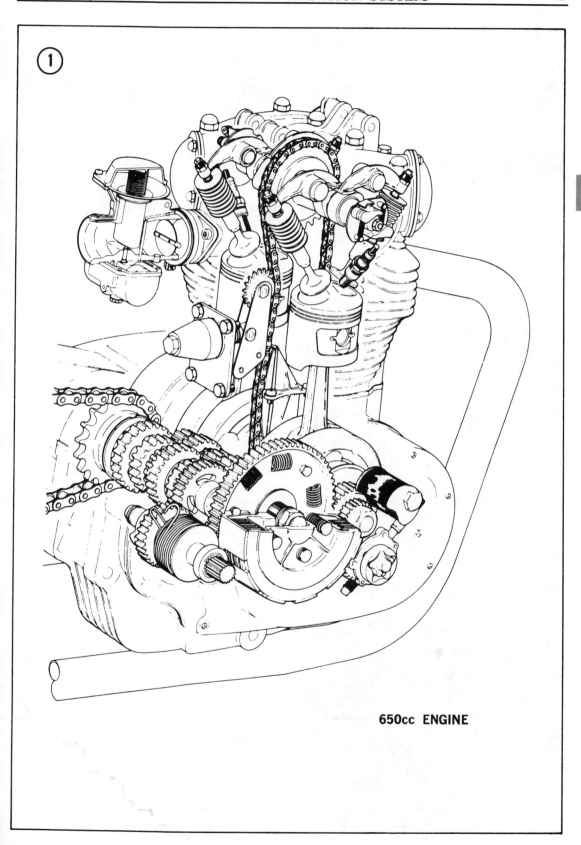

650cc ENGINE

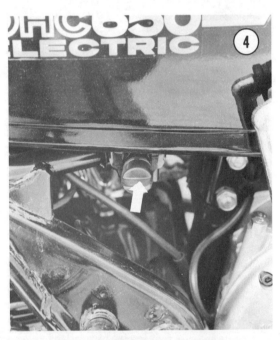

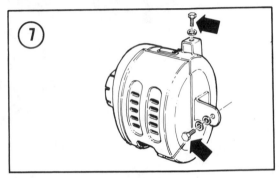

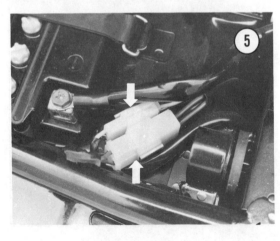

filter housing at the carburetor and at the frame mounting points. Then remove the entire air filter housing. On those models equipped with separate air filter units, remove the air filter mounting bolts as shown in **Figure 7**. Do not disconnect the filters at the carburetor.

8. Refer to **Figure 8**. Disconnect the fuel balance tube between the float bowls. Then loosen the carburetor-to-intake manifold attaching clamp. Repeat for opposite side. Remove the carburetors one at a time, beginning with the left one. Be careful not to damage the carburetor starter linkage. On those models equipped with separate air filter units, remove the carburetor with the air filter attached.

9. Disconnect the engine breather tube located above and between the carburetors.

10. Disconnect the neutral light lead on the engine cases. Refer to **Figure 9**.

11. Disconnect the spark plug leads.

12. On electric start models, remove the left front rocker cover and then the attached decompressor cable.

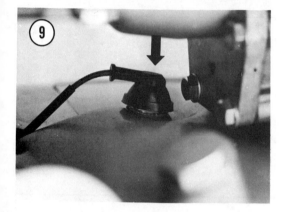

13. Disconnect the tachometer cable from the right front side of the engine as shown in **Figure 10**.

14a. Disconnect the point wires at the condenser and ignition switch connectors as shown. Refer to **Figure 11**. This wiring is routed along the main top frame tube.

14b. *On 1980 and later models:* disconnect the engine ground lead that goes to the top engine mount bracket.

15. Remove the horn and its bracket as a unit as shown in **Figure 12**.

16a. XS1, XS1B, XS2: Remove the left engine case cover for access to the drive chain and disconnect the chain master link. See **Figure 13**.

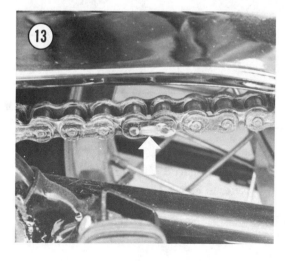

16b. All other models: After the master clip is removed, you will need a chain cutter to push out the press-fit master link. Using adapters shown in **Figure 14**, press the link out of its link plate by alternately pushing on both pins. See **Figure 15**.

> NOTE: *To install the chain, lay it over the sprockets so both loose ends meet just before the rear sprocket. Slide the link pins through both loose ends. Choose proper chain cutter adapters shown in* **Figure 16**. *Attach a new link plate and press it onto the link pins. Install a new master link clip.*

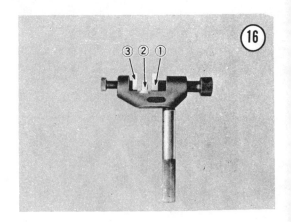

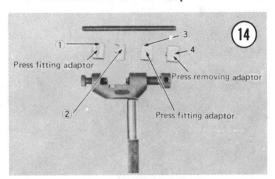

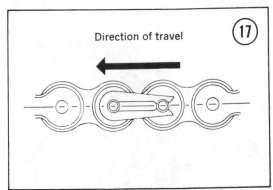

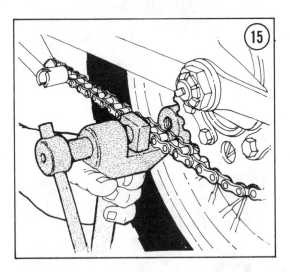

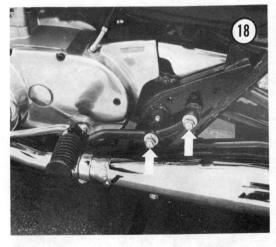

17. When the drive chain is reconnected, be sure the master link clip is replaced with its closed end toward the direction of chain travel as shown in **Figure 17**.

18. Refer to **Figure 18** and remove the left footpeg. A pair of rubber bushings will come off with the peg as it is removed. When replacing the footpeg, insert the bushings into the peg with the lip end of the bushings on the outside of the mounting hole.

19. Remove both exhaust pipes.

20. Remove the top engine mounting brackets as shown. Refer to **Figure 19**. If the brackets are removed at the points indicated in the photo, assembly will be easier than if the brackets are removed piece by piece.

4

21. Remove the brake pedal. See **Figure 20**.

22. Remove the remaining engine mounting bolts and brackets in the order shown. Refer to **Figure 21**. It is important that the bottom center bolt be removed last.

23. Lift the engine out from the left side as shown. Refer to **Figure 22**.

Installation

Install the engine in the reverse order of removal. Be sure the bottom middle engine mounting bolt is installed first. Torque 10mm bolts to 25-28 ft.-lb.; 8mm bolts to 14-18 ft.-lb.

CYLINDER HEAD COVER

Disassembly

Refer to **Figure 23** during the following procedure.

The engine must be removed from the frame for cylinder head cover removal or disassembly.

1. Remove the oil delivery line found on the front of the engine between the 2 cylinders.

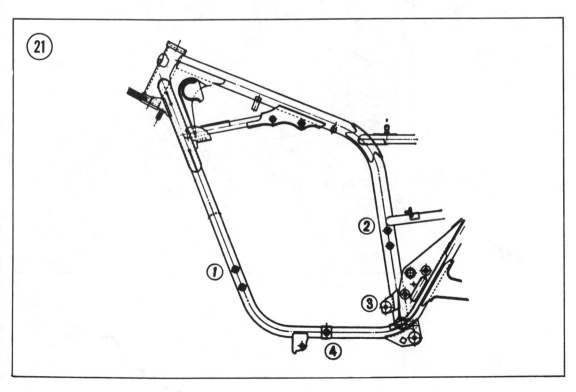

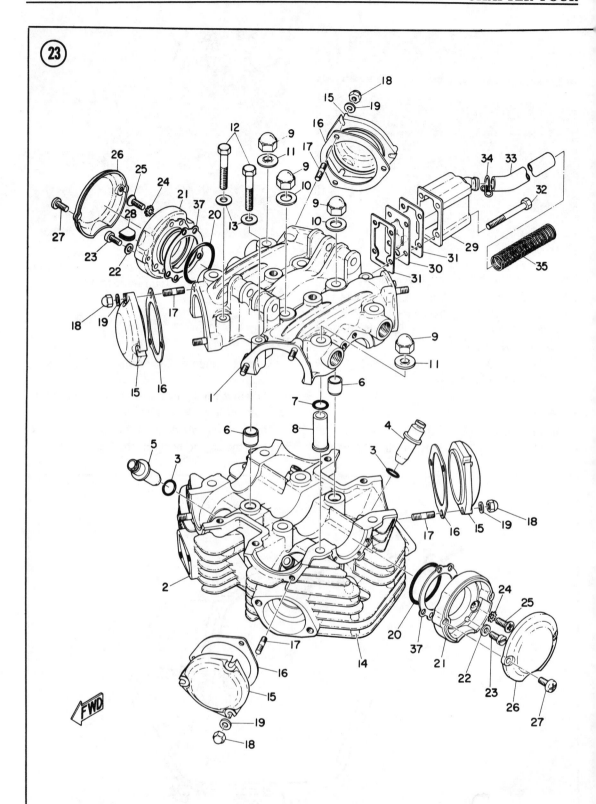

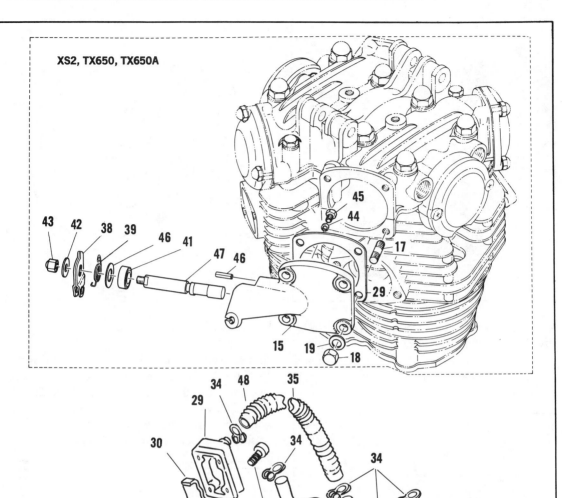

CYLINDER HEAD

1. Cylinder head cover
2. Cylinder head
3. O-ring
4. Intake valve guide
5. Exhaust valve guide
6. Dowel pin
7. O-ring
8. Cylinder head cover sleeve
9. Acorn nut
10. Plain washer
11. Washer
12. Bolt
13. Plain washer
14. Absorber
15. Cover
16. Gasket
17. Stud

18. Crown nut
19. Plain washer
20. O-ring
21. Breaker base plate
22. Plain washer
23. Breaker plate screw
24. Star washer
25. Flat head screw
26. Breaker cover
27. Screw
28. Plug
29. Breather cover assembly
30. Breather plate
31. Breather cover gasket
32. Bolt
33. Breather pipe
34. Pipe clamp

35. Balance pipe
   outer spring
36. Breather pipe
37. Breather cover gasket
38. Decompression lever
39. Decompression spring
40. Spring pin
41. Oil seal
42. Washer
43. Crown nut
44. Flat washer
45. Stopper bolt
46. Flat washer
47. Decompression cam
48. Support spring

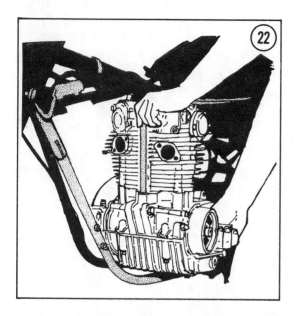

2. Remove the 4 tappet covers. Refer to **Figure 24** and remove the nuts and bolts in the sequence shown. Use a rubber mallet around the edges of the cover to break it loose if necessary.

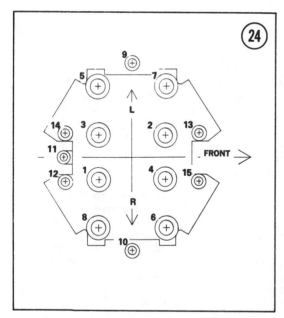

3. To remove the ignition point unit, remove the 2 slotted head screws holding the point assembly backing plate. Refer to **Figure 25**. Remove the 3 Phillips head screws to remove the point housing. Use a soft mallet to tap the housing loose if necessary.

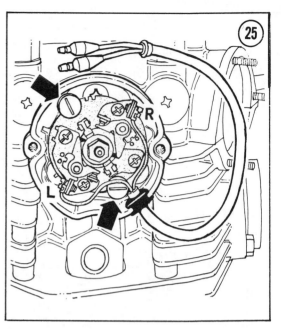

4. Disassemble the ignition advance unit. Refer to **Figure 26**. Remove the locknut and notched plate and pull the advance rod out from the left side. To avoid losing or mixing up these parts with others, reassemble the notched plate, lockwasher, and locknut on the advance rod.

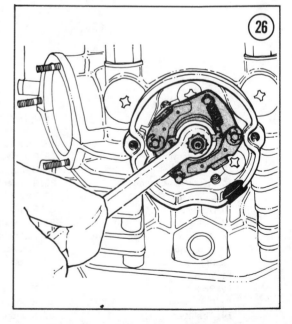

5. Use a punch and hammer as shown to loosen the ring nut holding the advance unit in place. Refer to **Figure 27**. Slide the advance unit out

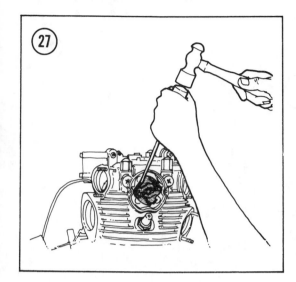

a little at a time as the ring nut is loosened to keep the nut from binding against the advance unit.

6. Remove the advance unit locating pin with needle-nosed pliers as shown in **Figure 28** and take out the 3 Phillips head screws securing the advance unit housing. Use a soft mallet to tap the housing loose if necessary.

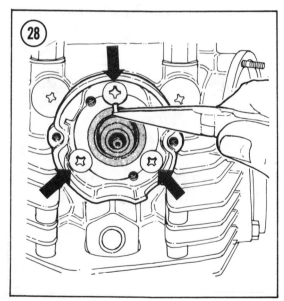

Assembly

1. Use 30-weight engine oil to lubricate all head cover retaining bolts and studs prior to torqueing them down. This must be done to avoid shearing them during reassembly.

2. Use a non-hardening gasket cement such as Yamaha Bond No. 4 on the head and cover mating surfaces and fit the head cover in place on the head. Tighten all nuts and bolts finger-tight. Refer to **Figure 29** and follow the sequence given when tightening nuts and bolts. A torque wrench must be used to tighten bolts to the torque figures found in Figure 29.

Go over the sequence several times, tightening the nuts and bolts a little at a time and as evenly as possible to prevent warping the head.

3. Install the ignition point housing and the centrifugal advance housing.

4. Install the advance locating pin. Refer to **Figure 30**.

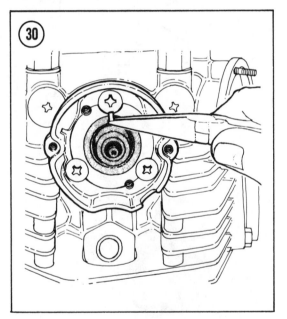

5. If a greasy deposit was found on the points when they were inspected, check the oil seal shown in **Figure 31** and replace if necessary. Use a new gasket between the housing and head covers if needed. Grease the lip of the oil seal before the housing is installed.

6. Install the centrifugal advance unit in its housing. Line up the notch in the back of the unit with the locating pin and screw the ring nut onto the camshaft end. Tighten the ring nut securely using a punch and hammer.

7. Install the notched disc and engage the weight arms into their proper slots on the disc. See **Figure 32**.

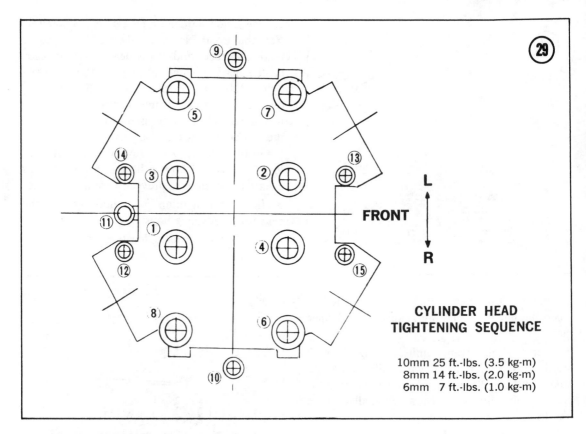

CYLINDER HEAD
TIGHTENING SEQUENCE

10mm 25 ft.-lbs. (3.5 kg-m)
8mm 14 ft.-lbs. (2.0 kg-m)
6mm   7 ft.-lbs. (1.0 kg-m)

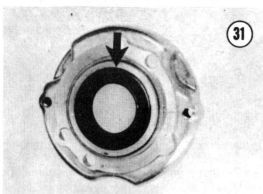

8. The disc surface has an arrow showing direction of rotation. This arrow must be visible. The color marks on the backing plate and disc must also match. The advance unit will not operate correctly if the disc is installed with the wrong side out or if it is installed 180 degrees out of phase.

9. Grease the needle bearings inside each end of the camshaft with light grease. This should be done each time this unit is disassembled. See **Figure 33**.

10. Insert the governor rod into the camshaft from the left side. Rotate the rod until the locating pin, which sticks up at the threaded end of the governor rod, slips into the inner notch in the governor unit disc. Install and tighten the locknut. See **Figure 34**.

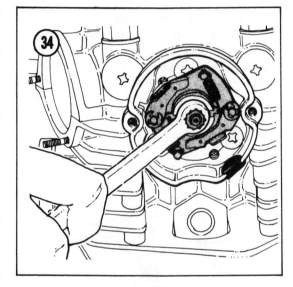

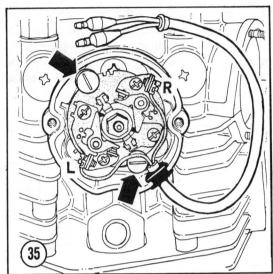

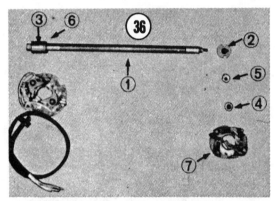

1. Governor rod
2. Disk
3. Point cam
4. Lockwasher
5. Nut
6. Shim(s)
7. Governor

11. Expand both sets of points so they fit over the point cam. An "R" (indicating right set of points) is stamped just below the points. This set must be installed at the top of the housing. Install and tighten both securing screws. See **Figure 35**. Check the point wire rubber grommet and replace if necessary. Install the point housing cover.

12. Install the oil delivery line at the front of the engine. After the engine has been warmed up, check the line for leaks at the attaching points.

ADVANCE ROD UNIT

Disassembly/Assembly

See *Cylinder Head Cover* procedure for removal. **Figure 36** shows the advance rod unit completely disassembled.

1. To completely disassemble the advance rod, refer to **Figure 37**. Remove the nut and washer holding the point cam. Some late models have a washer behind the cam.

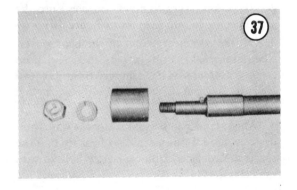

2. Note the location of the 2 pins pressed into the advance rod. These must be replaced if they fall out during handling. Refer to **Figure 38** for assembly procedure. The point cam fits over the longer machined area indicated in the drawing and the advance disc fits over the shorter machined area. The point cam and its spacing washer both have grooves which will line up with the locating pin.

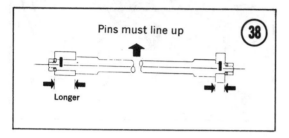

3. Use a 6mm screw or bolt screwed into the

Pins must line up

Longer

ROCKER ARM AND SHAFT

Removal/Installation

1. Take off the 4 rocker shaft covers. Refer to **Figure 39** and remove the shouldered sleeves and O-rings shown.

5. Check each rocker arm for wear at the points shown. Refer to **Figure 41**. Use an inside micrometer as shown in **Figure 42**. Measure the rocker shaft diameter. If the difference between the shaft diameter and the rocker I.D. is greater than 0.004 in. (0.10 mm), replace both.

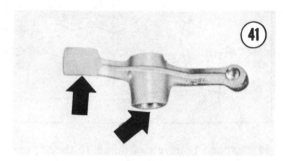

2. Use a 6mm screw or bolt screwed into the rocker shafts to pull them out (**Figure 40**).

3. Lift the rocker arms out of the head cover. Keep each rocker arm with its shaft and keep track of each unit as it is removed from the head cover so they can be reinstalled in their original positions.

4. When replacing the shafts, use the 6mm bolt or screw used for disassembly to ensure that the shafts are replaced with the screw hole toward the outside.

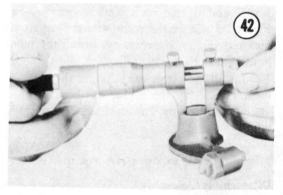

6. Check the cam lobe contacting surface indicated in **Figure 43** for grooves, scratches,

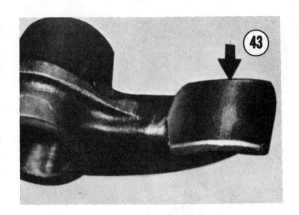

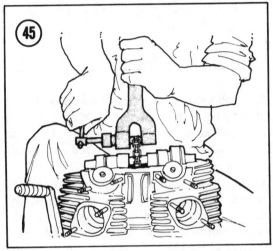

CYLINDER HEAD

Cam Chain Removal

Figure 44 shows the cylinder head and valves.

1. Use the Yamaha chain breaker as shown in **Figure 45**. Wrap a rag around the sprocket to keep metal chips from falling into the engine.

flaking, or discoloration of the metal from overheating. Check the cam lobes for the same problems.

7. Check the rocker shaft for grooving and discoloration. Replace if either is present and check the oil pump and oil passages if overheating is suspected.

8. Coat all parts with a light film of engine oil during assembly and proceed in the reverse order of disassembly. Replace the shaft hole covers.

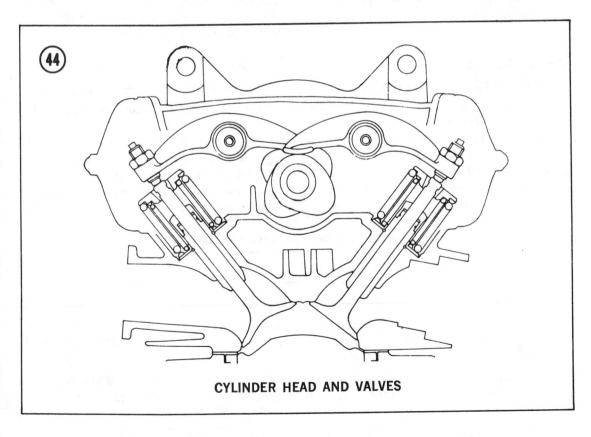

CYLINDER HEAD AND VALVES

2. **Figure 46** shows the master chain link which is to be separated. The rivet heads have punch marks and slots across their heads. Use a new link during assembly.

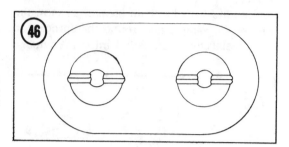

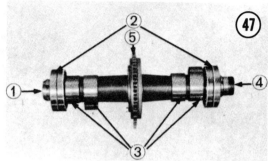

1. Needle bearing
2. Single row ball bearings (4)
3. Cam lobes
4. Governor mounting threads
5. Camshaft sprocket

3. Hook a wire through the chain on both sides of the link to be separated to keep the chain from falling down into the engine. Wrap the wire ends around a stud after the chain ends are free.

4. If only the chain is being serviced and the engine will not be disassembled completely, attach a piece of wire slightly longer than the chain itself to one end of the chain and pull it through so the chain can be easily replaced.

5. Clean the cam chain and check for excessive wear.

Camshaft Removal

See **Figure 47** for camshaft components.

1. Remove the cam chain or hold it out of the way as shown under *Cam Chain.*

2. Check the camshaft for signs of visible damage or wear. Look for discoloration, flaking, or pitting. If any of the above conditions are obvious, the camshaft will have to be replaced. If wear or damage is found, inspect the corre-

sponding rocker arm surface for a similar condition.

3. Even with no visible wear, check the cam lobes with a micrometer and refer to **Table 1** for permissible limits.

4. Clean the camshaft bearings in solvent.

5. Inspect the camshaft bearings for pitting, rusting, or chatter marks and replace if any damage is found. If the old bearings will be reused, grease them as soon as possible after inspection to keep them from rusting.

Camshaft Installation

Refer to **Figure 48** for following procedure.

1. Time the camshaft before the cam chain is secured.

2. Place the camshaft in position, with all bearings slid in toward the center of the camshaft and with the threaded end (**Figure 49**) to the right. Hold the cam bearings in toward the sprocket and move the camshaft back and forth

Table 1   CAM LOBE SPECIFICATIONS

	Cam Lift Standard Value	(A) Wear Limit
XS1; XS1B; XS2		
Intake	0.1561-0.1562 in. (39.58-39.68mm)	0.1550 in. (39.39mm)
Exhaust	0.1547-0.1548 in. (39.31-39.41mm)	0.1550 in. (39.39mm)
All other models		
Intake	0.1572-0.1576 in. (39.94-40.04mm)	1.569 in. (39.84mm)
Exhaust	0.1574-0.1578 in. (39.98-40.08mm)	1.570 in. (39.88mm)

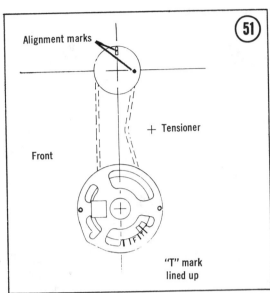

to line the camshaft sprocket up with the crankshaft sprocket. The sprockets will be lined up when the inner bearing on each side overlaps an equal distance from the inner edge of each of the camshaft bearing bosses.

3. Line up the rotor timing mark with the "T" mark on the stator as shown in **Figure 50**. This brings the pistons to top dead center (TDC). If the stator is off the engine, find top dead center by using the dowel pin method detailed in the *Valve Timing* section in this chapter. Be sure the piston is on its compression stroke (with intake and exhaust valves closed) and rotate the engine a few degrees forward and backward to ensure that all slack is taken up and the piston is ready to start downward.

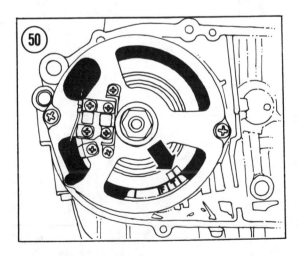

4. The groove in the left side of the camshaft sprocket must line up in a vertical direction with the sprocket centers. Refer to **Figure 51**. The punch mark on the camshaft sprocket should be parallel with the head and barrel surface. Check

by laying a straightedge across the head surface and compare the punch mark position.

5. The cam chain should be installed so it has no slack in the front run. Slack in the rear run (toward the back of the engine) will be taken up by the cam chain tensioner. Use a new link and connect the chain with a riveter as shown in **Figure 52**.

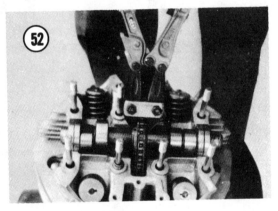

6. Adjust chain tension as detailed under *Cam Chain Tensioner Adjustment*.

7. Check the sprocket timing marks to ensure they are correct before proceeding.

Carburetor Manifold
Removal/Installation

1. Remove the Allen screws from each carburetor manifold.

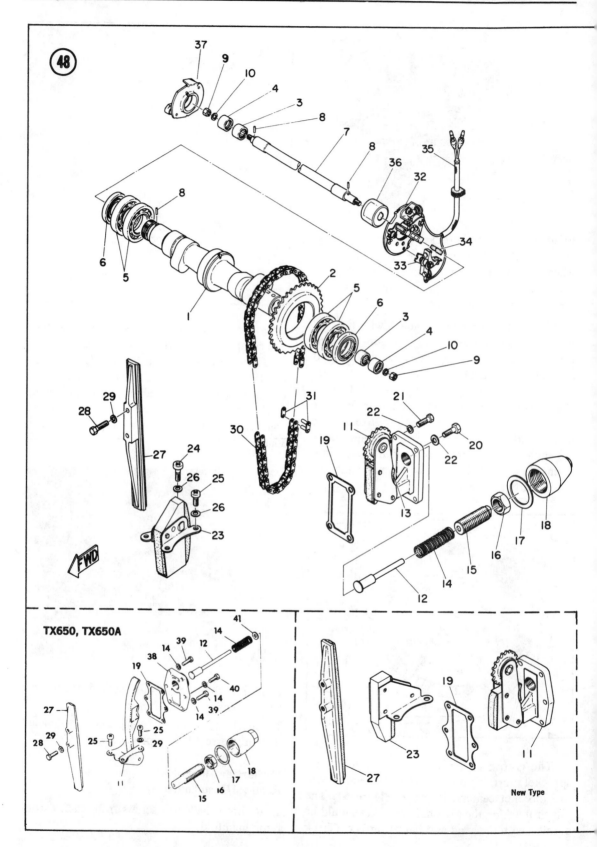

TX650, TX650A

FWD

New Type

CAMSHAFT
AND CHAIN TENSIONER

1. Camshaft
2. Sprocket
3. Breaker shaft bearing or bushing
4. Seal
5. Bearing
6. Oil seal
7. Breaker shaft
8. Dowel pin
9. Nut
10. Lockwasher
11. Tensioner arm assembly
12. Rod
13. Damper
14. Spring
15. Bolt
16. Locknut
17. Gasket
18. Cap
19. Tensioner case gasket
20. Reamer bolt
21. Bolt
22. Plain washer
23. Stopper guide
24. Reamer bolt
25. Pan head screw
26. Lockwasher
27. Stopper guide
28. Bolt
29. Holder gasket
30. Chain
31. Master link
32. Breaker plate assembly
33. Contact breaker
34. Lubricator
35. Lead wire
36. Cam
37. Governor assembly

TX650, TX650A

38. Tensioner holder
39. Bolt
40. Bolt
41. Rubber damper

2. Check the equalizer tube for cracking or collapsing and replace if necessary (XS1 and XS1B models). Refer to **Figure 53**.

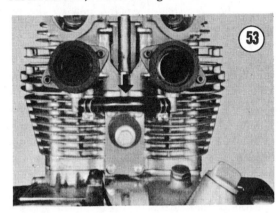

Be sure the coil spring originally fitted inside the tube is still in place.

Cylinder Head Removal/Installation

1. Refer to **Figures 54 and 55** for the remaining head bolts. Remove the 2 bolts beneath the spark plug holes and the single screw between the intake manifolds.

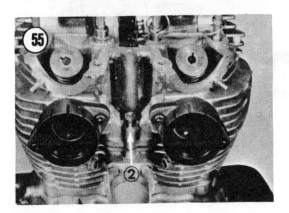

2. Hold the cam chain wires while a helper lifts the head up and off the studs.

NOTE
After the cylinder head is removed from the engine, tie the ends of the chain to the upper frame bar with wire.

3. Check the head for warping by cleaning it thoroughly and placing it on a surface plate. Severe warpage will be indicated if the head can be rocked in any direction. Try to insert a 0.001-0.002 in. feeler gauge between the head and surface plate all around the head. If the gauge can be inserted, the head must be machined.

4. Head milling must not exceed 0.010 in. or piston-to-head clearance will be affected.

5. A new head gasket must be used each time the head has been removed. Note that the gasket will fit only one way. As the cylinder head is being slipped in place, guide the camshaft chain securing wires up through their proper slots in the head so the chain can be pulled into place.

6. Replace and tighten both bolts under the spark plug holes and the screw between the intake manifolds. It is a good idea to lightly screw both spark plugs in place at this time to keep foreign matter from falling into the combustion chamber.

Valve Removal/Installation

1. Remove the valves as shown in **Figure 56** using an automobile valve spring compressor. Compress each valve spring and tap the collar to free the keepers.

2. Remove the compressor.
3. Remove the collar and springs.
4. Remove the valve stem seal. If the valves will not come out easily, check for expansion

at the stem tip or keeper grooves. Remove excess metal carefully with a fine file. Forcing the valve through the guide may damage the guide. Valve components are shown in **Figure 57**.

5. Reverse procedure to install.

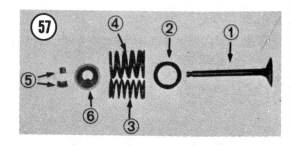

1. Valve
2. Valve spring seat
3. Inner valve spring
4. Outer valve spring
5. Keepers
6. Collar

Decarbonization

1. Use a carbon scraper and solvent to clean the combustion chambers, being careful to avoid scratching or otherwise damaging the metal surfaces.

2. Valves may be cleaned with a wire brush chucked in an electric drill.

Valve and Valve Seat Inspection

1. Check the valves for wear or damage. The valve stem end may show an indentation where it is constantly struck by the adjuster. If this indentation is more than 0.015-0.020 in. (0.4-0.5mm) deep, the tip must be carefully ground flat, removing only the minimum amount of metal necessary. Use of a commercial valve grinder is recommended.

2. Measure valve stem outside diameter and valve guide inside diameter. **Table 2** gives replacement specifications.

3. Check the valve for a bent stem by rolling it on a surface plate or sheet of glass. A bent valve must be replaced.

4. Check the portion of the valve which does the actual sealing against the valve seat for pits, scratches, and chipping. If damage is slight, the valve can often be made serviceable by lapping it to the valve seat.

Table 2   VALVE/GUIDE CLEARANCE

Valve	Minimum	Maximum
Intake	0.0008 in. (0.010mm)	0.004 in. (0.10mm)
Exhaust	0.0014 in. (0.035mm)	0.005 in. (0.12mm)

Valve Lapping

1. Lap a bad valve by applying a small quantity of valve lapping compound to the valve face and inserting the valve into its guide.

2. Use a vacuum cup type lapping handle (available from auto supply stores) to grip the valve head and rotate the tool between your palms. An alternate method is to use a piece of 5/16 in. inside diameter rubber tubing slipped over the valve stem after the valve is in place. Keep even pressure against the valve seat. Occasionally lift the valve off its seat, turn it ¼ turn and resume lapping. Begin with coarse grinding compound and end with fine.

3. Thoroughly clean all traces of grinding compound away according to directions on the container. Check the seat and valve face condition with blueing compound (Dykem). Apply the blueing to the valve face and rotate the valve completely in its seat. Blueing will remain in spots if the seat is not properly lapped. A matte surface completely around the valve seat indicates sufficient lapping.

4. Check seat condition further after the valves have been assembled (with springs, collars, and keepers all in place), by pouring solvent or kerosene into each intake and exhaust port in turn. The valve seats should allow no leakage. If they do, the lapping operation must be repeated.

Valve Cutting

1. If valve faces are heavily damaged they can be resurfaced with a mechanical grinder. After grinding they must be checked for sufficient margin thickness (**Figure 58**) and lapped to the valve seat as described previously.

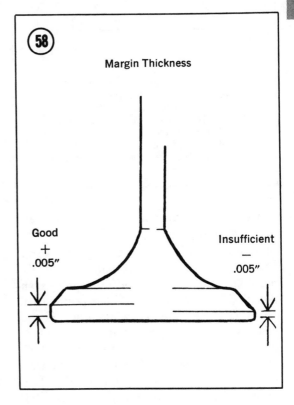

Margin Thickness

Good
+
.005"

Insufficient
—
.005"

2. Deep scratches in the valve stem will necessitate valve replacement.

3. If any valve seat is pitted or obviously worn, it will have to be resurfaced with a cutter. If a valve face has been recut, the valve seat will also need recutting. Whenever new valve guides are installed the valve seats should be checked.

4. Refer to **Figure 59** to determine the proper cutter to use for each portion of the valve seat.

5. Use blueing compound (Dykem) to measure valve seat width. Apply dye to the valve face

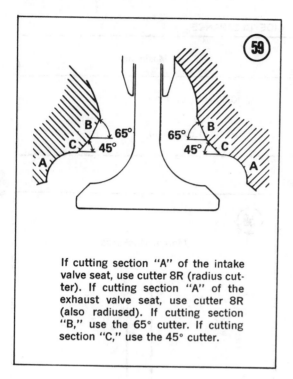

If cutting section "A" of the intake valve seat, use cutter 8R (radius cutter). If cutting section "A" of the exhaust valve seat, use cutter 8R (also radiused). If cutting section "B," use the 65° cutter. If cutting section "C," use the 45° cutter.

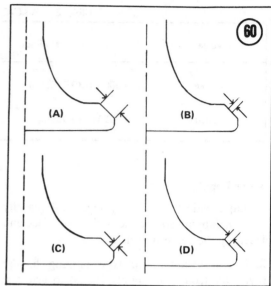

and apply a small quantity of lapping compound to the valve seat.

6. Insert the valve and rotate it quickly so the valve face comes in contact with the seat. Remove the valve and clean off the lapping compound. The valve seat width and position will be evident. Measure the width using vernier calipers. The valve seat should be uniform around the perimeter of the valve face, 0.051 in. (1.3mm) in width and centered on the valve face. Seat width can increase to 0.078 in. (2.0mm) before service is required, but 0.051 in. (1.3mm) is the desired dimension.

7. Refer to **Figure 60** and correct the valve seat width or positioning as follows: If the seat is centered but too wide as shown in drawing (A), use both "R" and 65 degree cutters to reduce seat width. If the seat is centered but too narrow as shown in drawing (B), use the 45 degree cutter to widen it to 0.051 in. (1.3mm). If the seat is narrow and too close to the valve margin as shown in drawing (C), use the "R" cutter and then the 45 degree cutter until the seat is centered and 0.051 in. (1.3mm) in width. If the seat is narrow and too near the bottom edge of the valve face as shown in drawing (D), use the 65 degree cutter and then the 45 degree cutter.

8. Remember the valves must be lapped to their seats if any cutting is required to valves or seats.

9. Valve stem seals (**Figure 61**) should be checked for hardening, cracking, or deterioration and replaced.

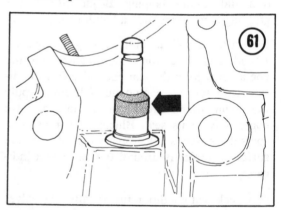

Valve Spring and Valve Guide Inspection

1. Valve springs must be checked individually for bending or cocking. They can be checked with a square while on a flat surface. The springs are ground so most of one coil on each end of the spring fits against either the collar or seat. If less than ¾ of either end coil is not flush against the seat or collar, the spring must be replaced.

2. Note that there are a pair of springs (inner and outer) with each valve. The springs should be measured and checked against the specifications given in **Table 3**.

Table 3   VALVE SPRING FREE LENGTH MINIMUM

Model	Outer	Inner
1970-1977	1.638 in. (41.69mm)	1.614 in. (41.00mm)
1978 and later	1.675 in. (42.55mm)	1.654 in. (42.00mm)

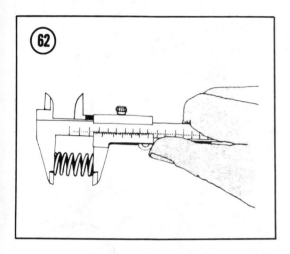

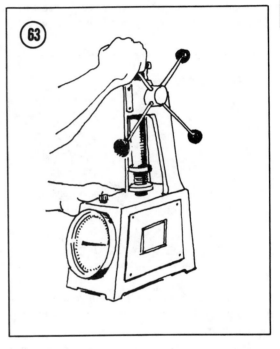

3. Measure the springs with vernier calipers as shown in **Figure 62**. If any spring's length is lowered more than 0.080 in. (2mm), it must be replaced.

4. A spring pressure gauge, such as the one shown in **Figure 63**, must be used for the pressure tests. Several readings should be taken on each spring and the results averaged. Refer this test to a dealer.

5. Valve guide specifications will be found in Table 2. If guides need to be replaced, heat the head in an oven to 200-400°F. Use the special drift available from Yamaha and a hammer as shown in **Figure 64** to drive out the old guide and drive in the new one.

> NOTE: *For proper interference fit, the valve guide must be 0.04mm larger than the hole in the head. If the guide is replaced due to natural wear, 1st and 2nd oversize (outside diameter of guide) are available from your dealer to install if the guide hole opens up slightly.*

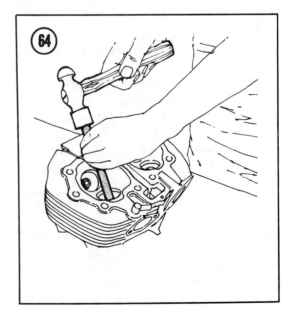

Valve Timing

A degree wheel can be used to check that valve timing is correct.

Be sure the cam chain tension is correct as detailed below before making this test.

1. Set intake and exhaust valves to 0.012 in. for all models. After valve timing is checked, set back to standard valve clearances.

2. Remove the left engine case cover.

3. Remove the stator and mount a degree wheel (**Figure 65**) on the rotor lock bolt as shown.

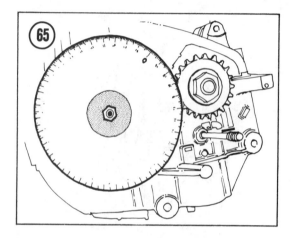

4. Remove both spark plugs and rotate the engine until both valves are closed to indicate top dead center.

5. Insert a dowel as shown in **Figure 66** and use it as an indicator to find true top dead center.

6. From the left side of the engine, turn the crank clockwise until the dowel starts to go down.

7. Turn the engine counterclockwise until the dowel rises as far as it will go.

8. Turn the engine slowly. Top dead center will be just as the dowel starts to go down again with the engine being rotated counterclockwise and with all the slack taken out. Mount a pointer so it matches the "0" on the degree wheel.

9. Mount a dial indicator as shown in **Figure 67** over an intake valve adjuster.

10. Rotate the engine counterclockwise until all slack in the drive chain is taken up and the dial indicator shows the intake valve just starting to open. The degree wheel should show the valve opening at 47 degrees before top dead center.

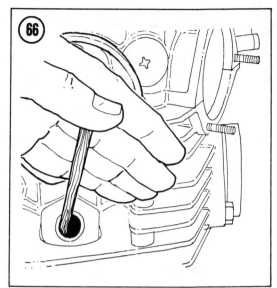

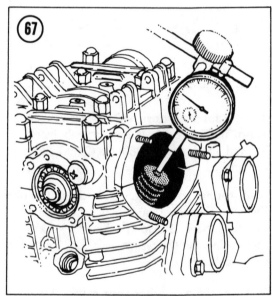

It is possible for the camshaft sprocket to be misaligned one tooth either way. If the sprocket is misaligned, the cam chain must be separated again and reconnected with the cam chain sprocket positioned correctly.

11. Adjust the valves (Chapter Two).

CYLINDER REMOVAL/INSPECTION

Refer to **Figure 68** during the following procedure.

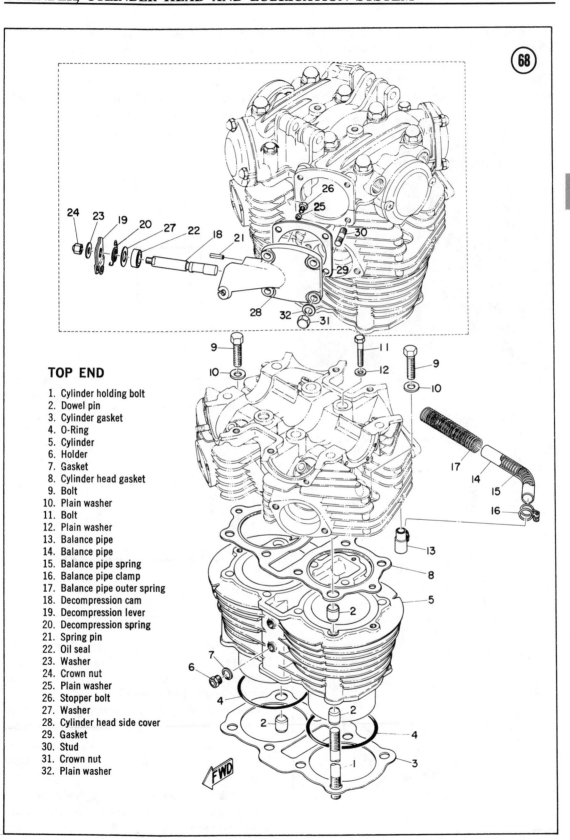

68

TOP END

1. Cylinder holding bolt
2. Dowel pin
3. Cylinder gasket
4. O-Ring
5. Cylinder
6. Holder
7. Gasket
8. Cylinder head gasket
9. Bolt
10. Plain washer
11. Bolt
12. Plain washer
13. Balance pipe
14. Balance pipe
15. Balance pipe spring
16. Balance pipe clamp
17. Balance pipe outer spring
18. Decompression cam
19. Decompression lever
20. Decompression spring
21. Spring pin
22. Oil seal
23. Washer
24. Crown nut
25. Plain washer
26. Stopper bolt
27. Washer
28. Cylinder head side cover
29. Gasket
30. Stud
31. Crown nut
32. Plain washer

1. The cylinder can be removed after the head cover and head have been disassembled as detailed previously. If the oil line fitting has not been removed during head cover removal, it should be taken off now as shown in **Figure 69**.

2. If the cylinder will not come free, tap it gently with a rubber mallet. As the cylinder is lifted up and off, exercise caution that the pistons do not fall against the front or rear of the crankcase. Clean rags placed in the crankcase opening will keep foreign matter from falling into the engine. See **Figure 70**.

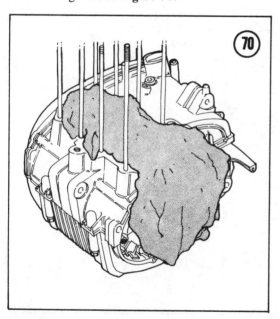

3. Refer to **Figure 71** for cylinder bore measurement procedures. Subtract the bottom bore measurement from the top bore measurement to obtain cylinder taper. Cylinder bore size should not exceed 2.954 in. (75.1mm) and taper should not exceed 0.002 in. (0.05mm).

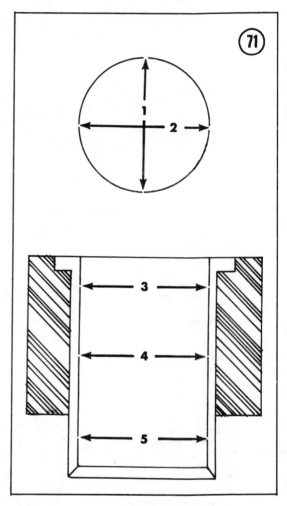

4. Little wear and/or light scratches or nicks can be taken care of by honing the bore with a commercial cylinder hone chucked in a variable speed electric drill run at low speed. The hone should be moved from top to bottom in the bore at an even speed to obtain a cross-hatch pattern.

5. Heavy wear or deep scratches will necessitate boring out the cylinder. Pistons are available in 4 oversizes.

6. Check the upper edge of the cylinder bore for a ridge and use a commercially available ridge reamer if necessary.

CAM CHAIN VIBRATION DAMPENER AND IDLER

1. The cam chain vibration dampener is located in the cavity between the cylinders. If the engine is run with the cam chain too loose, it may wear out the dampener. Two bolts at the front of the cylinder secure the dampener. See **Figure 72**.

2. The cam chain idler assembly sits in the top engine case half (**Figure 73**) and can be removed after the cylinders have been removed by taking out the 4 securing screws. Check for damage or excessive wear. Note the 2 slotted screws are installed on the right side and the 2 Phillips screws on the left side, as shown.

3. Reverse procedure to install.

CAM CHAIN TENSIONER

Removal/Installation

Figure 74 shows the cam chain tensioner.

1. Remove the 4 mounting bolts shown in **Figure 75** (6 bolts on later models) and pull the tensioner out.

> NOTE: *TX650 and TX650A are equipped with a tension bar instead of tension wheel.*

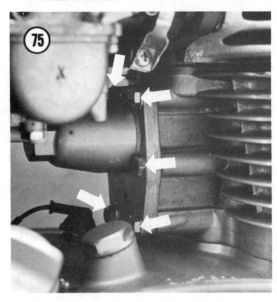

2. When replacing the tensioner, use a new gasket coated on both sides with gasket cement.

Adjustment

1. Rotate the engine in a counterclockwise direction (viewed from the left side) to take up slack in the front side of the chain.

2. Remove the cam chain tensioner cover and loosen the tensioner locknut.

3. Turn the adjuster in or out until the pushrod inside the adjuster is flush with the end of the adjuster (**Figure 76**).

4. Tighten the locknut and replace the cover. Cam chain adjustment should be checked according to the maintenance schedule.

PISTON, PINS, AND RINGS

Piston Removal/Inspection/Installation

1. Take out the outside circlip as shown in **Figure 77**. Push (do not hammer) the piston pin out with a soft drift.

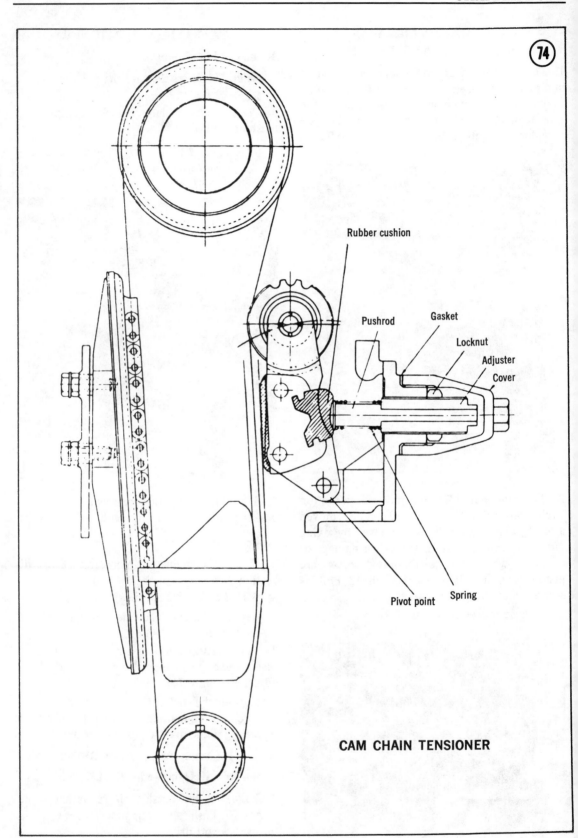

74

Rubber cushion

Pushrod   Gasket

Locknut

Adjuster

Cover

Pivot point   Spring

CAM CHAIN TENSIONER

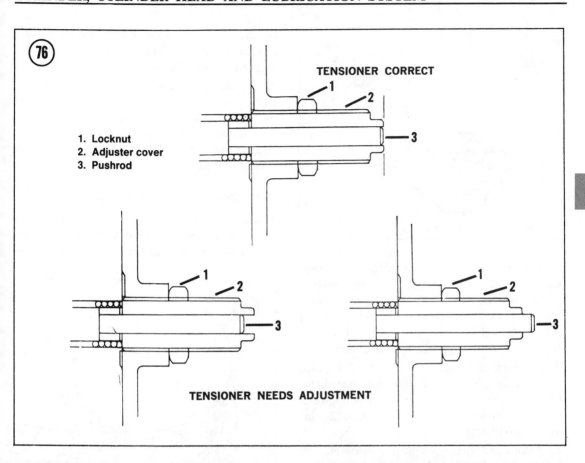

76

TENSIONER CORRECT

1. Locknut
2. Adjuster cover
3. Pushrod

1
2
3

1
2
3

1
2
3

TENSIONER NEEDS ADJUSTMENT

4

77

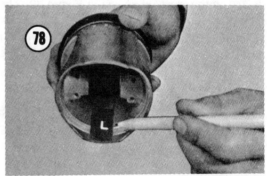

78

2. As each piston is disassembled from its connecting rod, keep the respective piston pin with the piston it came from and mark the pistons as shown in **Figure 78** so they can be replaced in the proper cylinder when the engine is reassembled.

3. Clean the pistons thoroughly, using a carbon scraper and solvent.

4. Look for cracks, signs of heat damage, score marks, or other damage. Score marks on the piston skirt which can be removed with emery cloth are not serious enough to warrant replacing the piston but indicate a failure in the lubrication system at some time or improper clearance when the pistons were fitted.

5. Measure the piston diameter as shown in **Figure 79**. Measure piston at right angles to the piston pin. Measure piston 0.394 in. (10mm) from the bottom on 1978 and later models; and 0.75 in. (20mm) from the bottom on earlier models.

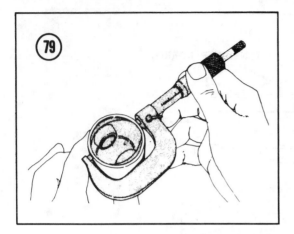

6. With maximum piston diameter and minimum cylinder bore measurement determined, piston-to-bore clearance can be calculated. Subtract maximum piston diameter from minimum cylinder bore diameter to arrive at the clearance. It should not exceed 0.0039 in. (0.10mm).

7. If clearance exceeds 0.0039 in. (0.10mm), the cylinder will have to be honed or bored and honed so the next oversize piston will give a standard clearance of 0.0020-0.0022 in. (0.050-0.055mm).

8. Pistons are stamped with a number and an arrow on the crown as shown in **Figure 80**. The number indicates piston size and the arrow shows the front of the piston. Pistons should always be installed with the arrow pointing toward the front of the engine.

> NOTE: The piston size number shown in Figure 80 is an abbreviation. It stands for 74.945mm. The '74' is always dropped. This piston is slightly smaller than the nominal bore size of 75mm.

9. Cylinder bore size is stamped on the bottom of the cylinder. It will be 75mm plus the number marked on the cylinder.

10. Install the pistons on their respective connecting rods. Oil the pins and push them into place. Note that the pistons are installed with the arrows on their crowns pointing forward. Always use new circlips whenever pistons have been removed.

Piston Ring Inspection/Installation

1. Use an old ring as shown in **Figure 81** to clean carbon from ring grooves. Check that oil relief holes (**Figure 82**) are not blocked.

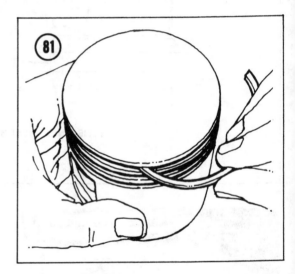

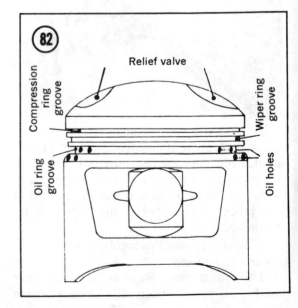

2. Piston rings are installed starting with the bottom, or oil control ring first. The oil control ring consists of 3 parts, shown in **Figure 83**.

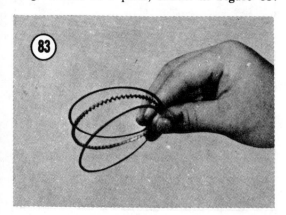

Start by installing the spacer portion in the bottom ring groove. The 2 remaining parts, called rails, are identical and have no particular top side. Insert one rail between the bottom part of the ring groove and the spacer and the other rail between the top part of the ring groove and spacer. Space the end gaps of the 3 ring components 120 degrees apart.

3. The middle and top rings are marked with an "R" as shown in **Figure 84** which must face up.

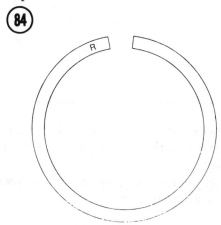

4. Place the middle ring end gap 120 degrees from the top rail gap of the oil control ring. Then place the top ring gap 120 degrees from the middle ring gap.

5. Top and middle rings are marked as shown in **Figure 85** to indicate oversizes.

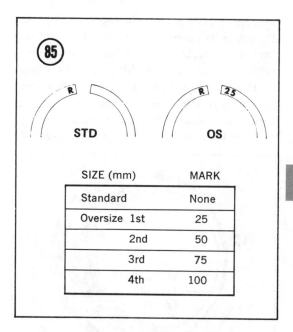

SIZE (mm)		MARK
Standard		None
Oversize	1st	25
	2nd	50
	3rd	75
	4th	100

6. Oil control ring components are all marked as indicated in **Figure 86** to identify oversizes.

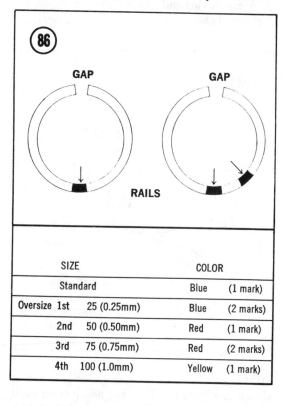

SIZE		COLOR	
Standard		Blue	(1 mark)
Oversize 1st	25 (0.25mm)	Blue	(2 marks)
2nd	50 (0.50mm)	Red	(1 mark)
3rd	75 (0.75mm)	Red	(2 marks)
4th	100 (1.0mm)	Yellow	(1 mark)

7. When checking rings for wear, be sure the rings and grooves are perfectly clean. All 3 rings should show the same type of wear so they

may be checked in the same fashion except that the expander component in the oil control ring cannot be checked for end gap. Instead, the 2 rails should be measured for proper end gap.

8. Use an inverted piston to push a ring down into the bore and place the cylinder over a white surface so a visual check can be made for gaps between the ring and cylinder wall (**Figure 87**).

9. Measure ring end gap as shown in **Figure 88**. Refer to **Table 4** for replacement specifications.

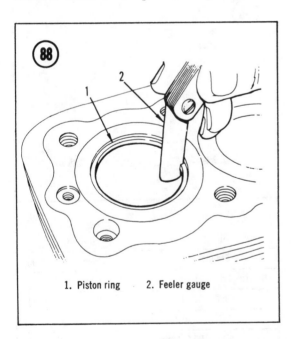

1. Piston ring   2. Feeler gauge

10. Check top and middle rings for side gap as shown in **Figure 89**. The ring and groove must be clean for this test. The wear limit is 0.006 in. (1.5mm). The oil control ring must have no side gap clearance.

Table 4   PISTON RING INSTALLED GAP

Model	Minimum	Maximum
Top and 2nd rings		
1970-1977	0.008 in. (0.2mm)	0.031 in. (0.8mm)
1978 and later	0.008 in. (0.2mm)	0.040 in. (1.0mm)
Oil ring		
All models	0.012 in. (0.3mm)	0.060 in. (1.5mm)

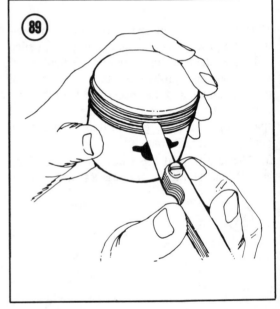

11. Replace the entire set of 3 rings if any of the tests detailed above show excess wear to any ring.

12. Rings must always be checked for proper end gap when installed.

Piston (Wrist) Pin Inspection

1. Refer to **Figure 90** in checking the piston pin for wear. Any noticeable grooving of the pin indicates a need for replacement but a dull finish at the center of the pin as shown in the photo is normal wear. As long as the dull area is not pitted, the pin can be reused.

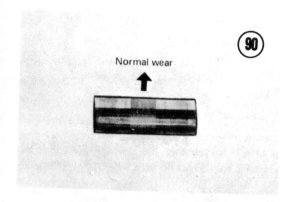

2. Blue discoloration caused by overheating means the pin should be replaced and the rod and lubrication system checked for a malfunction. If the pin is replaced, check the rod small end for wear. No bushing is fitted at this end.

> NOTE: *All models, except the early XS1, use no type of needle bearing in the rod top end. The rod is precision drilled and hardened. This is in effect a bushing type piston pin bearing. The piston pin must be a snug push fit thru the small rod hole.*

CYLINDER ASSEMBLY

1. With crankcase and cylinder surfaces clean, use a new base gasket (**Figure 91**) and new cylinder base O-ring if necessary (**Figure 92**) when replacing the cylinders.

2. Use a piston support plate or thin strips of wood across the crankcase mouth to support the pistons as the cylinder is fitted. Cushion the new base gasket with rags if necessary.

3. Apply clean engine oil or special engine assembly oil available from your dealer to the rings, pistons, and cylinder bores. Compress the rings with piston ring compressors and slip the cylinder down on the studs until it rests on the compressors. Work slowly and carefully to avoid breaking rings.

Rotate the engine to bring the pistons up into the bores at top dead center and remove the compressors and piston support plate or wood strips. Check that the base gasket has not been damaged and bring the cylinder down into place. See **Figures 93, 94, and 95.**

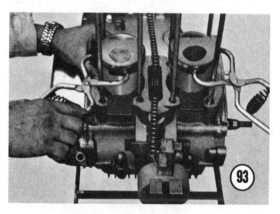

4. Before the engine is started, kick it over several times with the ignition off to pump oil into all passages.

PRIMARY CASE

Removal/Installation

1. Remove the primary case cover screws and the cover.

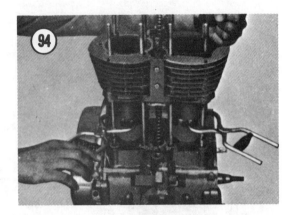

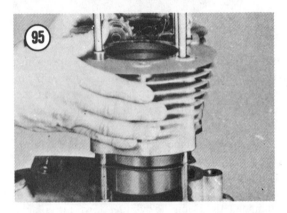

2. Unscrew the tachometer shaft locknut (1) as shown in **Figure 96** and drive the tachometer housing (2) out with a hammer and punch. Lift the gear (3) out.

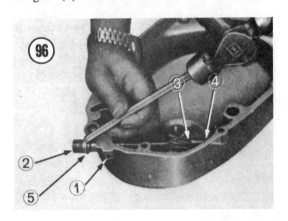

3. Assemble the tachometer drive mechanism in reverse order of disassembly. Check that the copper washer (4) is seated under the shaft and that the housing O-ring (5) is in good condition.

4. Install the case cover and screws.

OIL PUMP

Removal/Installation

Figure 97 is an exploded view of the oil pump.

1. Remove the tachometer drive gear. Take out the key on the shaft and remove the oil pump driven gear (**Figure 98**).

2. Remove the 3 set screws shown in **Figure 99** and pull up on the pump shaft as shown in **Figure 100** tapping the pump case as necessary with a soft mallet. Remove the inner and outer rotors.

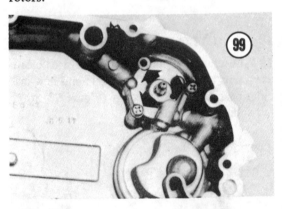

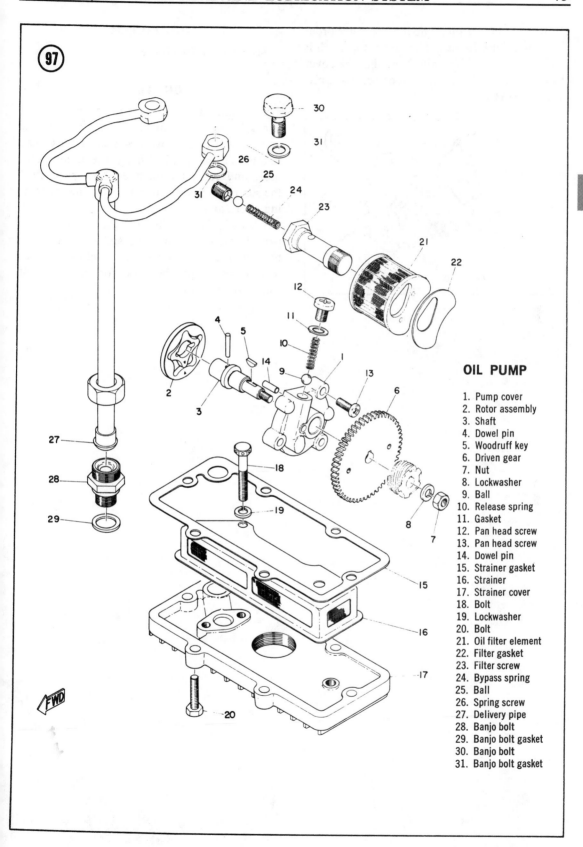

OIL PUMP

1. Pump cover
2. Rotor assembly
3. Shaft
4. Dowel pin
5. Woodruff key
6. Driven gear
7. Nut
8. Lockwasher
9. Ball
10. Release spring
11. Gasket
12. Pan head screw
13. Pan head screw
14. Dowel pin
15. Strainer gasket
16. Strainer
17. Strainer cover
18. Bolt
19. Lockwasher
20. Bolt
21. Oil filter element
22. Filter gasket
23. Filter screw
24. Bypass spring
25. Ball
26. Spring screw
27. Delivery pipe
28. Banjo bolt
29. Banjo bolt gasket
30. Banjo bolt
31. Banjo bolt gasket

3. Reassemble the oil pump in the reverse order of disassembly. Be sure the inner rotor notch is lined up with the shaft pin. Note that the cover has a locating pin to ensure correct assembly. See **Figure 101**.

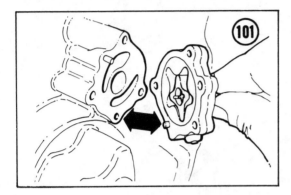

OIL FILTER

See Chapter Two for service.

BREAK-IN

A rebuilt engine requires the same care and break-in as a new engine because most of the parts are new. Never over-rev or allow the engine to labor at low speeds. Change the oil after 500 miles and clean the oil filter. New parts shed the scraps of metal which are left after machining operations.

Check ignition timing after the initial break-in period and tighten all nuts and bolts. If these few simple precautions are followed, your motorcycle should be good for thousands of trouble-free miles.

NOTE: If you own a 1978 or later model, first check the Supplement at the back of the book for any new service information.

CHAPTER FIVE

CLUTCH, TRANSMISSION, AND CRANKCASE

CLUTCH
Removal/Installation

Refer to **Figure 1** for the following procedure.

The clutch can be serviced with the engine in the motorcycle or on a workbench. Generally, most service operations are easier with the engine in the motorcycle because the engine is held firm when an impact driver is used to loosen the case screws and when the large nut on the basket and the pressure plate bolts are loosened and tightened.

1. Remove the right case cover.

2. Loosen the 6 clutch spring screws in a criss-cross pattern, a little at a time, until they are unscrewed and the pressure plate can be removed. See **Figure 2**.

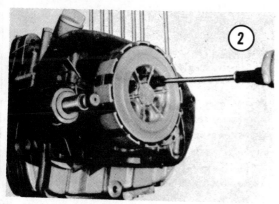

3. Remove the pushrod and ball bearing shown in **Figure 3** and the pushrod behind the ball. This pushrod may be more easily removed from the other end of the main shaft.

4. Construct a clutch holding tool by bolting a clutch driving plate and driven plate together so the clutch boss locknut can be loosened and removed as shown in **Figure 4**.

> NOTE: *Late model filter covers might be equipped with gasket instead of O-ring.*

5. Lift the clutch boss and plates and remove the 2 thrust washers and thrust bearing found behind the clutch boss. See **Figure 5**.

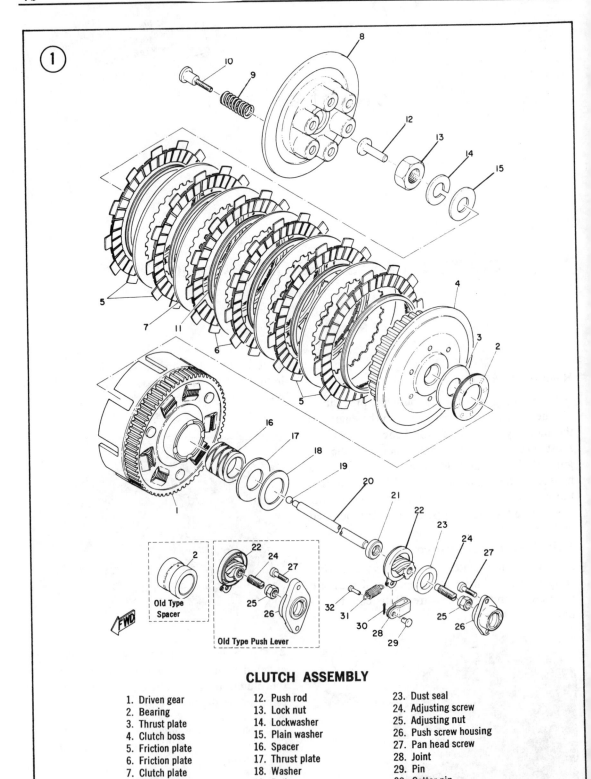

CLUTCH ASSEMBLY

1. Driven gear	12. Push rod	23. Dust seal
2. Bearing	13. Lock nut	24. Adjusting screw
3. Thrust plate	14. Lockwasher	25. Adjusting nut
4. Clutch boss	15. Plain washer	26. Push screw housing
5. Friction plate	16. Spacer	27. Pan head screw
6. Friction plate	17. Thrust plate	28. Joint
7. Clutch plate	18. Washer	29. Pin
8. Pressure plate	19. Ball	30. Cotter pin
9. Clutch spring	20. Pushrod	31. Return spring
10. Spring screw	21. Oil seal	32. Spring hook
11. Cushion ring	22. Push lever assembly	

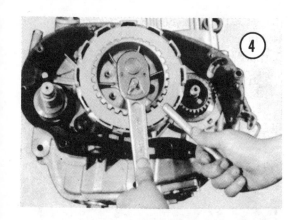

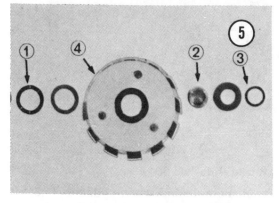

1. Thrust bearing and washers (between clutch boss and housing)
2. Spacer
3. Washers (right against axle bearing)
4. Clutch housing

6. Remove the clutch housing along with the clutch bushing spacer and thrust washer or washers found behind the housing. Refer to Figure 5.

7. Check clutch spring wear by measuring spring free length with vernier calipers. Standard free length is 1.350 in. (34.6mm) and if any spring is shorter by 0.04 in. (1mm) it should be replaced.

8. Measure friction plate wear as shown in **Figure 6**. Measure at several points on each plate and if the standard thickness of 0.140 in. (3.5mm) is decreased to 0.122 in. (3.1mm), replace the plate.

9. Check the clutch plates for warping by laying them on a machined surface plate or sheet of plate glass. If a 0.008 in. (0.2mm) feeler gauge can be inserted under the plate at any point, it should be replaced.

10. Roll the clutch pushrod on a flat surface. If it is bent or deeply grooved, replace it.

11. To reassemble the clutch, use heavy grease to hold the flat thrust bearing and the thrust washer closest to the clutch housing in place as the clutch boss is installed. Be sure both thrust washers are in place.

12. When the clutch friction plates and metal clutch plates are installed, follow the exploded view. Note that friction plates are alternated with metal clutch plates but that the friction plates are not identical. There are 4 fiber-backed plates and 2 aluminum-backed plates. Two fiber-backed plates are installed first, followed by the 2 aluminum-backed plates. There will be a metal clutch plate between every set of friction plates.

13. *On 1980 and later models:* When assembling the clutch, use a new lockplate under the clutch boss nut (13, **Figure 1**), and fold up an edge of the plate.

PRIMARY DRIVE GEAR

Removal/Installation

1. Take off the pump drive as detailed earlier and remove the nut and lockwasher from the crankshaft. Use a gear puller if necessary to remove the drive gear. There is a square key in the crankshaft keyway to keep the gear from spinning on the shaft.

2. When reinstalling the gear, be sure the key is in place and tighten the locknut to 85 ft.-lb. (12 kgm). There should be no visible tooth overlay between the drive gear and driven gear. If overlay exists, the clutch should be checked for improper installation.

3. Reverse procedure to install.

SHIFT SHAFT

Removal/Installation

1. Remove the circlip and washer on the shaft.
2. Pull the shift shaft assembly out (**Figure 7**).

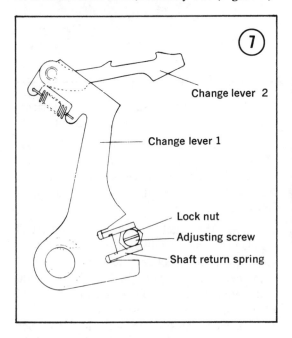

Change lever 2

Change lever 1

Lock nut

Adjusting screw

Shaft return spring

3. Reverse the order of disassembly to replace the shaft.

Adjustment

1. Check the shifting adjustment. Refer to **Figure 8**. Distances "A" and "AA" must be equal.

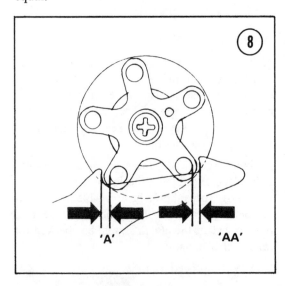

'A'   'AA'

2. Place the transmission in second, third, or fourth gear.

3. Loosen the screw locknut (2, **Figure 9**) and turn the eccentric screw (1) until "A" and "AA" (**Figure 8**) are equal.

4. Tighten the locknut and bend up the tabs of the locking washer. See **Figure 9**.

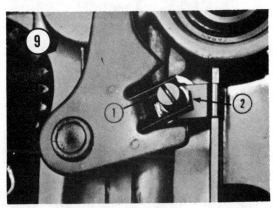

KICKSTARTER

Removal/Installation

1. Remove the kickstarter spring end from its anchor. Refer to **Figures 10** and **11**.

2. Pull the kickstarter assembly from the case.

3. Insert the assembly partially until the return return spring can be attached at its anchor point. Rotate the kick clip until it slips into the recessed area in the case and rotate the kick axle with the kickstarter level approximately one-half to three-quarters of a revolution so the axle can be pushed in and the kick stopper slips into its correct recessed area in the case. See **Figure 12**.

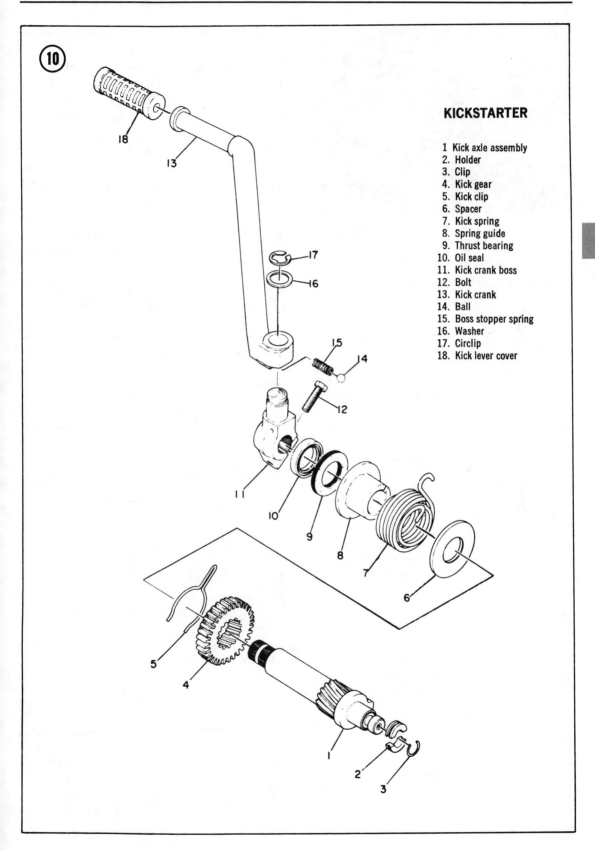

KICKSTARTER

1 Kick axle assembly
2. Holder
3. Clip
4. Kick gear
5. Kick clip
6. Spacer
7. Kick spring
8. Spring guide
9. Thrust bearing
10. Oil seal
11. Kick crank boss
12. Bolt
13. Kick crank
14. Ball
15. Boss stopper spring
16. Washer
17. Circlip
18. Kick lever cover

5

1. Kick clip   2. Kick stopper   3. Return spring

ELECTRIC STARTER

Removal/Repair/Installation

Figure 13 is an exploded view of the electric starter used on all models. Refer to **Table 1** for maintenance standards and specifications for electric starter service.

1. Drain the engine oil as described in Chapter Two.

2. Tilt the machine to the left as shown in **Figure 14** and remove the 4 mounting bolts so the motor can be pulled straight back from its mounting location. Tighten the mounting bolts in gradual stages until you reach 14 ft.-lb. (2.0 kgm) during installation.

3. Check the commutator surface and clean with No. 600 sandpaper as shown in **Figure 15** if necessary. Clean with electrical contact cleaner after sanding.

4. Mica insulation should be between 0.5-0.8mm below the commutator segments. See **Figure 16**.

5. Check commutator segments for resistance between each one and the others. The armature should be replaced if one of the segments shows an open circuit or if any segment shows less than 3 megohms resistance between it and the

Table 1   STARTER SPECIFICATIONS

Component	Item	Maintenance Standards	Remarks
MOTOR			
Fields	Resistance	0.05 ohms (20°C)	
Brush	Limit length	0.175 in. (4.5mm)	
Armature	Resistance	0.055 ohms (20°C)	No grounded core
STARTER SWITCH			
	Core gap	0.059-0.074 in. (1.5-1.88mm)	
	Point gap	0.035-0.044 in. (0.88-1.11mm)	
	Magnet windings	3.5 ohms (20°C)	
	Cut in voltage	6.5V	
	Cut out voltage	4.0V	
	Coil circuit	4A Draw. (20°C)	
SAFETY SWITCH			
	Yoke gap	0.008 in. (0.2mm)	
	Core gap	0.020-0.024 in. (0.5-0.6mm)	
	Point gap	0mm	
	Cut out voltage	2.5V or less	
MISCELLANEOUS			
Starter motor draw:		35A 12V (20°C); no load	
Feature standards			
Load		8.3V 100A 3,800 rpm	
Constraint		4V 300A or less	
Nominal engine rpm		300 rpm at 75A or less	
		(When the decompression lever is squeezed,	
		at 20°C)	

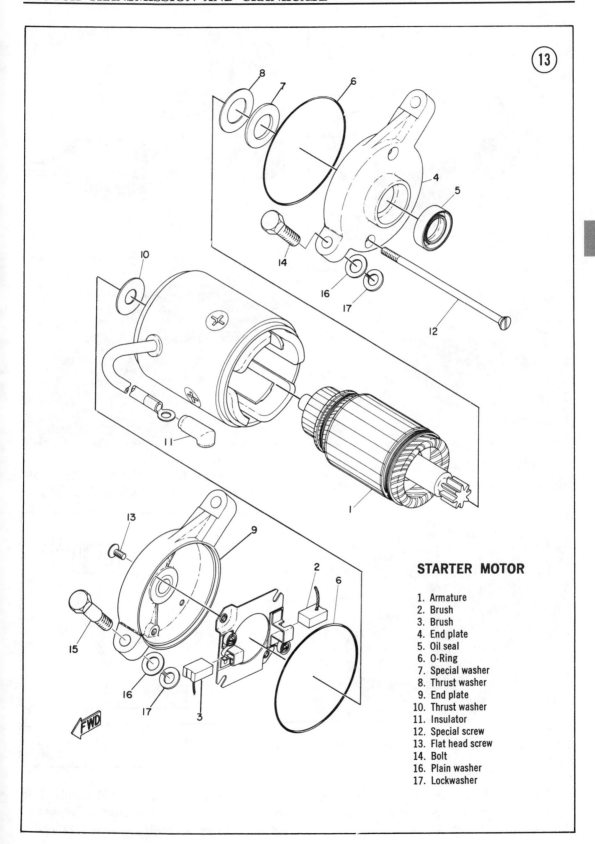

STARTER MOTOR

1. Armature
2. Brush
3. Brush
4. End plate
5. Oil seal
6. O-Ring
7. Special washer
8. Thrust washer
9. End plate
10. Thrust washer
11. Insulator
12. Special screw
13. Flat head screw
14. Bolt
16. Plain washer
17. Lockwasher

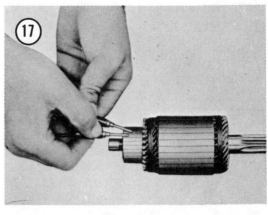

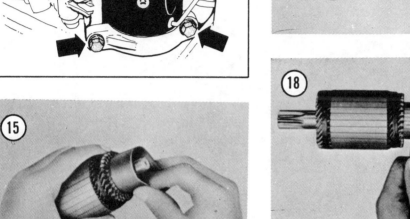

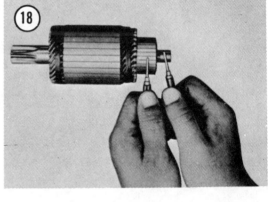

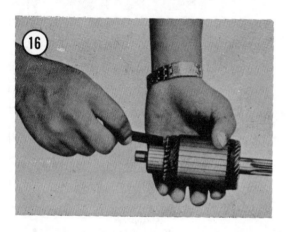

7. Check brush length. Refer to **Figure 19**. Brushes at or near the limits should be replaced.

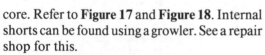

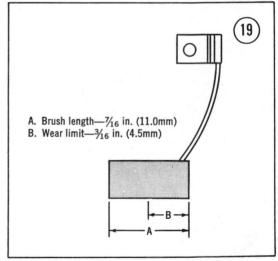

A. Brush length—$7/16$ in. (11.0mm)
B. Wear limit—$3/16$ in. (4.5mm)

core. Refer to **Figure 17** and **Figure 18**. Internal shorts can be found using a growler. See a repair shop for this.

6. Have a mechanic check the cover bearings, armature electrical properties, starter amperage draw and rpm, and the brushes.

8. Clean brush holders and yoke with clean solvent or electrical contact cleaner. Be sure all parts are dry before testing or reassembling.

9. Check yoke-to-coil resistance as shown in **Figure 20**. It should read 0.045-0.055 ohms. The yoke should not show leakage to ground.

10. Check the oil seals for hardening, cracking, wear, or deterioration. Lube the seals with white grease.

11. Clean the bearings and check them for proper rotation and the presence of damaged balls or races. All non-sealed bearings should be lubed with 20 or 30W motor oil.

12. To disassemble the starter reduction gears shown in **Figure 21**, refer to the appropriate section of the engine disassembly chapter to accomplish the following. Drain the engine oil and remove the left crankcase cover, the gear train cover and the idler gear. Remove the right crankcase cover and the clutch. Remove the stopper plate mounting bolt and plate as shown in **Figure 22**.

13. Remove gear 2 as shown and then remove the circlip as shown in **Figure 23**.

14. Refer to the exploded view to remove gears 4 and 5 and the starter wheel. See **Figure 24**.

15. Check gears for wear and damage; replace as necessary. Gear 4 receives the most wear.

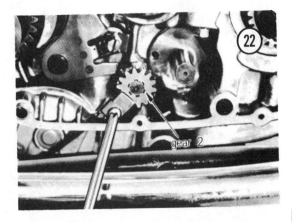

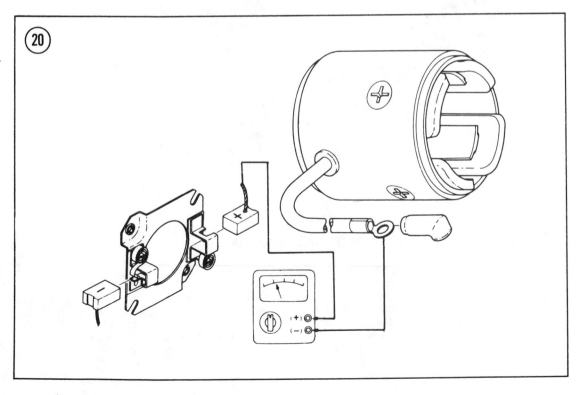

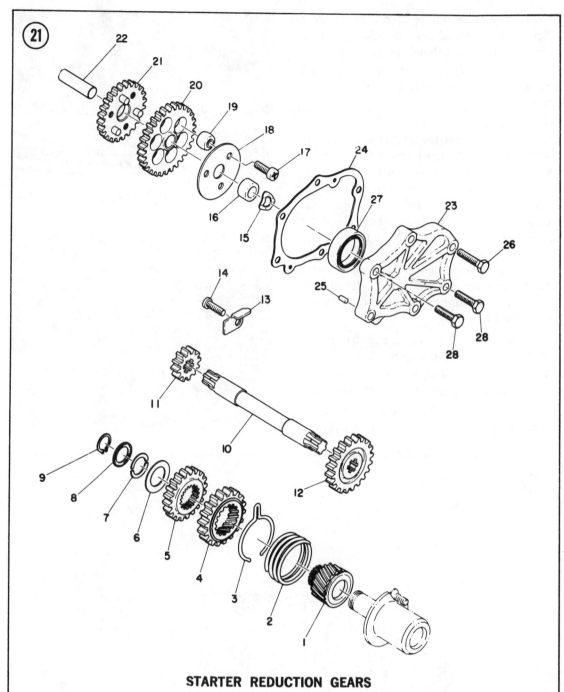

STARTER REDUCTION GEARS

1. Starter wheel	8. Clip holder	15. Lockwasher	22. Shaft #1
2. Return spring	9. Circlip	16. Collar #1	23. Gear train cover
3. Starter clip	10. Shaft #2	17. Phillips head screw	24. Gasket
4. Gear #4 (25 teeth)	11. Gear #2 (14 teeth)	18. Idler gear plate	25. Dowel pin
5. Gear #3 (24 teeth)	12. Gear #1 (24 teeth)	19. Dampener	26. Bolt
6. Flat washer	13. Stopper plate	20. Idler gear #1 (36 teeth)	27. Oil seal
7. Clip	14. Phillips head screw	21. Idler gear #2 (26 teeth)	28. Bolt

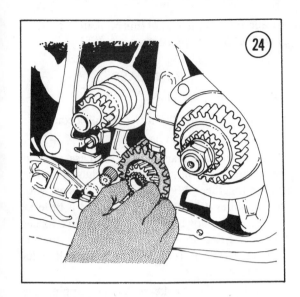

16. Check that the return spring provides positive return.

17. Reverse procedure for assembly. Check that the starter clip (**Figure 25**) is correctly fitted in the crankcase as shown.

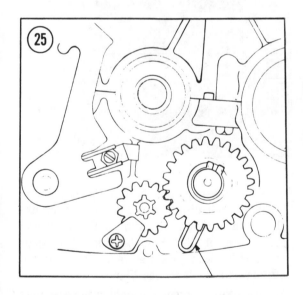

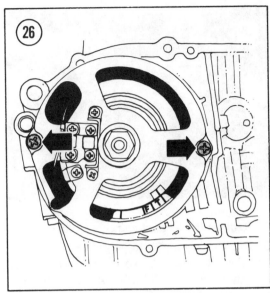

4. Refer to **Figure 27**; remove the rotor key as shown.

5. When installing the rotor, lubricate the shaft with light grease, install the key, line up the slot and push the rotor on the shaft. Install the lockwasher, nut, and stator.

ALTERNATOR STATOR AND ROTOR

Removal/Installation

1. Remove the 2 screws shown to remove the stator. Refer to **Figure 26**. Slide the stator off carefully to avoid damage to the wiring.

2. Remove the rotor securing nut and washer.

3. Use a rotor pulling tool, available from Yamaha, to remove the rotor.

DRIVE SPROCKET

Removal/Installation

The drive sprocket can be easily removed with the engine still in the frame. It needs to be removed only for transmission disassembly or replacement of the sprocket itself.

1. Bend down the locking tabs of the washer and place the transmission in gear to keep the shaft from turning. See **Figure 28**.

2. Remove the locknut and the sprocket.

3. Refer to **Figure 29** to help determine if the sprocket is worn. A worn drive chain will quickly wear both the drive sprocket and the rear wheel sprocket. Check all components for wear.

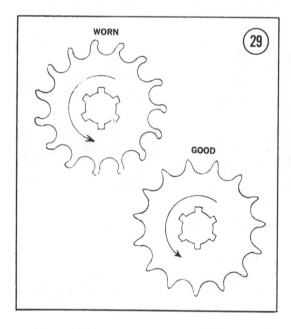

4. Replace the sprocket and bend up the washer tabs after the locknut has been tightened.

DRIVE AXLE

Oil Seal Replacement

In 1980, Yamaha redesigned the transmission drive axle oil seal to allow it to be replaced without removing and disassembling the engine. If the drive axle oil seal on any model 650 motorcycle is leaking, refer to the

supplement at the end of this book under *Drive Axle, Oil Seal Replacement.*

CRANKCASE

Disassembly/Assembly

Refer to **Figure 30** during this procedure.

1. Remove the cam chain.

2. Numbers are stamped on the case next to each nut and bolt which holds the crankcase halves together. When disassembling, start with bolt number 18 and loosen them all a little at a time going down to number 1. Don't forget the case bolts around the dipstick. A quarter turn at a time is recommended until all bolts and nuts are loose.

3. Separate the crankcase halves, tapping the top case with a rubber hammer if necessary. **Figure 31** shows the case cover mounting flange. Do not hammer on it.

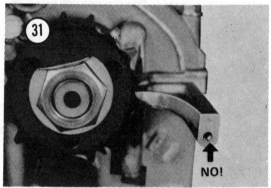

4. When reassembling the case halves, fit the shifting mechanism, transmission, and crankshaft in the top case half. Apply a non-hardening gasket cement (like Yamaha Bond No. 5) to thoroughly clean gasket surfaces and slide the bottom half in place. See **Figure 32**.

5. Use a torque wrench to tighten the case nuts and bolts to 14 ft.-lb. (2 kgm). Start with number 1 and go to number 18, in 3 stages to keep from warping the case halves. See **Figure 33**.

TRANSMISSION

CAUTION
When replacing transmission gears and shafts, make sure to write down your motorcycle's engine number and

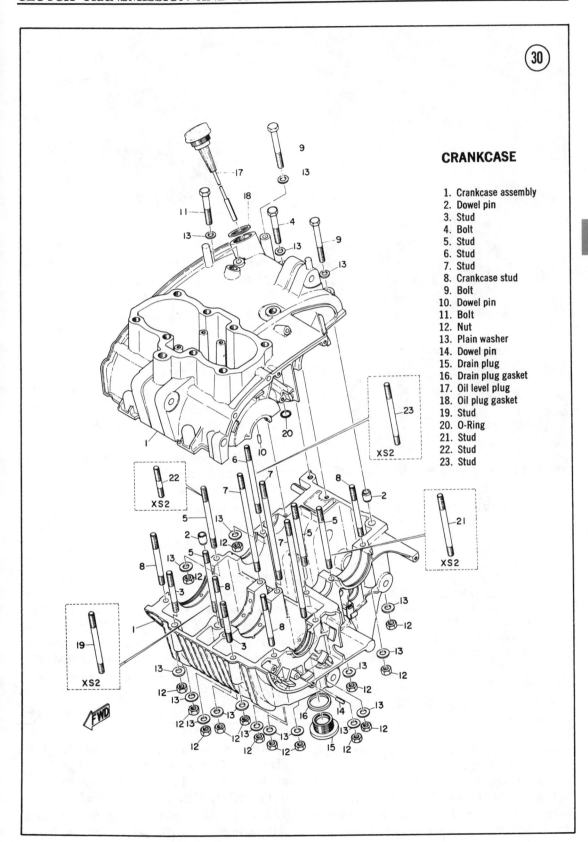

30

CRANKCASE

1. Crankcase assembly
2. Dowel pin
3. Stud
4. Bolt
5. Stud
6. Stud
7. Stud
8. Crankcase stud
9. Bolt
10. Dowel pin
11. Bolt
12. Nut
13. Plain washer
14. Dowel pin
15. Drain plug
16. Drain plug gasket
17. Oil level plug
18. Oil plug gasket
19. Stud
20. O-Ring
21. Stud
22. Stud
23. Stud

5

purchase parts from a Yamaha dealer. Starting with XS650D models (engine number 1T3-721262), the transmission gear and shaft splines have been changed to provide quieter operation. Because the new spline design changes the bearing surface and clearances of all parts, the parts are not interchangeable with previous models. Mixing the transmission parts will cause transmission failure and possible rider accident.

Removal/Installation

Figure 34 is an exploded view of the transmission.

1. Refer to **Figure 35** and remove the transmission assembly by tapping gently with a rubber hammer as shown.

2. Inspect the gears at the wear points indicated in **Figure 36**. Look for chipped teeth, rounded edges at the engagement dogs and slots, and blue discloration in the sliding gear fork grooves.

Replace components if necessary. It may be necessary to replace parts as a set if engagement dogs are damaged. Check mating gears carefully when damage is found.

> NOTE: *Bearing No. 9 in Figure 34 has a 30mm outside diameter dimension after XS1 engine No. 1235. All other models have the smaller bearing with an* OD *of 31mm.*

3. To fit the transmission assembly back in the case, assemble both shafts, complete with bearings and seals. Place the shift drum in neutral, fit the assembly into the top case. Check that shaft circlips are fitted to the bearings and circlips are in their grooves. The shift fork should easily slip over the sliding gears.

4. Before reassembly, check that all engaging dogs engage completely and that the transmission shifts easily through all the gears.

5. To remove the shift drum assembly, bend down the locking tabs so the shift drum stopper plate screws can be removed and remove the screws and plate. Pull out the fork guide bar. Roll the bar on a surface plate or piece of sheet glass to check it for straightness. Replace if necessary. Refer to exploded view (**Figure 37**).

6. Remove the neutral detent as shown. Refer to **Figures 38 and 39**.

7. Remove the cotter pin in each cam follower as shown in **Figure 40**.

8. Remove the shift drum stopper. Refer to **Figure 41**. Release the stopper spring as shown at No. 1 and bend down tabs shown at No. 2 so the locking plate can be removed.

9. Pull the shift drum out and remove the 3 shift forks from the case. Don't lose the 3 cam

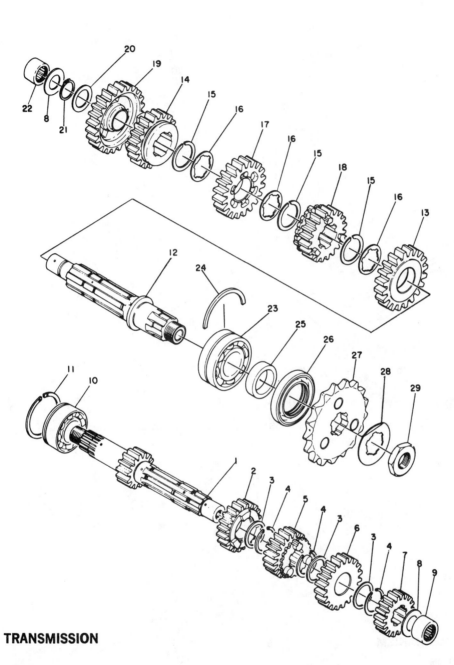

TRANSMISSION

1 Main axle
2. 4th pinion gear
3. Gear hold (5) washer
4. Circlip
5. 3rd pinion gear
6. 5th pinion gear
7. 2nd pinion gear
8. Drive axle shim

9. Bearing
10. Bearing
11. Circlip
12. Drive axle
13. 2nd wheel gear
14. 4th wheel gear
15. Circlip

16. Gear hold (3) washer
17. 3rd wheel gear
18. 5th wheel gear
19. 1st wheel gear
20. Gear hold washer
21. Circlip
22. Bearing

23. Bearing
24. Circlip
25. Distance collar
26. Oil seal
27. Drive sprocket
28. Lockwasher
29. Lock nut

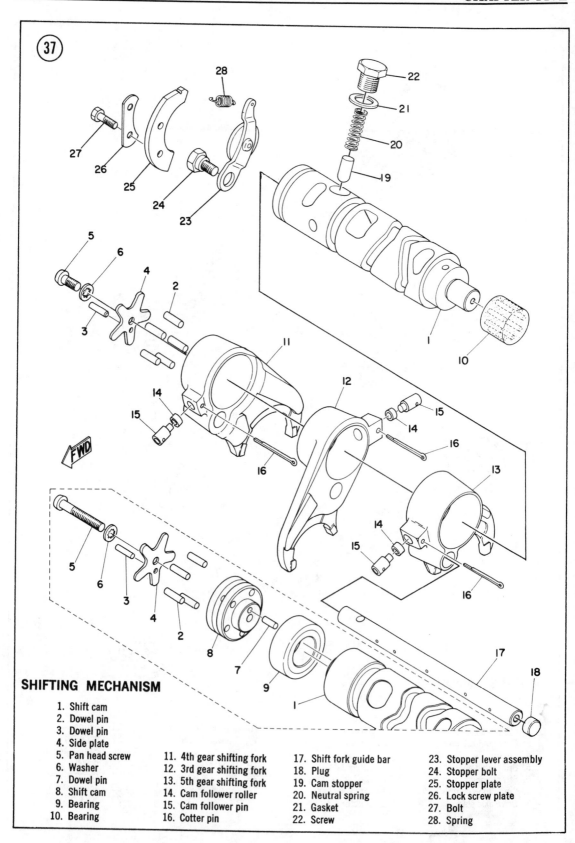

SHIFTING MECHANISM

1. Shift cam
2. Dowel pin
3. Dowel pin
4. Side plate
5. Pan head screw
6. Washer
7. Dowel pin
8. Shift cam
9. Bearing
10. Bearing

11. 4th gear shifting fork
12. 3rd gear shifting fork
13. 5th gear shifting fork
14. Cam follower roller
15. Cam follower pin
16. Cotter pin

17. Shift fork guide bar
18. Plug
19. Cam stopper
20. Neutral spring
21. Gasket
22. Screw

23. Stopper lever assembly
24. Stopper bolt
25. Stopper plate
26. Lock screw plate
27. Bolt
28. Spring

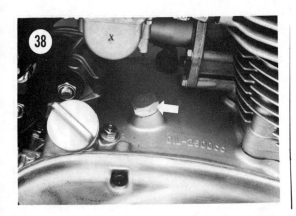

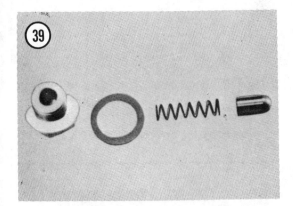

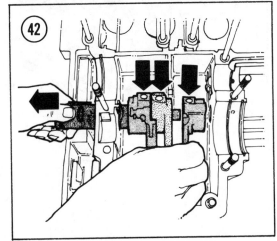

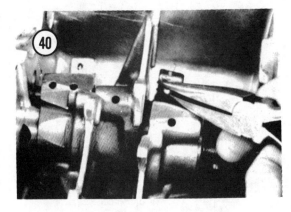

5

cate the shift drum and forks and use new cotter pins in the cam followers. Bend the cotter pin ends so they cannot drag and check the forks for smooth movement on the drum after assembly.

CRANKSHAFT

Crankshaft measuring and dismantling should not be attempted unless prior knowledge of the procedures and the correct tools are available. Your dealer can quickly and accurately perform all crankshaft services.

Removal

1. See **Figure 43**. Remove the crankshaft by tapping with a rubber mallet as necessary to loosen it.

2. Crankshaft bearings should be carefully checked for wear and damage. Clean them in solvent and blow dry immediately. Lubricate

follower rollers that rest in the grooves in the drum. See **Figure 42**.

10. Keep track of the shift forks and refer to the exploded view to ensure they are correctly installed. The fifth gear shift fork and fourth gear shift fork both have notches machined in one side so they can clear the neutral light button and the neutral position stopper respectively. If they are incorrectly installed, the neutral light button and neutral stopper will not fit. Lubri-

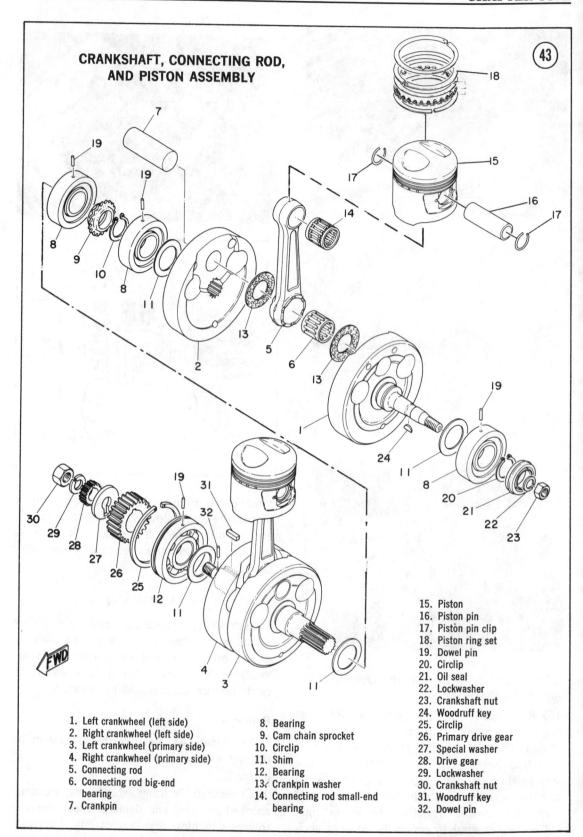

CRANKSHAFT, CONNECTING ROD, AND PISTON ASSEMBLY

1. Left crankwheel (left side)
2. Right crankwheel (left side)
3. Left crankwheel (primary side)
4. Right crankwheel (primary side)
5. Connecting rod
6. Connecting rod big-end bearing
7. Crankpin
8. Bearing
9. Cam chain sprocket
10. Circlip
11. Shim
12. Bearing
13. Crankpin washer
14. Connecting rod small-end bearing
15. Piston
16. Piston pin
17. Piston pin clip
18. Piston ring set
19. Dowel pin
20. Circlip
21. Oil seal
22. Lockwasher
23. Crankshaft nut
24. Woodruff key
25. Circlip
26. Primary drive gear
27. Special washer
28. Drive gear
29. Lockwasher
30. Crankshaft nut
31. Woodruff key
32. Dowel pin

them as soon as possible after inspection to avoid rusting. Pitting, scratching, chatter marks or rusting indicate new bearings are needed.

3. Keep the big end bearing from sliding back and forth on the crankshaft and rock the small end of the crankshaft as shown in **Figure 44**. If there is more than 0.078 in. (2mm) play at the small end of the crankshaft, it should be disassembled and the connecting rod, crank pin and needle bearing should be inspected carefully for wear. After new parts are installed, small end play should not exceed 0.04 in. (1.0mm).

Table 2 CRANKSHAFT SPECIFICATIONS	
Connecting rod big end side clearance	
1970-1977	0.012-0.024 in. (0.3-0.6mm)
1978 and later	0.006-0.016 in. (0.15-0.4mm)
Crankshaft runout (maximum)	
1970-1977	0.001 in. (0.03mm)
1978 and later	0.002 in. (0.05mm)

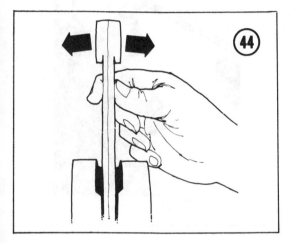

4. Connecting rod big end side play is measured by sliding the rod to one side of the crankpin and inserting a feeler gauge between the crankwheel and the connecting rod. Refer to **Figure 45** and **Table 2**. If clearance is excessive, refer crankshaft to a dealer for repair.

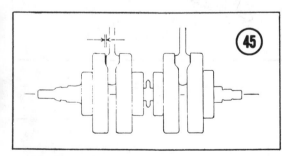

5. Mount the crankshaft as shown in **Figure 46** and check for excessive runout with a dial indicator. It should not exceed specifications in **Table 2**.

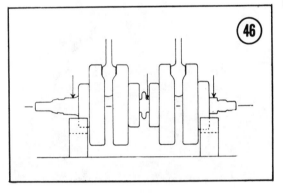

Installation

1. Be sure the left crank seal is installed with its Teflon lip to the outside and that all crank bearings are lubricated. Lay the crankshaft into the top case. Fit each main bearing outer race over its locating pin in the case. Line up the bearing outer race punch mark with the crankcase mating surface so the race fits in the locating pin. See **Figure 47**.

CAUTION
Failure to locate main bearing holes over locating pins will result in damaged cases and bearings when cases are torqued together.

2. Install the cam chain over the sprocket. Refer to **Figure 48**. Tie off each end of the chain to prevent its dropping into the cases.

3. The oil strainer, located in the bottom case, can be removed for cleaning by removing the 6 bolts as in **Figure 49**. Gasket surfaces must be clean and a new gasket installed along with gasket cement.

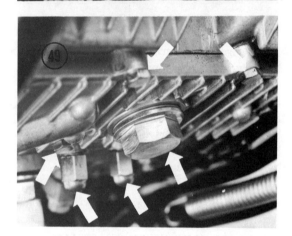

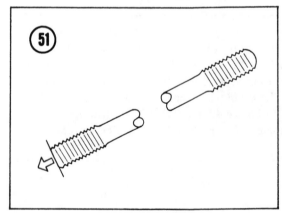

CYLINDER STUDS

Cylinder studs can be removed if necessary with a stud remover as shown in **Figure 50**. Refer to **Figure 51** and replace studs with their flat ends screwed into the case as shown. Two nuts tightened together or a vise grip can be used in place of a stud remover.

NOTE: If you own a 1978 or later model, first check the Supplement at the back of the book for any new service information.

CHAPTER SIX

ELECTRICAL SYSTEM

The electrical system includes the battery, ignition system, charging system, lighting, and horn. Wiring diagrams are given at the end of this chapter. Specifications for service and replacement parts are given in Appendix.

Any part of the electrical system may be repaired with a minimum of special tools by following the procedures described.

BATTERY

Very little maintenance is required on battery systems. Batteries must be checked occasionally for water level and state of charge.

Excessive battery water usage is an indication of overcharging. Most common causes of overcharging are high battery temperatures or a high voltage regulator setting. No appreciable usage of water over a period of 2 or 3 months of average use could indicate an under-charged battery condition. A poor cable connection is the most common cause for this condition.

Most battery failures can be prevented by systematic battery service.

Cleaning

It is particularly important to keep the battery clean and free of corrosion. Dirt provides a leakage path between terminals and causes the battery to discharge. Wash the battery with a weak solution of baking soda or ammonia, then rinse thoroughly with clean water. Be sure to keep all vent plugs tight so that no ammonia or baking soda solution enters the cells.

Electrolyte Level

The liquid level of the battery should be checked frequently. A monthly check is recommended but check more frequently during hot weather especially if many long trips are made. All batteries have some sort of "full" mark indicator, usually a split ring or triangle, under each cell cap. Add distilled water as required to bring the electrolyte level up to the "full" indicator. See **Figure 1**. Never overfill a battery. Overfilling results in loss of electrolyte, terminal corrosion and short battery life. Never put anything into a battery except pure water. Distilled water, which is available at any supermarket, is best. It is sold for use in steam irons and is inexpensive. In an emergency only, odorless, colorless drinking water may be substituted for distilled water.

Never allow the liquid level in any cell to drop below the top of the plates. This results in permanent damage to the battery and reduced battery performance.

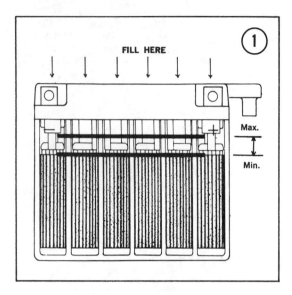

FILL HERE

Max.

Min.

It is most important to maintain batteries in a fully charged state during cold weather. See **Table 1**. Not only do starting loads increase as engine oil thickens, but battery capacity decreases at the same time. Assuming battery capacity to be 100 percent at 80°F., **Table 2** shows the charged conditions at lower temperatures. At 20°F., the power required for starting is 3½ times that required at 80° but only 30 percent of battery power is available.

Table 1   BATTERY CONDITION

Specific Gravity	Percent Charged
1.110-1.130	Discharged
1.140-1.160	Almost discharged
1.170-1.190	One-quarter charged
1.200-1.220	One-half charged
1.230-1.250	Three-quarters charged
1.260-1.280	Fully charged

Table 2   BATTERY CAPACITY

Temperature	Battery Capacity Available	Cranking Power Required
80°F	100%	100%
32°F	68%	165%
−20°F	30%	350%

Another reason for keeping batteries fully charged during cold weather is that a fully charged battery freezes at a much lower temperature than does one which is partially discharged. Freezing temperature depends on the electrolytes specific gravity. See **Table 3**.

Table 3   BATTERY FREEZING TEMPERATURES

Specific Gravity	Freezing Temperature	
1.100	18°F	− 7.7°C
1.120	13°F	−10.5°C
1.140	8°F	−13.3°C
1.160	1°F	−17.2°C
1.180	− 6°F	−21.1°C
1.200	−17°F	−27.2°C
1.220	−31°F	−35.0°C
1.240	−50°F	−45.5°C
1.260	−75°F	−59.4°C
1.280	−92°F	−68.8°C

Because freezing may ruin a battery, protect it by keeping it in a charged condition.

All motorcycles use the same type of battery. Refer to **Figure 2** for battery construction.

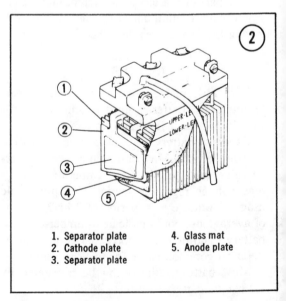

1. Separator plate
2. Cathode plate
3. Separator plate
4. Glass mat
5. Anode plate

Removal

1. Remove the retaining strap. Disconnect the ground, or negative (−) cable first, then the positive (+) cable.

2. Lift the battery from the mounting, noting the location of the terminal covers, mounting pads and breather tube for reinstallation later.

Safety Precautions

When working with batteries, use extreme care to avoid spilling or splashing the electrolyte. The electrolyte is sulphuric acid which can ruin clothing and cause serious chemical burns. If any electrolyte is spilled or splashed on clothing or skin, immediately neutralize it with a solution of baking soda and water, then flush with an abundance of clean water.

> **WARNING**
> *Electrolyte splashed into the eyes is extremely dangerous. Safety glasses should always be worn while working with batteries. If electrolyte is splashed into the eye, call a physician immediately, force the eye open, and flood with cool, clean water for approximately 5 minutes.*

If electrolyte is spilled or splashed onto any surface, it should be neutralized immediately with baking soda and water solution and then rinsed with clean water.

While batteries are being charged, highly explosive hydrogen gas forms in each cell. Some of this gas escapes through filler openings and may form an explosive atmosphere in and around the battery which may persist for several hours. Sparks, an open flame, or a lighted cigarette can ignite this gas, causing an internal battery explosion and possible serious personal injury. The following precautions should be taken to prevent an explosion:

a. Do not smoke or permit any open flame near any battery being charged or which has been recently charged.

b. Do not disconnect live circuits at battery terminals, because a spark usually occurs when a live circuit is broken. Care must always be taken when connecting or disconnecting any battery charger; be sure its power switch is off before making or breaking connections. Poor connections are a common cause of electrical arcs which cause explosions.

Battery Inspection and Service

1. Measure the specific gravity of the battery electrolyte with a hydrometer. See Table 1. The specific gravity is calibrated on the hydrometer float stem. The reading is taken at the fluid surface level with the float buoyant in the fluid (see **Figure 3**).

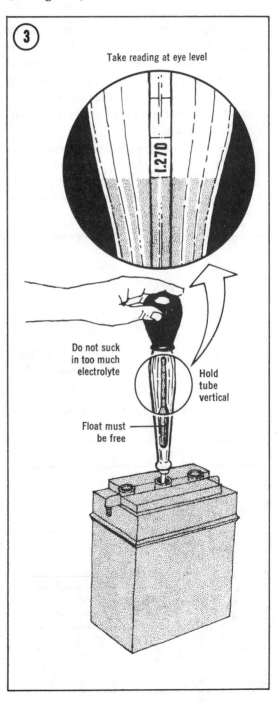

③ Take reading at eye level

1.270

Do not suck in too much electrolyte

Hold tube vertical

Float must be free

6

2. If the reading is less than 1.20 with the temperature corrected to 68°F, recharge the battery (see **Figure 4**).

3. If any cell's electrolyte level is below the lower mark on the battery case, fill with distilled water to the upper mark.

4. Replace the battery if the case is cracked or damaged.

5. Corrosion on the battery terminals causes leakage of current. Clean them with a wire brush or a solution of baking soda and water.

6. Check the battery terminal connections. If corrosion is present, the connection is poor. Clean the terminal and connector and coat with Vaseline and reinstall.

7. Vibration causes the corrosion of the battery plates to flake off, forming a paste on the bottom and battery failure (see **Figure 5**). Replace the battery when it no longer holds a satisfactory charge.

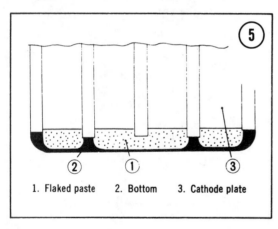

1. Flaked paste   2. Bottom   3. Cathode plate

Battery Charging

Batteries are not designed for high charge or discharge rates. For this reason, it is recommended that a battery be charged at a rate not exceeding 20 percent of its ampere-hour rating. For example, never exceed 1 amp for a 4.5 ampere-hour battery or 0.5 amperes for a 2.5 ampere-hour battery. The charging rate should continue for 5 hours if the battery is completely discharged, or until the specific gravity of each cell is up to 1.260-1.280, corrected for temperature and approximately 12.6 volts. If after prolonged charging, specific gravity of one or more cells does not come up to at least 1.230 and 12.4 volts, the battery will not perform as well as it should, but it may continue to provide satisfactory service for a short time.

Some temperature rise is normal as a battery is being charged. Do not allow the electrolyte temperature to exceed 110°F. If the temperature reaches that figure, discontinue charging until the battery cools, then resume charging at a reduced rate.

If possible, always slow-charge a battery. Quick-charging will shorten the battery service life. Refer to **Table 4**.

If a quick-charge must be used, the rate should be no more than 10.0 amperes.

1. Hook the battery to a charger by connecting the positive (+) lead to the positive terminal on the battery and the negative (−) lead to the negative terminal. To do otherwise could cause severe damage to the battery and could result in injury if the battery explodes.

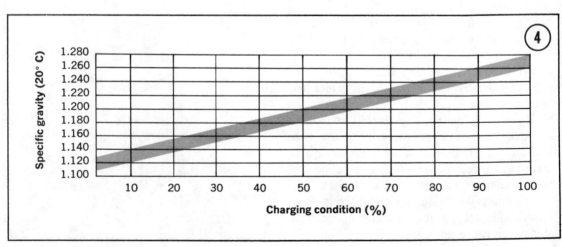

Table 4   BATTERY CHARGE

	Normal Charge	Rapid Charge
Charging current rate	2.0 ampere-hours	10.0 ampere-hours maximum
Checking for full charge	① Specific gravity: 1.260-1.280 68°F (20°C) maintained constant. ② 7.5-8.3 volts at terminals. Check with voltmeter.	① Specific gravity: 1.260-1.280 maintained at 68°F (20°C). ② Voltage: When a large volume of gas is emitted from the battery (in about 2-3 hours for fully discharged battery) reduce charging rate to 2.0 amperes. ③ Battery is fully charged when a voltage of 7.5 volts is maintained.
Charging duration	A battery with specific gravity of electrolyte below 1.220 at 68°F (20°C) will be fully charged in approximately 12-13 hours.	A battery with specific gravity of electrolyte below 1.220 at 68°F (20°C) will be fully charged in approximately 1-2 hours.
Remarks		When required, the quick charging method may be used, however, the recommended charging current rate should be under 2.0 amperes.

6

2. The electrolyte will begin bubbling, signifying that explosive hydrogen gas is being released.

WARNING
Make sure the area is adequately ventilated and that there are no open flames.

3. It will take at least 5 hours to bring the battery to full charge. Test the electrolyte periodically with a hydrometer to see if the specific gravity is within the standard range of 1.260-1.280. If the reading remains constant for more than an hour, the battery is charged. See Table 1.

Installation

NOTE
If installing a new battery, make sure the breather tube was cut at the bottom of the tube.

1. Wash the battery with water to remove spilled electrolyte.
2. Coat the terminals with Vaseline or light grease before installing.
3. Connect the positive terminal first, then the negative terminal. Do not overtighten the clamps.
4. Remeasure the specific gravity of the electrolyte with a bulb hydrometer, reading it as described in this chapter.

CAUTION
If the battery's breather tube was removed with the battery or if a new battery is installed, make sure to route the tube correctly when installing the battery to prevent damage to the motorcycle.

Battery Storage

1. Remove the battery and thoroughly clean the case with a baking soda solution.
2. Inspect battery holder and surrounding area for damage caused by spillage of battery acid. Wash the area with a solution of baking soda and warm water.

CAUTION
Keep cleaning liquid out of the battery cells or the electrolyte will be seriously weakened.

3. Clean battery terminals with a stiff wire brush or one of the many tools made for this purpose.
4. Examine battery case for cracks.
5. Fill cells to full mark with distilled water.
6. Recharge the battery with a battery charger. Do not use the engine's charging system for charging a discharged battery.
7. Check the specific gravity of each cell as described previously.

8. Lightly smear battery terminals with petroleum jelly (Vaseline).

9. Store the battery in a cool, dry place. Do not leave the battery where there is a risk of freezing. Never leave a battery stored on a concrete or dirt floor or the charge will bleed off overnight. Put the battery on wood blocks.

> NOTE: *If possible, recharge the battery once a month.*

10. Disconnect and clean the terminals on the starter and generator or alternator. Reconnect wires and lightly smear with petroleum jelly (Vaseline).

BATTERY CHARGERS

Types

The 2 basic types of battery chargers are "unregulated" and "regulated."

Unregulated battery chargers or "trickle" chargers are designed for motorcycle use. These inexpensive chargers continue to charge the battery at a slow rate even after the battery is fully charged. If left unattended, the battery could be permanently damaged.

Regulated chargers are more suitable for safe use. Two types are available. The automatic charger shown in **Figure 6** is representative. This type will automatically shut off when the battery is fully charged.

Make sure the charger you select carries the label of the Underwriter's Laboratory.

Capacity

Charger capacity is the maximum current the charger can deliver measured in amperes. The charger should be able to recharge the batteries in less than a 24-hour period.

SPARK PLUGS

See *Spark Plugs* section in Chapter Two.

IGNITION TIMING

See *Ignition Timing* in Chapter Two.

BREAKER POINTS

See *Breaker Point Service* section of Chapter Two for removal and installation of breaker points.

CONDENSER

See *Condenser* section in Chapter Two.

COILS

See *Coils* section in Chapter Two.

ROTOR AND STATOR

See *Rotor and Stator* section of Chapter Five for removal and installation.

IGNITION SWITCH

1. Remove the headlight as indicated in **Figure 7**.

2. Reach inside the shell, disconnect the main switch connector, and remove the switch.

3. Reverse procedure to install.

VOLTAGE REGULATOR

Removal/Installation

1. Disconnect the multiple wiring connector.

2. Remove the mounting screws shown in **Figure 8** to remove the regulator. Voltage regulator service is covered in Chapter Three.

3. Reverse procedure to install.

HEADLIGHT

Removal/Installation

1. The headlight is a sealed beam unit. To replace, remove screw as shown in **Figure 9**.

2. Unhook spring (D) and pull out the defective lamp.

3. Assemble in reverse order of disassembly.

Adjustment

Proper headlight adjustment is essential to safe night riding. If the light is set too low, the road will not be visible. If set too high, it will blind oncoming vehicles. Headlight adjustment is controlled by screws and bolts (A) and (B) in **Figure 10**. Screw (A) is turned in or out to center the headlight and bolt (B) is loosened to move the headlight up or down and then retightened. Adjustment is very simple; proceed as follows.

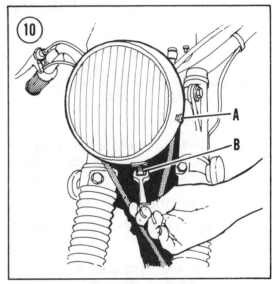

1. Place the machine approximately 16 ft. from a white or light-colored wall. Refer to **Figure 11.**

2. Make sure the bike and wall are on level, parallel ground and that the machine is pointing directly ahead.

3. Measurements should be made with one rider sitting on the bike and both wheels on the ground.

4. Draw a cross on the wall equal in height to the center of the headlight.

5. Switch on the high beam. The cross should be centered in the concentrated beam of light.

6. If the light does not correspond to the mark, loosen the bolts and adjust. Tighten the bolts and recheck positioning.

6

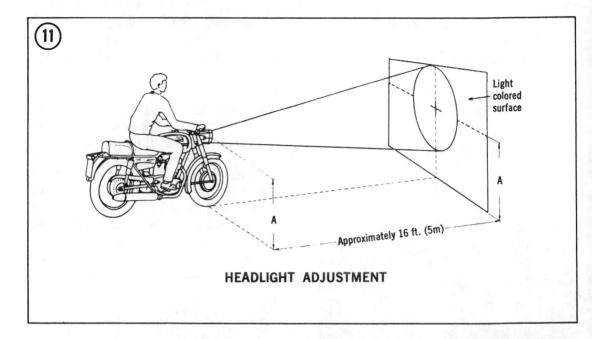

Light
colored
surface

A

Approximately 16 ft. (5m)

A

A

HEADLIGHT ADJUSTMENT

TAILLIGHT, FLASHER LIGHTS, AND HORN

Removal/Installation

Removal and installation of the taillight, flasher lights and horn are straightforward jobs and do not require step-by-step procedures.

ELECTRIC STARTER

See Chapter Five under the heading of *Electric Starter*.

ALTERNATOR BRUSH REPLACEMENT

Poor brush condition or worn brush springs cause poor brush contact, which is one of the most frequent causes of low alternator output. To gain access to the alternator brushes, remove the stator cover screws (**Figure 12**) and remove the cover. Remove the brush protector plate screws and plate. Then remove the screws securing the brushes to the stator plate and remove the brushes (**Figure 13**). Measure the brush length (**Figure 14**). New brush length is 9/16 in. (14.5mm). If a brush is worn to less than 1/4 in. (7mm), install a new brush. If an old brush is of the correct length, install the brush and check to see that the spring presses the brush firmly against the rotor. If not, install a new brush and spring.

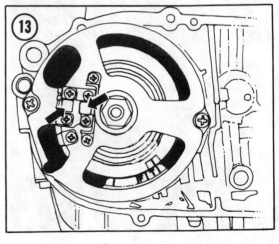

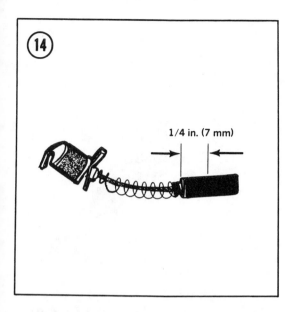

1/4 in. (7 mm)

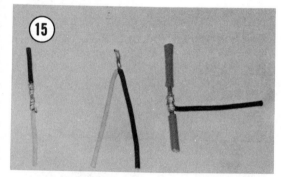

REPAIRING AND SPLICING WIRING

The most frequent cause of electrical system malfunctions is a defective connection. Frequently, troubles are traced to a hastily twisted, poorly insulated wire connection. Such connections eventually loosen and corrode, then become useless. The 2 best types of connections are soldered and crimped.

Soldered Connections

Soldering is easy and it takes only a little practice to make perfect permanent connections. All that is needed it a 75-100 watt soldering iron, rosin-core solder, and plastic electrical tape. Do not use acid-core solder which is corrosive. Wire cutters and strippers are also handy for this type of work.

The 3 common types of splices, butt, pigtail and tee, are illustrated left to right, respectively, in **Figure 15**. They differ only in the way that the wires are connected. The soldering technique is the same for all. Note that butt and pigtail splices connect the ends of 2 wires together. The tee splice is used when it is necessary to tap into an existing wire.

1. Strip approximately 1 in. from the end of each wire to be connected (**Figure 16**). Be careful not to nick any strands.

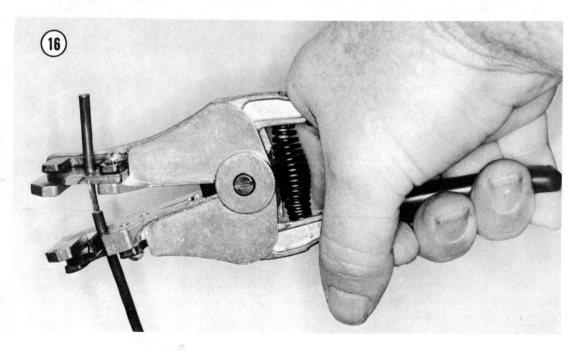

NOTE
Always use stranded wire for all wiring.
Solid wire will eventually break under
vibration.

2. Twist the 2 stripped ends together firmly, as shown in **Figure 17**. Mechanical strength of the solder joint depends on this twisting. Be sure that fingers are clean during this operation, otherwise solder will not adhere to the wire.

3. Be sure that the soldering iron is well tinned, then hold its tip under the twisted wires to heat the joined wires (**Figure 18**).

4. When the joint is heated, apply solder slowly to the joint (not to the iron itself). Melted solder will flow smoothly throughout the joint (**Figure 19**). Then remove the solder and soldering iron. Allow the joint to cool completely before moving it. A properly soldered connection will be bright and shiny with shapes of individual wires still visible (**Figure 20**).

5. Cut off any excess wire (**Figure 21**) from the connection.

6. Protect and insulate the connection with plastic electrical tape (**Figure 22**). Be sure to use at least 2 layers, and carry the tape at least an inch on either side of the connection.

Crimped Connections

Crimped connections are faster and easier than soldered ones but are also considerably more expensive. **Figure 23** illustrates various types of crimp connections and the tools required to make them. Crimped connections are small, neat and desirable in cramped locations. Crimp connectors are usually color coded to denote wire sizes with which they may be used. See **Table 5**.

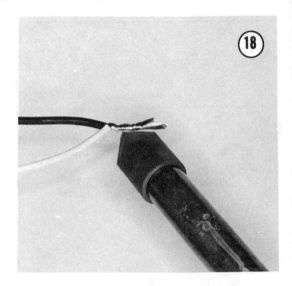

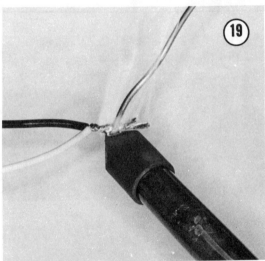

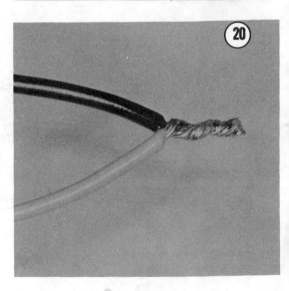

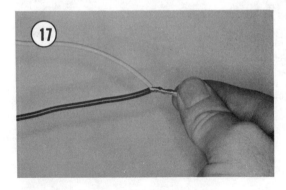

Table 5   CRIMP CONNECTOR SIZES

Color	Wire Size
Yellow	10 and 12
Blue	14 and 16
Red	16 and 18

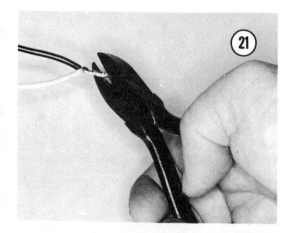

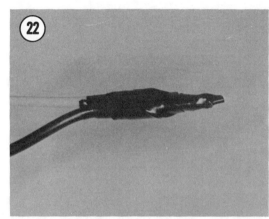

6

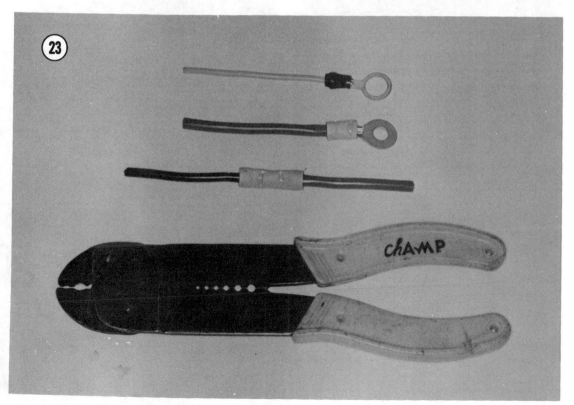

1. Strip approximately 5/16 in. of insulation from the end of the wire to be connected. This distance will vary slightly for each connector and can best be determined by experience. The distance is correct when the shoulder formed by the remaining insulation bottoms in the terminal and the stripped end of the wire just emerges from the crimping portion of the terminal (**Figure 24**).

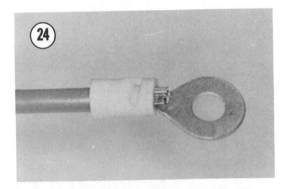

2. Squeeze the terminal with the crimping tool (**Figure 25**) until the jaws are closed. A little practice with a few spare terminals and pieces of scrap wire beforehand will ensure good connections every time.

Wiring

Occasionally damaged wiring must be replaced or new wires installed for additional lights or other accessories. Several precautions should be observed when such wiring is done.
1. Be sure that any new circuits are protected by a fuse of appropriate size.
2. Be sure that all wiring is adequately supported and protected against chafing, in particular in areas where it passes over or through metal parts. Rubber grommets are available for such installations.

Avoid placing wires near a hot exhaust pipe. Whenever possible, attach any additional wiring to existing wire harnesses by the use of plastic insulation tape.

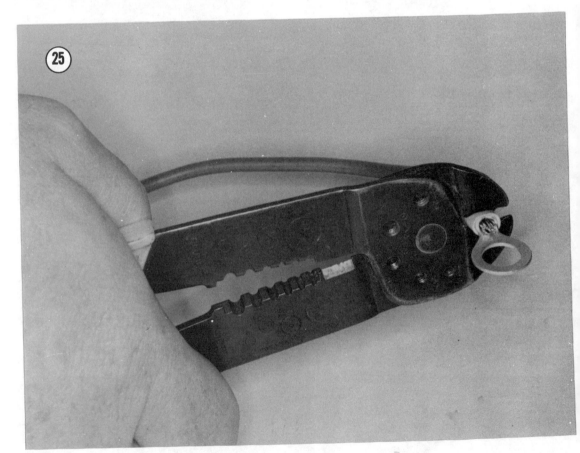

Table 6 WIRE AND FUSES

Wire Size (AWG)	Current Capacity (Amperes)	Fuse Size (Amperes)
10	25	30
12	20	14
14	15	14
16	6	9
18	3	9

3. Always use good quality wire designed for automotive applications. Such wire is available at any auto parts store either in bulk or on handy spools. Never use rubber-insulated wire. Automotive wire has either plastic or Teflon insulation which is highly resistant to abrasion.

4. Be sure to use wire of adequate size. **Table 6** lists current carrying capacities of various wire sizes.

WIRING DIAGRAMS

Wiring diagrams are at the end of the book.

6

NOTE: If you own a 1978 or later model, first check the Supplement at the back of the book for any new service information.

CHAPTER SEVEN

FUEL SYSTEM

For correct operation, a gasoline engine must be supplied with fuel and air mixed in proper proportions by weight. A mixture in which there is an excess of fuel is said to be rich. A lean mixture is one which contains an insufficient amount of fuel. It is the function of the carburetor to supply the correct fuel/air mixture to the engine under all operating conditions.

Yamaha's 650cc engines are equipped with slide valve carburetors. The carburetor incorporates 4 subsystems: starting, fuel feed, main control, and idling.

Trace fuel system problems from the gas tank, though the petcocks, fuel lines, and finally the carburetors. **Figure 1** shows the tank and petcocks. Chapter Three has troubleshooting procedures.

PETCOCKS

1. Petcocks can be removed from the gas tank by removing the 2 Phillips head screws shown in **Figure 2**.

2. Check the O-ring in the groove in the petcock-to-tank mating surface for damage or deterioration and replace if necessary.

3. Cleaning of the petcocks can be accomplished without removing them from the tank. Remove the bolt shown in **Figure 3** to allow

water and sediment to drain. A screw-held plate at the opposite end of the fuel outlet can be removed to clear the petcock of large obstructions.

CARBURETOR

Removal

See Chapter Four under *Engine Removal*.

Disassembly/Assembly

Refer to **Figures 4 and 5** during the following procedure.

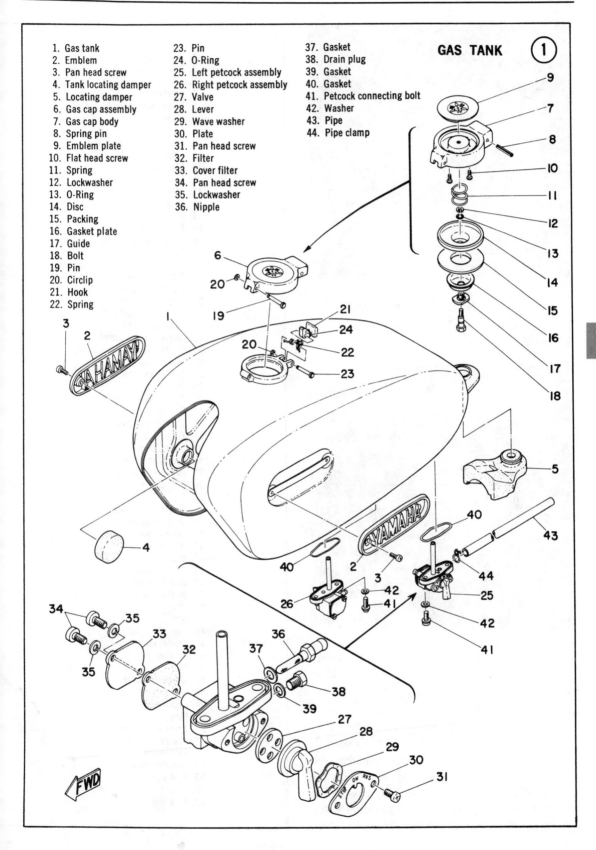

GAS TANK (1)

1. Gas tank
2. Emblem
3. Pan head screw
4. Tank locating damper
5. Locating damper
6. Gas cap assembly
7. Gas cap body
8. Spring pin
9. Emblem plate
10. Flat head screw
11. Spring
12. Lockwasher
13. O-Ring
14. Disc
15. Packing
16. Gasket plate
17. Guide
18. Bolt
19. Pin
20. Circlip
21. Hook
22. Spring
23. Pin
24. O-Ring
25. Left petcock assembly
26. Right petcock assembly
27. Valve
28. Lever
29. Wave washer
30. Plate
31. Pan head screw
32. Filter
33. Cover filter
34. Pan head screw
35. Lockwasher
36. Nipple
37. Gasket
38. Drain plug
39. Gasket
40. Gasket
41. Petcock connecting bolt
42. Washer
43. Pipe
44. Pipe clamp

7

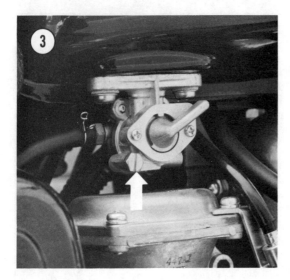

1. Remove the vacuum chamber cover.

2. Unscrew the 4 Phillips head screws. See **Figure 6**.

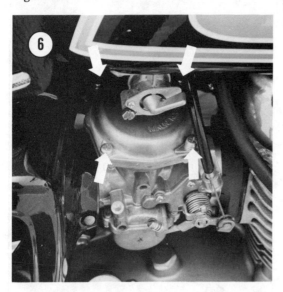

3. Lift off the chamber cover. When the cover is replaced be sure the throttle cable anchor bracket is positioned correctly. Refer to the exploded view drawings.

4. Remove the spring, jet needle retainer, jet needle, and vacuum piston as shown in **Figure 7**.

5. Insert the vacuum piston into the carburetor body and line up the small projection on the outer edge of the rubber diaphragm with the notch on the outer edge of the carburetor top mating surface. See **Figure 8**.

1. Body assembly (left)
2. Main nozzle
3. O-Ring
4. Washer
5. Valve seat assembly
6. Float
7. Float pin
8. Float chamber packing
9. Float chamber body
10. Pilot jet
11. Main jet
12. Washer
13. Plug screw
14. Plate
15. Pan head screw
16. Diaphragm assembly
17. Needle
18. Clip
19. Set needle plate
20. Diaphragm spring
21. Diaphragm cover
22. Throttle bracket (left)
23. Pan head screw
24. Starter body assembly
25. Starter plunger
26. Plunger spring
27. Set lever starter spring
28. Washer
29. Plunger cap
30. Plunger cap cover
31. Throttle stop ring
32. Throttle stop screw
33. Starter packing
34. Flat head screw
35. Pilot screw spring
36. Pilot screw
37. Cap
38. Throttle assembly shaft
39. Throttle spring
40. Throttle lever
41. Washer
42. Nut
43. Throttle valve
44. Oval head screw
45. Starter shaft
46. Clip
47. Seal
48. Cap
49. Starter lever
50. Washer
51. Nut
52. Connector lever
53. Lockwasher
54. Lockwasher
55. Ring
56. Lever assembly
57. Pan head screw
58. Lockwasher
59. Overflow pipe
60. Fuel pipe
61. Spring
62. Pipe clip

TYPICAL CARBURETOR

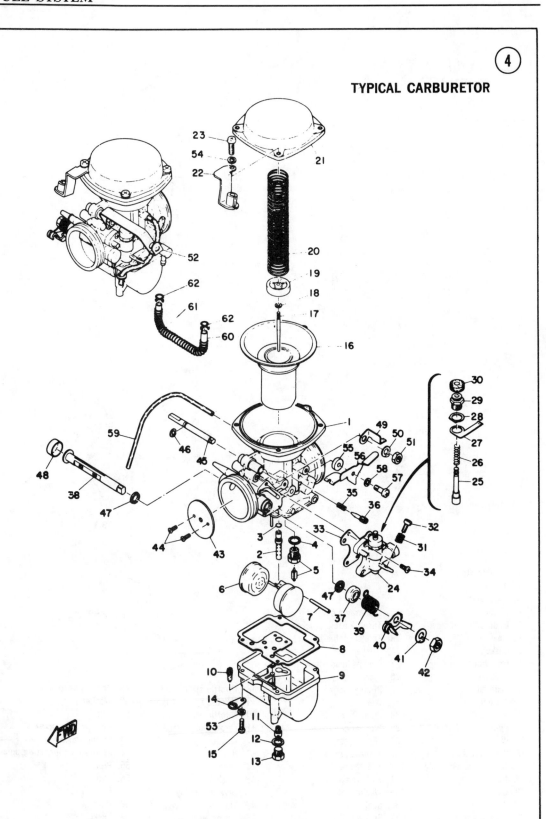

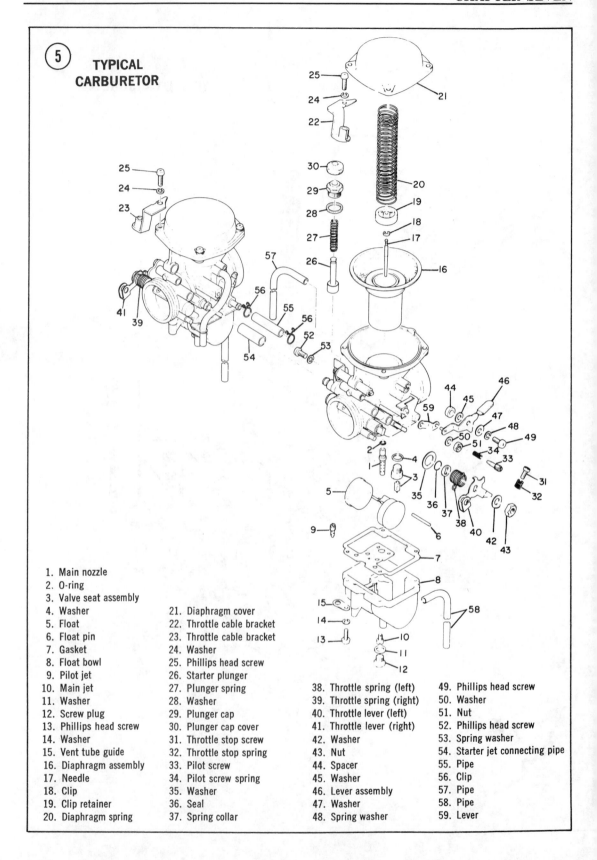

⑤   **TYPICAL CARBURETOR**

1. Main nozzle
2. O-ring
3. Valve seat assembly
4. Washer
5. Float
6. Float pin
7. Gasket
8. Float bowl
9. Pilot jet
10. Main jet
11. Washer
12. Screw plug
13. Phillips head screw
14. Washer
15. Vent tube guide
16. Diaphragm assembly
17. Needle
18. Clip
19. Clip retainer
20. Diaphragm spring

21. Diaphragm cover
22. Throttle cable bracket
23. Throttle cable bracket
24. Washer
25. Phillips head screw
26. Starter plunger
27. Plunger spring
28. Washer
29. Plunger cap
30. Plunger cap cover
31. Throttle stop screw
32. Throttle stop spring
33. Pilot screw
34. Pilot screw spring
35. Washer
36. Seal
37. Spring collar

38. Throttle spring (left)
39. Throttle spring (right)
40. Throttle lever (left)
41. Throttle lever (right)
42. Washer
43. Nut
44. Spacer
45. Washer
46. Lever assembly
47. Washer
48. Spring washer

49. Phillips head screw
50. Washer
51. Nut
52. Phillips head screw
53. Spring washer
54. Starter jet connecting pipe
55. Pipe
56. Clip
57. Pipe
58. Pipe
59. Lever

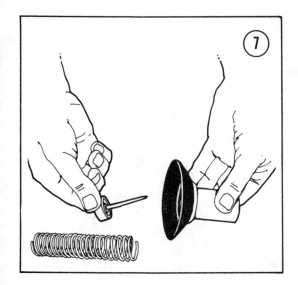

6. **Figure 9** shows carburetor inlet passage (1) and the air passage to the starter jet (2).

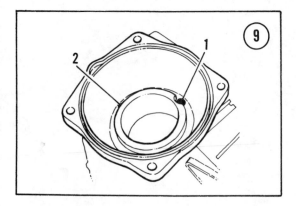

7. Remove the 3 Phillips head screws shown in **Figure 10** to disassemble the starter jet housing.

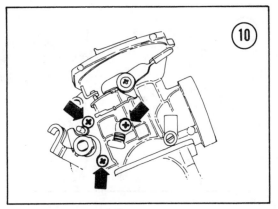

8. Remove the 4 retaining screws on the bottom of the main housing to remove the float bowl.

9. Remove the float chamber body and the bowl gasket.

10. Invert the mixing chamber body and slowly lower the float until the float just contacts the top of the float needle. Be careful that you don't compress the float needle spring.

11. Refer to **Figure 11** and measure the distance (A) indicated. It should be as specified in **Table 1**. Bend the tang which contacts the inlet needle to get the correct measurement. Both floats should have the same measurement. Bend the connecting bar to level the floats if necessary.

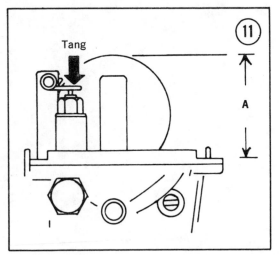

Tang

A

12. The pilot jet and main jet are screwed into orifices in the float bowl. See **Figure 12**. The pilot jet is accessible from the inside while the main jet can be removed after a cover screw is removed from the bottom.

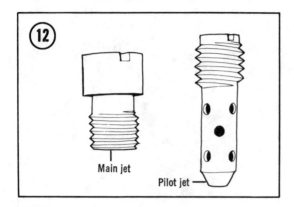

Main jet

Pilot jet

13. Pull out the float pivot pin. Note the float valve just under the float adjustment tang. It should be removed when the float is taken out to avoid losing it.

14. Remove needle jet as shown in **Figure 13** by pulling it out with your fingers.

15. Reverse the procedure for assembly.

AIR FILTER

See Chapter Two for details. **Figures 14 and 15** show construction of the filters.

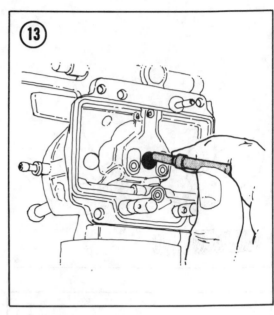

Table 1   CARBURETOR FLOAT LEVEL

1970-1979	0.95 in.	(24mm)
1980 and later	1.07 in.	(27.3mm)

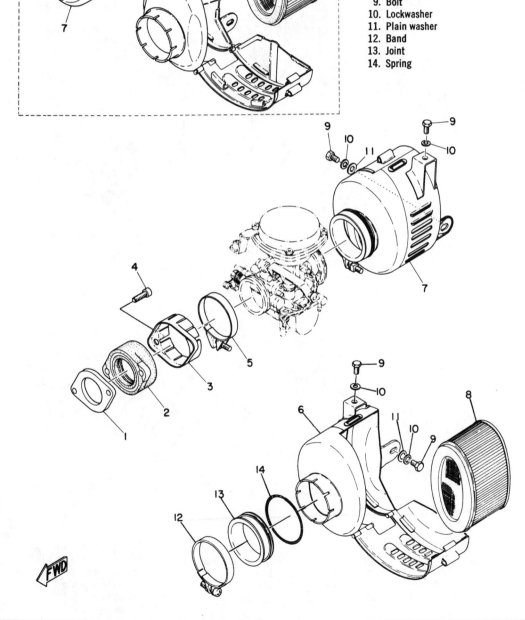

**AIR FILTER
WITH PAPER
FILTER ELEMENT**
1. Joint gasket
2. Carburetor joint
3. Joint cover
4. Bolt
5. Band
6. Air cleaner left case
7. Air cleaner right case
8. Air filter
9. Bolt
10. Lockwasher
11. Plain washer
12. Band
13. Joint
14. Spring

7

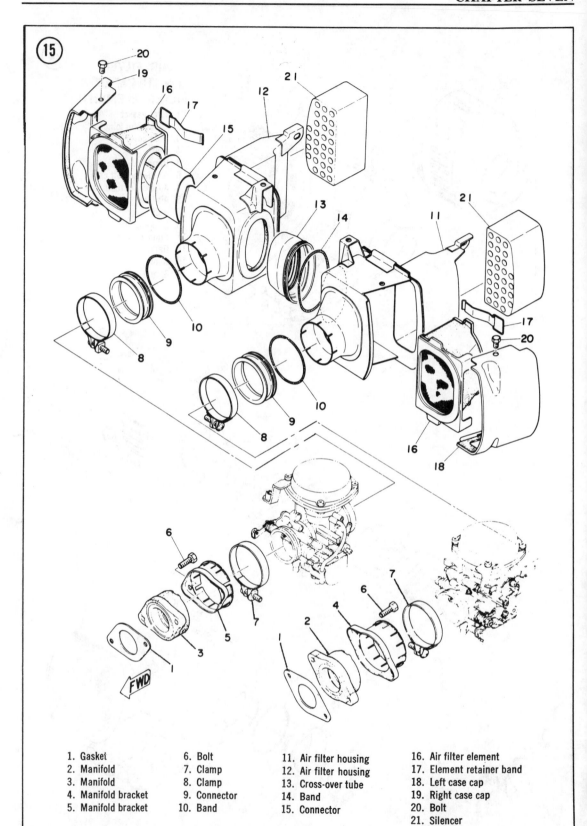

1. Gasket
2. Manifold
3. Manifold
4. Manifold bracket
5. Manifold bracket
6. Bolt
7. Clamp
8. Clamp
9. Connector
10. Band
11. Air filter housing
12. Air filter housing
13. Cross-over tube
14. Band
15. Connector
16. Air filter element
17. Element retainer band
18. Left case cap
19. Right case cap
20. Bolt
21. Silencer

NOTE: If you own a 1978 or later model, first check the Supplement at the back of the book for any new service information.

CHAPTER EIGHT

CHASSIS

This chapter covers frame component service, suspension unit service, and wheel and brake service and maintenance.

The front wheel and brake are very critical components on any motorcycle. No matter how well the motorcycle is running, if it can't be ridden safely it is useless.

The front brake must supply more braking effort than the rear to stop in the shortest possible distance. Proper maintenance will assure these operate safely.

Balance and shimmy are more critical on the front wheel than the rear. The front wheel affects all other handling aspects of the bike. The front wheel should be checked for balance, shimmy (side-to-side play), wobble, out-of-round, run-out, and proper tire inflation. Many of these problems go unnoticed at low speeds but become dangerous at high speeds.

Frames are of welded steel tubing (**Figure 1**). Service on the frame is limited to inspection for bending of the frame members or cracked welds. Examine the frame carefully in the event that the machine has been subjected to a collision or hard spill.

SEAT

Removal/Installation

1. To remove the seat, lift it as illustrated in **Figure 2**.

2. Disconnect the seat support bracket and remove the rear pivot pin nut.

3. Slide the seat forward to remove.

4. Reverse procedure to install.

BATTERY AND TOOL BOX

1. Disconnect flasher unit wiring under the box.

2. Refer to **Figure 3** and remove the 2 retaining bolts shown.

3. Slide the box forward so the anchor pins clear the bushings and lift the box up and out.

4. Reverse procedure to install.

8

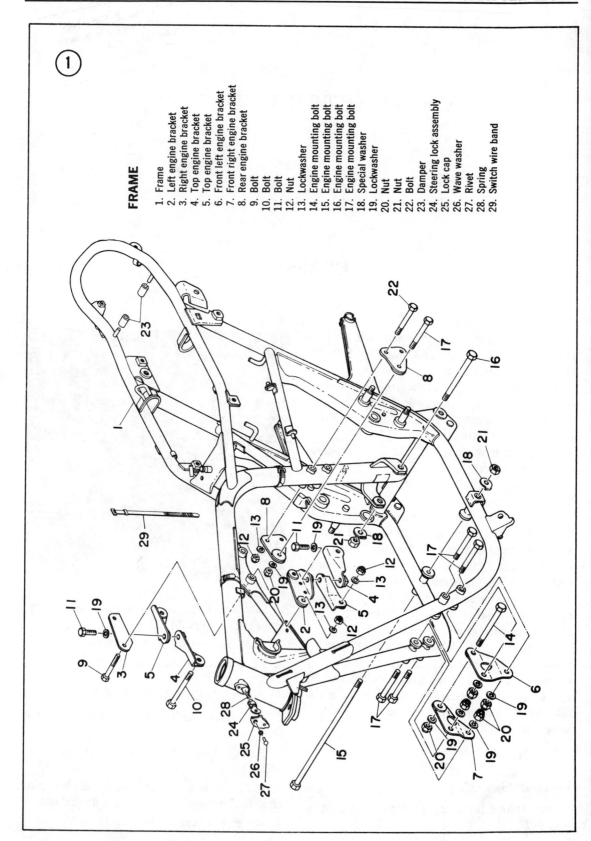

FRAME

1. Frame
2. Left engine bracket
3. Right engine bracket
4. Top engine bracket
5. Top engine bracket
6. Front left engine bracket
7. Front right engine bracket
8. Rear engine bracket
9. Bolt
10. Bolt
11. Bolt
12. Nut
13. Lockwasher
14. Engine mounting bolt
15. Engine mounting bolt
16. Engine mounting bolt
17. Engine mounting bolt
18. Special washer
19. Lockwasher
20. Nut
21. Nut
22. Bolt
23. Damper
24. Steering lock assembly
25. Lock cap
26. Wave washer
27. Rivet
28. Spring
29. Switch wire band

1. Drain fork oil as detailed in Chapter Two.

2. Pull up the dust seal as shown in **Figure 8**.

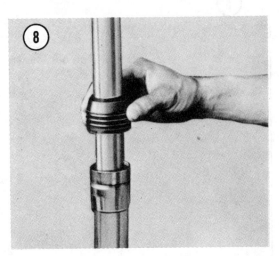

COIL

Each coil is mounted with 2 nuts on a frame bracket. Remove the gas tank wiring loom connections and nuts as shown in **Figure 4**. See Chapter Two under *Coils* for more detail.

3a. On XS1 and XS1B, use a strap wrench as shown in **Figure 9** to unscrew the outer nut. Inserting the axle will help grip the leg to keep it from turning during this operation. Use a piece of inner tube to protect the outer nut's chromed surface.

3b. On all models except XS1 and XS1B, remove the Allen head bolt from the bottom of each fork leg (30, Figure 7).

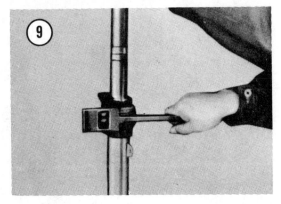

FRONT FORK

Removal/Disassembly

Refer to the exploded view drawings (**Figures 5, 6, and 7**) during fork service. A few details are different among the forks used on different models but service procedures are basically the same.

4. Pull the outer tube down and off as shown in **Figure 10**.

5. If fork leg disassembly is not necessary, both the inner and outer tubes can be removed as a unit. Loosen the handlebar mounting bolts as shown and pull the handlebars downward. See **Figure 11**.

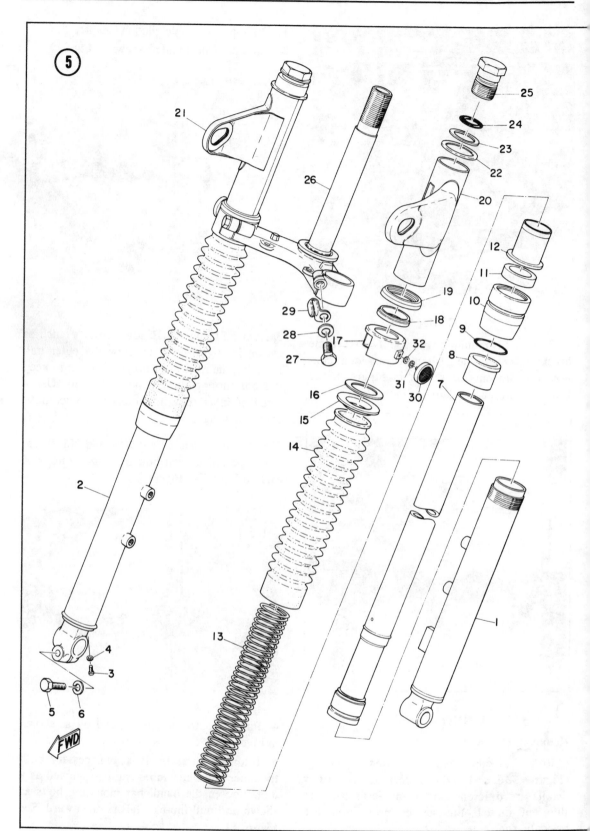

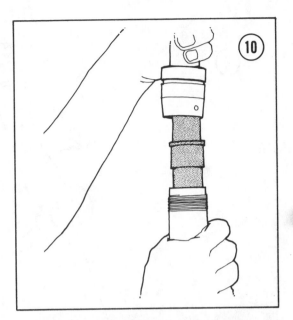

FRONT FORK — XS1

1. Outer left tube
2. Outer right tube
3. Drain plug
4. Drain plug gasket
5. Bolt
6. Lockwasher
7. Inner tube
8. Slide metal
9. O-Ring
10. Outer nut
11. Oil seal
12. Spring lower seat
13. Fork spring
14. Boot
15. Spring upper seat
16. Oil seal washer
17. Outer cover
18. Lamp bracket packing
19. Cover under guide
20. Upper left cover
21. Upper right cover
22. Cover upper guide
23. Cap washer
24. O-Ring
25. Cap bolt
26. Triple clamp
27. Triple clamp bolt
28. Lockwasher
29. Wire holder
30. Reflector
31. Lockwasher
32. Plain washer

6. Remove the cap bolts and loosen the pinch bolts. Refer to **Figure 12**.

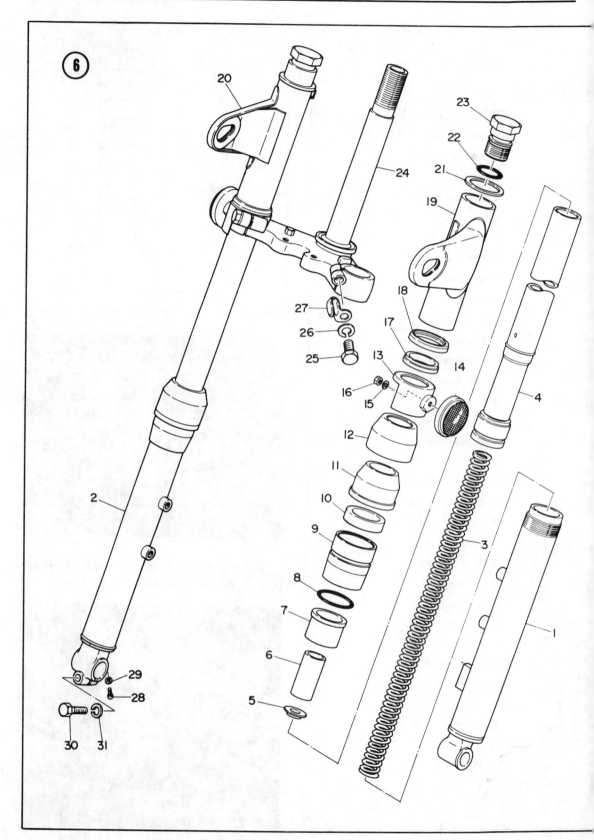

FRONT FORK – XS1B

1. Outer left tube
2. Outer right tube
3. Fork spring
4. Inner tube
5. Spring upper seat
6. Spacer
7. Metal slide
8. O-Ring
9. Outer nut
10. Oil seal
11. Dust seal
12. Dust seal cover
13. Outer cover
14. Reflector
15. Lockwasher
16. Nut
17. Packing (lamp stay)
18. Lower cover guide
19. Upper left cover
20. Upper right cover
21. Upper cover guide
22. Packing
23. Cap bolt
24. Under bracket
25. Under bracket bolt
26. Lockwasher
27. Wire holder
28. Drain plug
29. Drain plug gasket
30. Bolt
31. Lockwasher

7. Loosen the lower pinch bolts as shown in **Figure 13**.

8. Pull the inner fork tubes out of the mounting brackets as shown in **Figure 14**.

9. Disassemble the fork tubes as shown in **Figure 15**.

10. Check the inner fork tube for excessive wear, damage, or bends. Deep grooves or

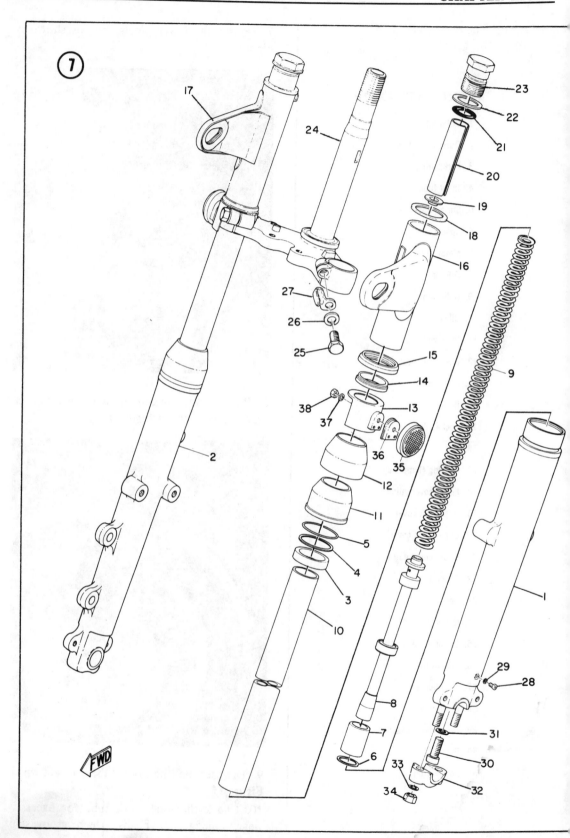

FRONT FORK
(ALL OTHER MODELS)

1. Outer left tube
2. Outer right tube
3. Oil seal
4. Oil seal washer
5. Oil seal circlip
6. Circlip
7. Piston
8. Cylinder
9. Spring
10. Inner tube
11. Dust seal
12. Dust seal cover
13. Outer cover
14. Packing
15. Guide
16. Upper left cover
17. Upper right cover
18. Guide
19. Seat
20. Spacer
21. Packing
22. Cap washer
23. Cap bolt
24. Triple clamp
25. Bolt
26. Lockwasher
27. Wire holder
28. Drain plug
29. Drain plug gasket
30. Bolt
31. Packing
32. Axle holder
33. Lockwasher
34. Nut
35. Reflector
36. Reflector stay cover
37. Lockwasher
38. Nut

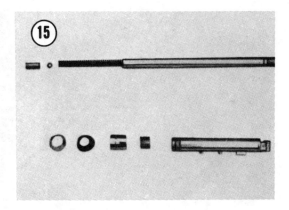

scratches can wear seals out quickly. Replace the inner tube if necessary. **Figure 16** is an exaggerated example of possible fork tube damage. Replacement is recommended for bent tubes but straightening may be possible in some cases. Consult your dealer if there is any doubt.

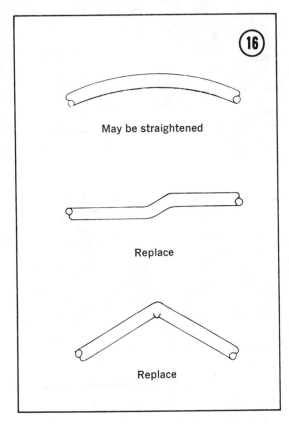

May be straightened

Replace

Replace

11. Check the bushing shown in **Figure 17**. It is identified as a metal slide in the exploded view drawings. If clearance between the bushing and inner fork tube exceeds 0.020 in. (0.5mm), the

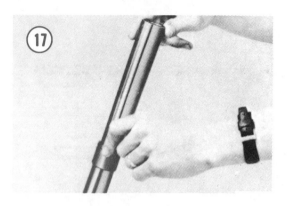

bushing should be replaced and the fork tube checked for excessive wear.

12. The front fork oil seals should be replaced each time the forks are disassembled. See **Figures 18 and 19**.

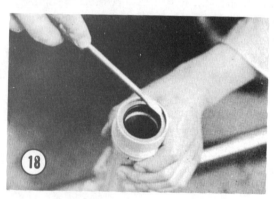

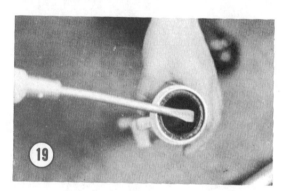

13. Check the rubber boot and O-rings around the fork seals for wear or deterioration and replace as necessary.

Triple Crown and Steering Head Service

1. Remove the handlebar retaining nuts and the holders and rubber cushions. See **Figure 20**.

1. Nut   2. Rubber cushion

2. Remove the steering dampener as shown in **Figure 21**. Pull out the dampener rod after its cotter pin has been removed.

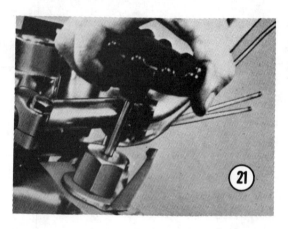

3. Loosen the triple crown pinch bolt. **Refer** to **Figure 22**. Unscrew the steering stem nut and remove the front fork cap bolts. The triple clamp will now come off.

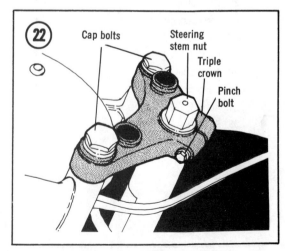

Cap bolts   Steering stem nut

Triple crown

Pinch bolt

4. Remove the stem ring nut shown in **Figure 23** carefully, supporting the bottom triple clamp.

5. Examine the ball bearings and their races. Pitting, rusting, or wear indicates replacement of all balls.

6. Grease the balls to keep them in place during assembly. Refer to **Figures 24, 25, and 26**.

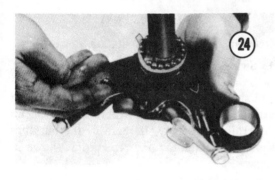

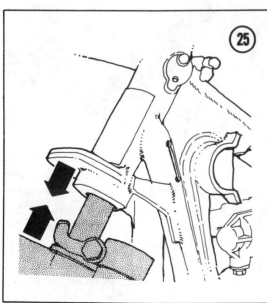

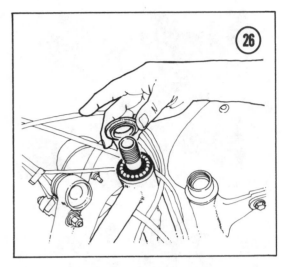

7. Tighten the stem nut so there is no free play in the steering head.

8. Check for any signs of binding as the handlebars are turned from lock to lock. The stem nut adjustment is critical.

9. Assemble the steering head in the reverse order of disassembly.

> NOTE: *If binding is evident, loosen the steering ring nut slightly until the forks swing freely from lock to lock, but without any up-down free play.*

Fork Installation

1a. On XS1 and XS1B, assemble the slide bushing, outer nut, bottom spring retainer, spring, rubber protector, top spring retainer, and flat metal washer over the inner tube.

1b. On all models except XS1 and XS1B, slide outer tube up over inner tube, then install and tighten Allen screw in bottom of each fork leg.

2. Install the inner tube as shown in **Figure 27**. The fork tube cap bolt must be tightened first. Use a strap wrench to keep the tube from turning. After the cap bolt is fully tightened, tighten the bottom triple clamp pinch bolts.

3. Slide the outer tubes up over the inner tubes and tighten the outer nut with a strap wrench as shown in **Figure 28**.

4. Check fork oil as described in Chapter Two.

8

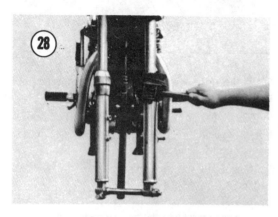

SHOCK ABSORBER

Removal/Inspection/Installation

1. Remove the top and bottom mounting bolts as shown in **Figure 29**.

2. Check shock absorber action by compressing the shock fully as shown in **Figure 30** and then quickly taking all weight off it. A worn shock will quickly return to its full length. A good shock will quickly return to half its full length and then slowly extend the rest of the way.

3. Reverse procedure to install.

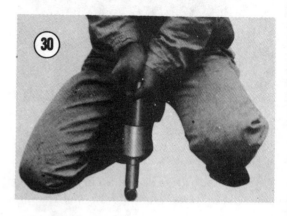

SWING ARM

Removal/Inspection/Installation

1. Swing arm bushings can be checked for wear with the swing arm in place and the rear wheel and shock absorbers removed. Twist the swing arm to detect free play. There should be no discernible free play. If there is, the bushings should be driven out and replaced as shown in **Figure 31**.

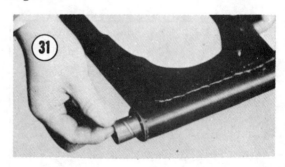

2. Remove the rear wheel as detailed in this chapter. See **Figure 32**.

3. Flatten the locking tabs on the pivot shaft lockwasher as shown. Refer to **Figure 33**. Remove the locknut and pull out the pivot shaft.

> NOTE: *Bronze swing arm bushings for greater durability and swing arm stability are available from your*

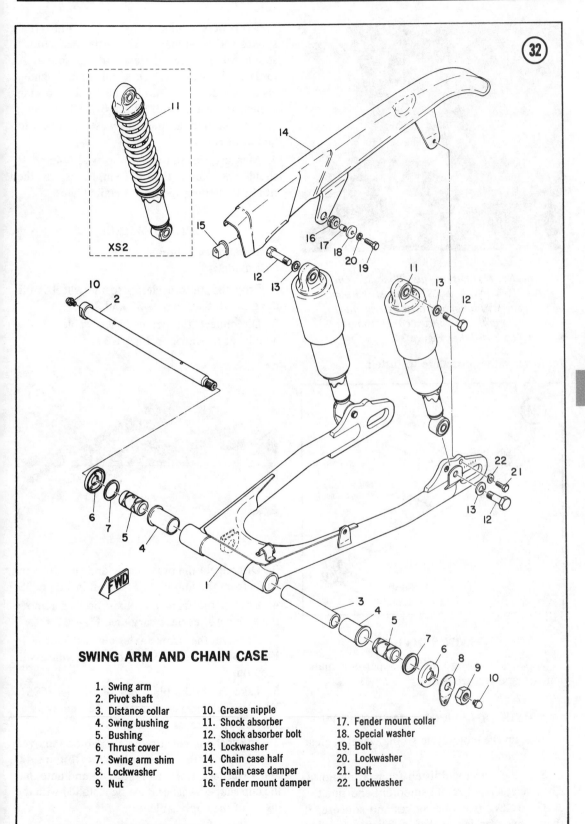

SWING ARM AND CHAIN CASE

1. Swing arm
2. Pivot shaft
3. Distance collar
4. Swing bushing
5. Bushing
6. Thrust cover
7. Swing arm shim
8. Lockwasher
9. Nut
10. Grease nipple
11. Shock absorber
12. Shock absorber bolt
13. Lockwasher
14. Chain case half
15. Chain case damper
16. Fender mount damper
17. Fender mount collar
18. Special washer
19. Bolt
20. Lockwasher
21. Bolt
22. Lockwasher

dealer. *This bushing fits all models. On XS1, XS1B, and XS2 models, the old spacer, bushing, and thrust cover must be discarded, and thrust cover from the TX650 used. See* **Figure 34**.

4. Reverse the procedure to install.

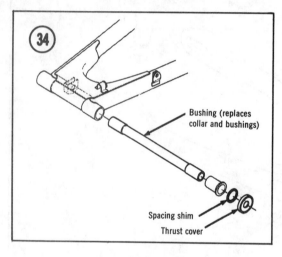

Bushing (replaces collar and bushings)

Spacing shim
Thrust cover

CHAIN SERVICE

See Chapter Two for details of periodic maintenance and replacement.

WHEEL AND SPOKE INSPECTION

1. Jack up the motorcycle so the wheel is clear of the ground.

2. Spin the wheel and listen for bearing noise. The wheel should rotate smoothly and quietly.

3. Grasp 2 consecutive spokes and squeeze. If they move, tension is not sufficient. Another

method for checking is to rap the individual spokes with a wrench or key. A properly tuned spoke will produce a clean ringing sound. A loose spoke will produce a dull thud. Tighten each loose spoke ¼ turn at the nipple, working around the wheel until all are tight. Tightening each spoke fully at first will cause the wheel to be out-of-round.

4. Measure rim runout with a fixed pointer. It should not be more than 1/16 in. If it is, true the rim by tightening spokes as detailed later.

FRONT WHEEL

Removal/Installation
(All models)

1. Prop the motorcycle up so the wheel is off the ground. See **Figures 35 and 36**.

2. Disconnect the front brake cable at the handlebar as shown in **Figure 37**.

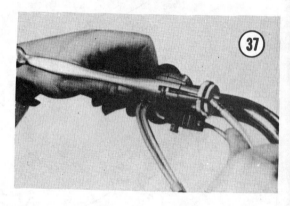

3. Disconnect the brake cable and speedometer cable from the hub plate as shown in **Figure 38**.

4. Loosen the front axle lock bolt or remove the axle caps, as necessary. See **Figure 39**.

5. Remove the front axle nut as shown in **Figure 40** and pull the axle out. The wheel will drop out.

6. Take the brake plate out of the hub (XS1, XS1B). The brake shoes can be removed as shown in **Figure 41**.

7. The speedometer drive gear can be removed by taking out the circlip shown in **Figure 42**, and 2 washers. Refer to **Figure 43** and note that the cup shaped washer must be installed with the inside of the cup visible.

8. To install, reverse the preceding steps.

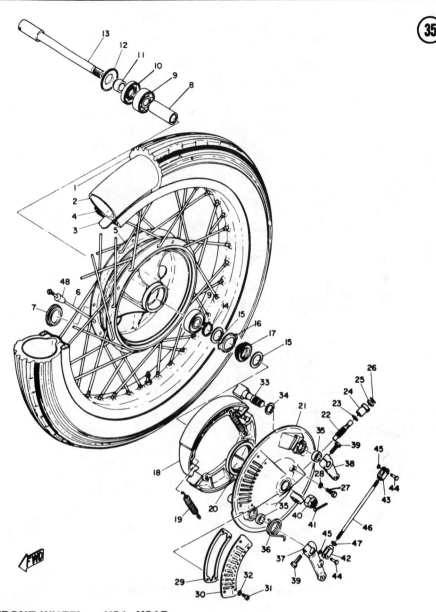

FRONT WHEEL — XS1, XS1B

1. Tire	13. Wheel shaft	25. Oil seal	37. Camshaft lever
2. Tube	14. Circlip	26. O-Ring	38. Camshaft lever
3. Rim band	15. Thrust washer	27. Bolt	39. Bolt
4. Rim	16. Speedometer clutch	28. Lockwasher	40. Shaft nut
5. Hub	17. Drive gear	29. Plate dust seal	41. Cotter pin
6. Spoke set	18. Brake shoe	30. Plate dust cover	42. Rod end
7. Blind plug	19. Shoe return spring	31. Pan head screw	43. Rod end
8. Bearing spacer	20. Oil seal	32. Lockwasher	44. Rod end pin
9. Bearing	21. Brake shoe plate	33. Camshaft	45. Circlip
10. Oil seal	22. Speedometer gear	34. Camshaft shim	46. Connecting rod
11. Wheel shaft collar	23. Thrust washer	35. Camshaft seal	47. Nut
12. Hub dust cover	24. Bushing	36. Lever return spring	48. Wheel balancer

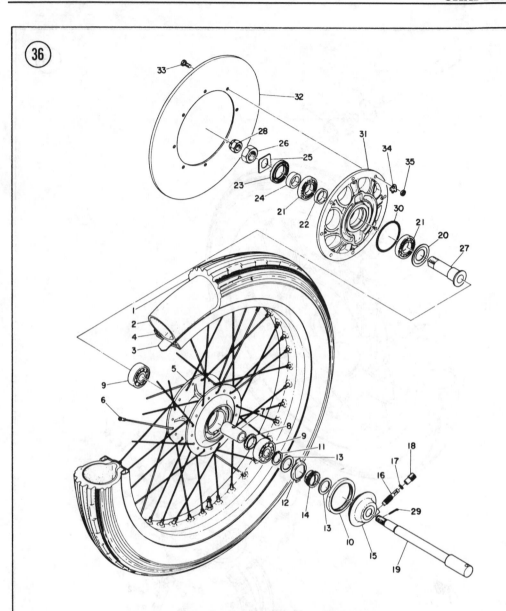

FRONT WHEEL — XS2, TX650, TX650A

1. Front tire	10. Oil seal	20. Dust cover	29. Cotter pin
2. Tube	11. Circlip	21. Bearing	30. O-Ring
3. Rim band	12. Meter clutch	22. Bearing spacer	31. Disc bracket
4. Rim	13. Thrust washer	23. Oil seal	32. Brake disc
5. Front hub	14. Drive gear	24. Shaft collar	33. Fitting bolt
6. Spoke set	16. Meter gear	25. Special washer	34. Lockwasher
7. Bearing spacer	17. Washer	26. Shaft nut	35. Nut
8. Spacer flange	18. Bushing	27. Disc shaft	
9. Bearing	19. Wheel shaft	28. Shaft nut	

8

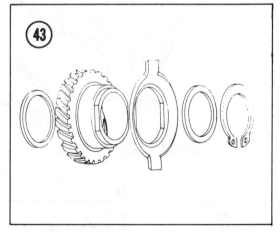

REAR WHEEL

Removal/Installation

1. See **Figure 44**. Prop the motorcycle up so the wheel is off the ground.

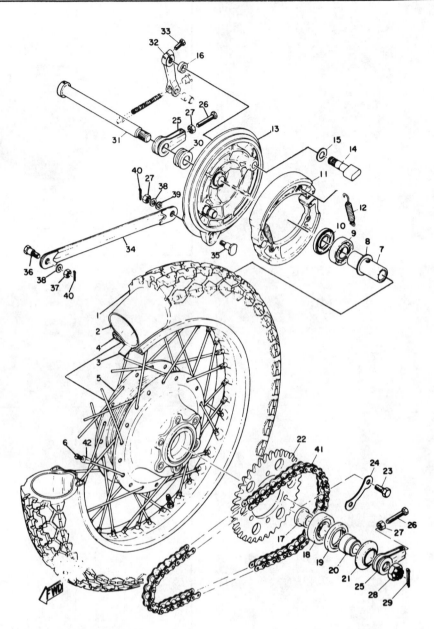

REAR WHEEL — ALL MODELS

1. Tire	12. Return spring	23. Fitting bolt	33. Bolt
2. Tube	13. Brake shoe plate	24. Lockwasher	34. Tension bar
3. Rim band	14. Cam shaft	25. Chain puller	35. Tension bar bolt
4. Rim	15. Cam shaft shim	26. Chain puller bolt	36. Tension bar bolt
5. Hub	16. Cam shaft seal	27. Nut	37. Nut
6. Spoke set	17. Collar	28. Shaft nut	38. Lockwasher
7. Bearing spacer	18. Bearing	29. Cotter pin	39. Plain washer
8. Spacer flange	19. Oil seal	30. Wheel shaft collar	40. Cotter pin
9. Bearing	20. Shaft collar	31. Wheel shaft	41. Chain
10. Oil seal	21. Dust cover	32. Camshaft lever	42. Wheel balancer
11. Brake shoe	22. Sprocket wheel gear		

2. Remove the cotter pin and disconnect the tension bar as shown in **Figure 45**. It must be reassembled correctly, so pay attention to the way it is replaced.

3. Disconnect brake rod. See **Figure 46**.

4. Loosen the chain adjustment bolts on both sides. See **Figure 47**.

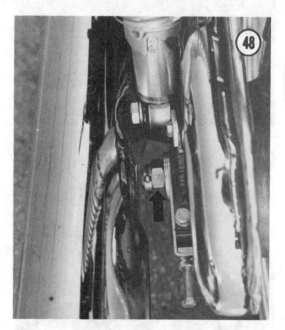

5. Remove the rear axle nut cotter pin and the rear axle nut. See **Figures 48 and 49**.

6. Remove the right chain adjuster and spacer. Refer to **Figure 50**.

7. Remove brake plate. See **Figure 51**.

8. Slip the chain off the rear sprocket, tilt the motorcycle to the left until the wheel can be removed as shown in **Figure 52**.

9. Brake shoes can be removed as shown in **Figure 53**.

10. Reverse procedure for installation.

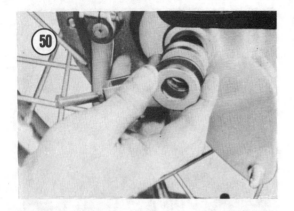

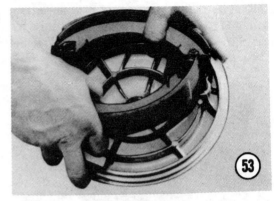

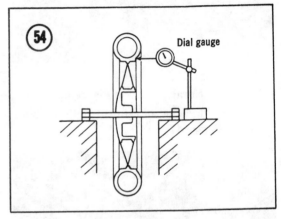

WHEEL TRUEING

1. Remove the tire, tube, and rim rubber from the wheel.

2. Install the wheel in a trueing stand or in the forks. See **Figure 54**.

3. Position a dial indicator as shown in Figure 54. A piece of wire, bent to touch the rim at its maximum point of runout, can be used as a substitute for approximate trueing.

4. Observe the dial indicator as the wheel is rotated through one complete revolution. Runout should not exceed 0.12 in. (3.0mm).

5. Tighten 3 or 4 spokes on each side of the rim at the high spot to reduce eccentricity.

6. Spin the wheel and check eccentricity again.

7. If more than 1 or 2 turns are required to lower the high spot, loosen the spokes on the opposite side to prevent flattening the rim.

8. Repeat Steps 3-7 until eccentricity is within 1/64-1/32 in.

9. For side-to-side rim wobble, loosen the spokes on one side and tighten those on the other. Work slowly and evenly.

10. Replace the tire, tube, and rim rubber. See *Tire Changing and Repair* in this chapter.

WHEEL LACING

1. To replace the rim only, tape each pair of spokes together and remove the rim. Install the new rim over the spokes and hub.

2. Install the spoke nipples beginning at the valve hole and working around the rim. Turn until 4 threads show at the bottom of the nipple.

3. Tighten each nipple one turn, working around the wheel from the valve side.

4. When the spokes are fairly tight, true the wheel as detailed before.

5. If hub or spokes require replacing, lay new hub, spokes, and rim on the bench. The hooked ends of the spokes have different radii, so use the correct ones during assembly.

6. Install a spoke through a flange hole in the hub. Repeat until 9 spokes are installed. See **Figures 55 and 56**.

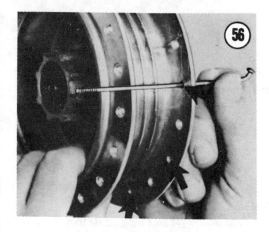

7. Set the hub face down on the bench with the spoke heads seated against the flange and set the rim over the spokes.

8. The rim spoke hole left of the valve hole should be angled up and to the left. Install a spoke in this hole and install the nipple. See Figures 55, 56, and **Figure 57**.

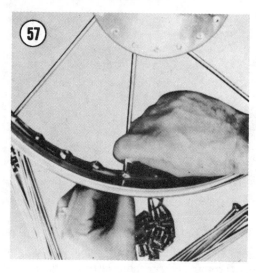

9. Install the next spokes in the fourth hole to the right of the first spoke. Repeat with every fourth hole until the next 9 spokes are fastened to the rim.

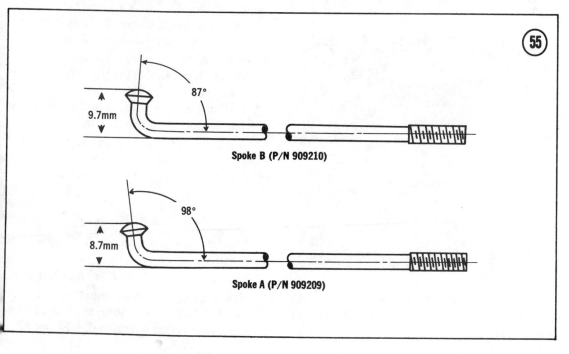

87°

9.7mm

Spoke B (P/N 909210)

98°

8.7mm

Spoke A (P/N 909209)

10. Turn the assembly over and install a spoke in a hole in the top flange and move the spoke to the right, crossing over 2 spokes in the opposite flange. Install the spoke in the next hole left of a spoke from the opposite flange. See Figures 55, 56, 57, and **Figure 58**.

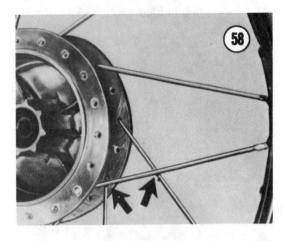

11. Work to the left on the hub, installing the other 8 spokes in every other hole in the flange and through the rim hole left next to a spoke from the lower flange.

12. Install other spokes in any hole in the top flange and move to the left, crossing over 2 spokes. See Figures 55 through 58 and **Figure 59** and install in the rim. Install 9 spokes in the holes on this flange.

13. Turn the wheel over and repeat the process on the other side. See Figures 55 through 59 and **Figure 60**.

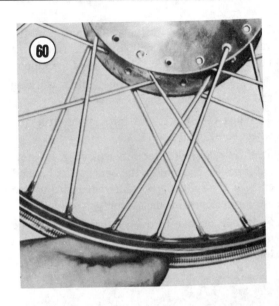

14. Tighten the spoke nipples until 4 threads remain on the spoke. Tighten each spoke around the wheel one turn until all are tight.

15. True the wheel as detailed in this chapter.

WHEEL BALANCING

1. The wheels must revolve freely to balance them properly. Loosen the axle nuts and remove the rear chain to eliminate friction.

2. Spin the wheel and let it coast to a stop. Mark the top of the wheel with a piece of chalk. Repeat several times to ensure that this spot is the lightest. A perfectly balanced wheel will stop in random spots.

3. Weights are available to attach to the spokes where the wheel needs balancing. See **Figure 61**. After adding each weight, spin the wheel and proceed as indicated in Steps 1 and 2.

4. Check the tightness of the valve stem. A loose stem, as shown in **Figure 62**, can shift and be torn loose causing the tire to deflate.

WHEEL ALIGNMENT

1. Measure the width of the 2 tires at their widest points.

2. Subtract smaller dimension from larger.

3. Nail a piece of wood, equal to the figure obtained in Step 2, to a straight piece of wood approximately 7 feet long. See (D), **Figure 63**.

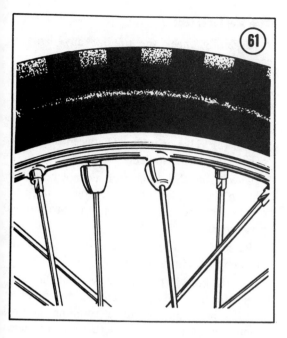

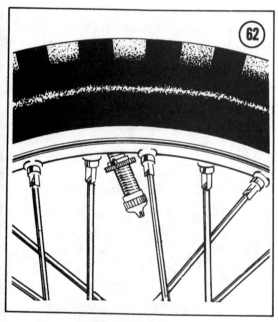

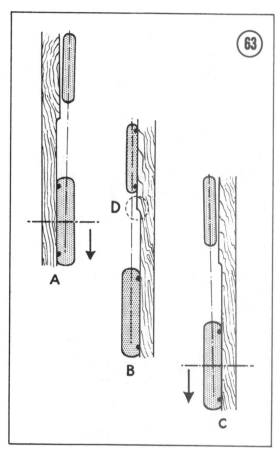

4. Lay the straight edge on blocks 6 in. high and place against the tires. If the wheels are aligned, the board will touch each wheel at 2 points as shown in (B), Figure 63.

5. If the wheels are not aligned as in (A) or (C), Figure 63, the rear wheel must be shifted to correct the situation. The chain adjuster must cause the wheel to move toward the rear on the side shown for the error indicated in Figure 63.

6. If the frame has been bent, this may not correct the misalignment. Replace the frame or have it aligned by an expert.

TIRE CHANGING AND REPAIR

1. Remove the valve cover to deflate the tire.

2. Press the entire bead on both sides of the tire into the center of the rim.

3. Lubricate the beads with soapy water.

4. Insert the tire iron under the bead next to the valve. Force the bead on the opposite side of the tire into the center of the rim and pry the bead over the rim with the tire iron (**Figure 64**).

5. Insert a second tire iron next to the first to hold the bead over the rim. Then work around the tire with the first tire iron, prying the bead over the rim. See **Figure 65**. Be careful not to pinch the inner tube with the tire irons.

6. Remove the valve from the hole in the rim and remove the tube from the tire. Lift out and lay aside.

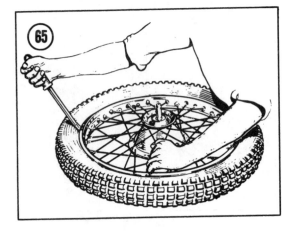

Tire Replacement

1. Carefully check the tire for any damage, especially inside.

2. A new tire may have balancing rubbers inside. These are not patches and should not be disturbed. A white spot near the bead indicates a lighter point on the tire. This should be placed next to the valve or midway between the 2 rim locks if they are installed.

3. Check that the spoke ends do not protrude through the nipples into the center of the rim to puncture the tube. File off any protruding spoke ends.

4. Be sure the rim rubber tape is in place with the rough side toward the rim.

5. Put the core in the tube valve. Put the tube in the tire and inflate just enough to round it out. Too much air will make installing the tire difficult, and too little will increase the chances of pinching the tube with the tire irons.

6. Lubricate the tire beads and rim with soapy water. Pull the tube partly out of the tire at the valve. Squeeze the beads together to hold the tube and insert the valve into the hole in the rim (**Figure 67**). The lower bead should go into the center of the rim with the upper bead outside it.

7. Stand the tire upright. Insert a tire iron between the second bead and the side of the rim that the first bead was pried over. See **Figure 66**. Force the bead on the opposite side from the tire iron into the center of the rim. Pry the second bead off the rim, working around as with the first bead.

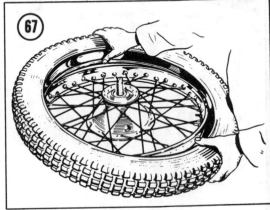

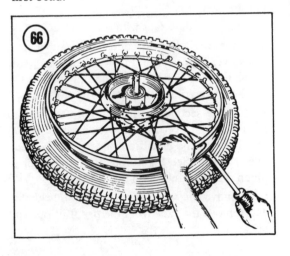

7. Press the lower bead into the rim center on each side of the valve, working around the tire in both directions. See **Figure 68**. Use a tire iron for the last few inches of bead (**Figure 69**).

8. Press the upper bead into the rim opposite the valve. Pry the bead into the rim on both sides of the initial point with a tire iron, working around the rim to the valve. See **Figure 70**.

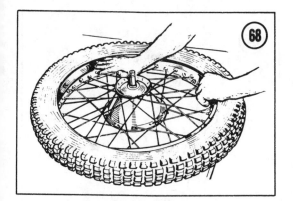

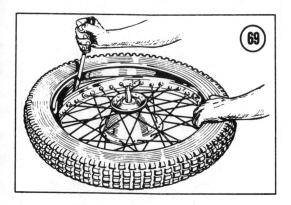

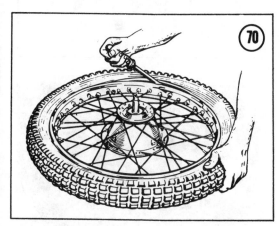

9. Wriggle the valve to be sure the tube is not trapped under the bead. Set the valve squarely in its hole before screwing on the valve nut to hold it against the rim.

10. Check the bead on both sides of the tire for even fit around the rim. Inflate the tire slowly to seat the beads in the rim. It may be necessary to bounce the tire to complete the seating. Inflate to the required pressure. Balance the wheel as described previously.

SEALS AND BEARINGS

Removal/Installation

Seal and bearing service is identical for front and rear hubs except the rear hub has a seal outside both bearings.

Wheel hub seals must be replaced each time they are removed.

1. Remove the wheel bearings as shown in **Figure 71**. Use a punch to move the spacer between both bearings to one side so the punch can be placed against the bearing. Tap the bearing out.

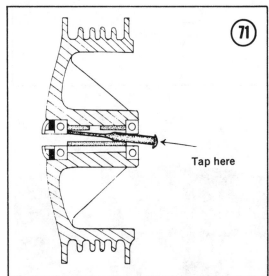

Tap here

2. A rod with bent end can be used as shown in **Figure 72**. The spacer has a hole at its midpoint and can be used to drive out the bearing.

3. Check the bearings for smooth rotation. Clean them in solvent and blow dry with compressed air.

4. Grease them with good quality bearing grease and inspect again for smooth action. Replace if necessary.

5. Use bearing installation tool to avoid cocking the bearing to one side and bending the seals.

REAR SPROCKET

Removal/Installation

1. Bend down the lockwasher tabs as shown in **Figure 73**. Remove the mounting bolts to free the sprocket.

8

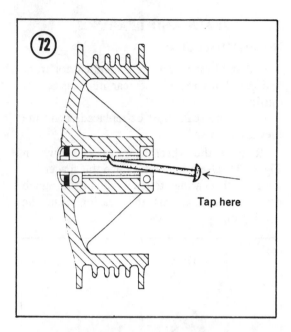

Tap here

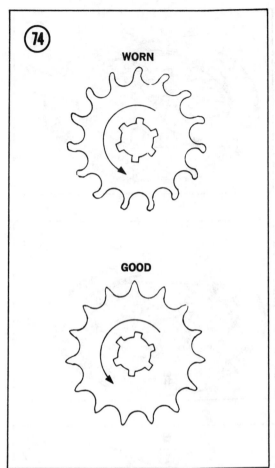

WORN

GOOD

2. Check the sprocket for wear as detailed in **Figure 74**.

3. When the sprocket is replaced, be sure bolts are tightened properly and the locking tabs are all in good shape and bent against the bolt flats.

DRUM BRAKES

1. Measure the brake shoes as a set as shown in **Figure 75** to obtain outside diameter. Measure the lining thickness and compare the figures against specifications found in **Table 1**. Replace the shoes as a set if necessary.

2. High spots on the linings which cause uneven contact with the drum can be removed with a file or emery cloth.

3. Glazing lowers braking efficiency. Rough up the lining surface with a file or emery cloth if necessary.

4. During brake servicing, care should be used to avoid getting grease or oil on the brake drum or shoe. Clean away any grease with solvent before reassembly.

Table 1   BRAKE SHOE SPECIFICATIONS

	Front		Rear	
	Standard	Wear Limit	Standard	Wear Limit
Shoe outside diameter	7.556 in. (192mm)	7.400 in. (188mm)	6.772 in. (172mm)*	6.612 in. (168mm)*
Lining thickness	0.160 in. (4mm)	0.080 in. (2mm)	0.160 in. (4mm)	0.080 in. (2mm)

*On 1977 and later models, standard diameter is 7.09 in. (180 mm); wear limit is 6.93 in. (176 mm).

5. Slight ridges in the brake drum can be removed with emery cloth. Deep ridges may necessitate drum replacement.

DISC BRAKES

Disassembly

1. See **Figure 76**. Remove the brake line as shown in **Figure 77**. Wrap the line with a plastic bag as shown in **Figure 78** to keep it clean.

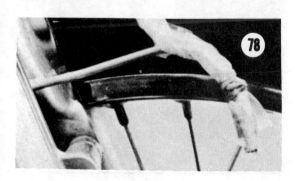

2. Use a heavy rubber band to keep the brake lever squeezed after the line has been disconnected. This will prevent the loss of brake fluid during servicing. See **Figure 79**.

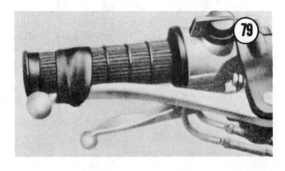

3. Remove the caliper mounting bolts and nuts and rotate the caliper assembly upward as shown in **Figure 80** to remove it.

4. Remove the pads from their seats as shown in **Figure 81**.

5. Remove the 2 bridge bolts and 2 hex bolts as shown in **Figure 82**. Remove the caliper pistons and seals. Refer to **Figure 83** and remove the caliper seal.

6. Use compressed air as shown in **Figure 84** to force the piston from the caliper cylinder.

8

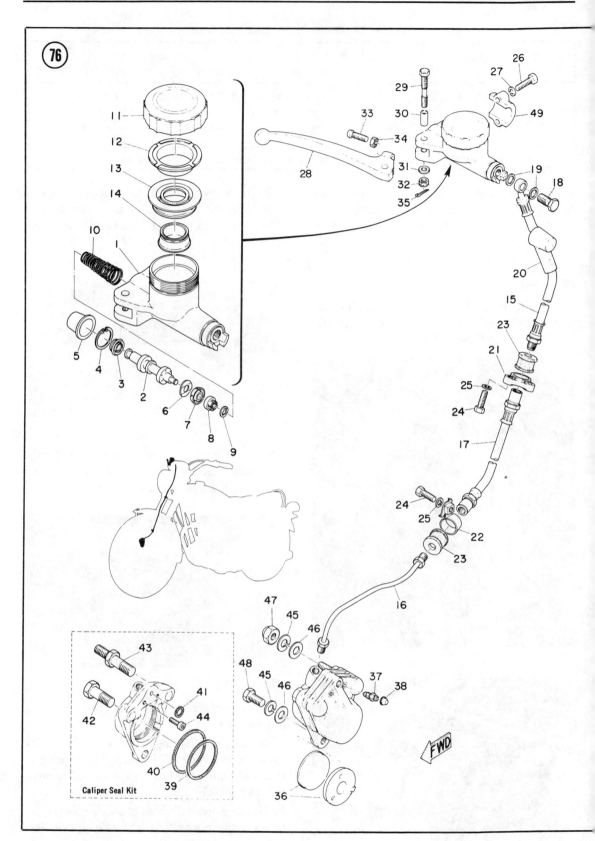

Caliper Seal Kit

MASTER CYLINDER AND CALIPER ASSEMBLY

1. Master cylinder body
2. Piston
3. Cup
4. Snap ring
5. Boot
6. Piston cup spacer
7. Cup
8. Spring retainer
9. Circlip
10. Spring
11. Cap
12. Diaphragm bushing
13. Diaphragm
14. Float
15. Brake hose
16. Brake pipe
17. Brake hose
18. Oil bolt
19. Oil bolt washer
20. Master cylinder boot
21. Brake hose holder
22. Brake hose holder
23. Brake hose rubber
24. Bolt
25. Lockwasher
26. Bolt
27. Lockwasher
28. Lever
29. Lever fitting screw
30. Lever collar
31. Plain washer
32. Slotted nut
33. Adjusting screw
34. Nut
35. Cotter pin
36. Brake pad
37. Bleed screw
38. Cap
39. Dust seal
40. Piston seal
41. Caliper seal
42. Bridge bolt
43. Bridge bolt
44. Bridge bolt
45. Lockwasher
46. Plain washer
47. Crown nut
48. Bolt
49. Master cylinder mounting clamp

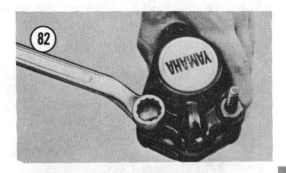

8

CAUTION
Never try pushing pistons out by any other means or they may be damaged.

7. Remove the piston seal and dust seal from each caliper body. Refer to **Figure 85**. Keep these parts free from gasoline, kerosene, or oil.

8. Remove the stoplight switch and the brake lever. Refer to **Figure 86**.

9. Disconnect brake line as shown in **Figure 87**.

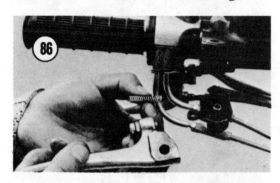

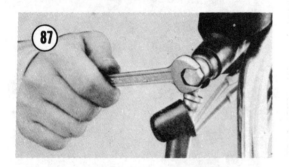

10. Remove the master cylinder mounting bolts as shown in **Figure 88** and remove the master cylinder.

11. Take off the reservoir tank cap and remove the diaphragm. Drain the hydraulic fluid from the reservoir.

12. Remove the master cylinder boot as shown in **Figure 89**.

13. Remove piston circlip. Refer to **Figure 90**.

14. Pull the piston out as shown in **Figure 91**.

15. Remove the master cylinder spring as shown in **Figure 92**.

16. Remove the clip as shown in **Figure 93** and take off the cylinder cup. See **Figure 94**.

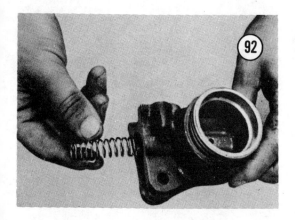

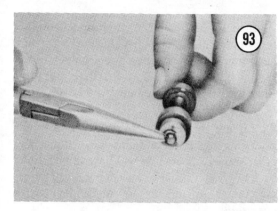

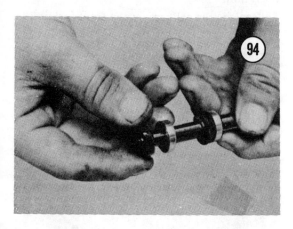

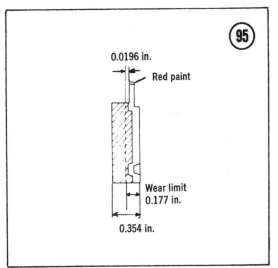

18. On earlier models, refer to **Figure 95** to determine brake pad wear. On newer models, pad wear limit is marked by a groove and red line on the pad.

19. Piston and dust seals should be replaced every 2 years or any time they show wear or damage.

20. Bridge bolts (refer to the exploded view) should be replaced each time they are removed,

whether damaged or not. They are included in the caliper seal kit available from a dealer.

21. Check the master cylinder for streaks or grooves worn in the wall. Check the outlet end for scratching or denting. Replace it if either condition is found. Check the compensating port for clogging and look for foreign matter in the cylinder or reservoir tank.

22. Check the cylinder cups for streaking or grooving on their contacting surface and replace if found. Swollen cylinder cups should be replaced along with all other seals and rubber parts. The cylinder cups should be replaced every 2 years as a matter of course.

23. The reservoir diaphragm and master cylinder boot should be checked for damage, cracks, and aging. If any signs of swelling are found, again replace all seals and rubber parts. They, like the cylinder cups, should be replaced every 2 years.

24. Check the conical spring for breakage and obvious wear.

25. Check the brake hose and line for leaks or damage. The brake hose should be replaced every 4 years.

Disc Inspection

1. Refer to **Figure 96** and check the brake disc for runout as shown. More than 0.006 in. (0.15mm) runout indicates service to the disc or bearings is needed.

2. Measure the disc thickness as shown in **Figure 97**. Minimum allowable disc thickness is 0.26 in. (6.5mm).

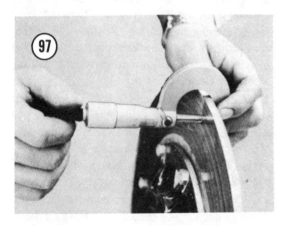

Assembly

1. Follow these instructions carefully when assembling disc brake components. All removed parts should be washed in new brake fluid before reassembly. No other liquid can be used. If another fluid (such as mineral oil) is introduced into the hydraulic system by mistake, the piston cups and seals should be replaced and all lines, ports, and passages must be thoroughly flushed with clean, new brake fluid.

2. Place the piston seal and dust seal in their seats in the caliper cylinder. Coat the cylinder walls and piston with new brake fluid and carefully insert the piston into the cylinder. See **Figure 98**.

3. Install a new caliper seal and put the inner and outer calipers together. Be sure the mating surfaces are clean. Use new bridge bolts. Tighten the 2 hex bolts to 43-72 ft.-lb. (6-10 mkg) and then tighten the bridge bolts to 53.5-68 ft.-lb. (7.5-9.5 mkg).

4. Replace the pads in their seats. If the pads are being replaced by themselves without any other service, the pistons will have to be pushed back by hand. Loosen the bleeder screw if necessary, to bleed off excess fluid during this operation.

5. Replace the calipers on the front fork in the reverse order of disassembly. Tighten mounting bolts to 28-36 ft.-lb. (4-5 mkg). Replace the brake line and tighten the fitting to 9-13 ft.-lb. (1.3-1.8 mkg).

6. Dip the cylinder cup in new brake fluid and install it on the piston as shown in **Figures 99 and 100**. Use care to avoid scratching the cup and piston.

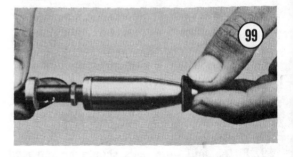

7. Refer to **Figure 101** and install the spacer as shown.

8. Replace the cup, retainer, and circlip shown in **Figure 102**.

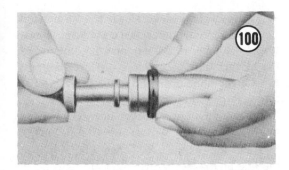

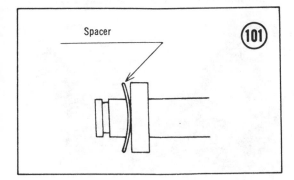

Spacer

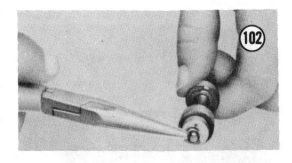

9. Insert the spring into the master cylinder as shown in **Figure 103**.

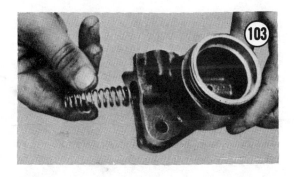

10. Carefully insert the piston into the cylinder. Do not force it under any circumstances. Install the circlip and replace the boot, with one end

in the master cylinder groove and the other end in the piston groove.

11. Replace the master cylinder on the handlebars and adjust the piston/pushrod clearance as shown in **Figure 104**. Tighten the adjusting screw locknut.

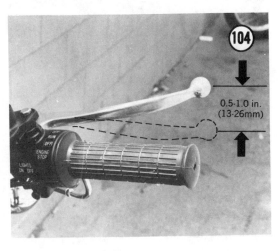

0.5-1.0 in. (13-26mm)

12. Connect the brake hose to the master cylinder, using new gaskets if necessary.

13. Add brake fluid (DOT 3) to the reservoir. Bleed the system as described in the following procedure.

Bleeding Hydraulic System

1. Bleed the system any time hydraulic lines are disconnected. Fill the reservoir to the top mark. Install the diaphragm as shown in **Figure 105**.

2. Connect a piece of neoprene tubing to the bleeder fitting shown in **Figure 106**.

3. The other end of the tubing must be submerged slightly in a clean cup of brake fluid as shown in **Figure 107**.

4. Apply the brake lever slowly a few times and loosen the bleeder screw while the lever is held under pressure. Fluid and air will come out of the bleeder tube. Just before the lever bottoms against the handlebar grip, tighten the bleeder screw. Repeat this operation until no more bubbles show up in the bleeder line. Tighten the bleeder screw to 4½-6½ ft.-lb. (0.6-0.9 mkg).

5. Refill the reservoir with new brake fluid to the line and reset the diaphragm to its original position as shown in **Figures 108 and 109**.

APPENDIX

SPECIFICATIONS

This chapter contains specifications for the Yamaha models covered by this book. Since there are differences between the various models, be sure to consult the correct table for your motorcycle.

SPECIFICATIONS — XS1 AND XS1B

Dimensions:

Overall length	85.4 in. (2,170mm)
Overall width	35.6 in. (905mm)
Overall height	45.3 in. (1,150mm)
Wheelbase	55.5 in. (1,410mm)
Minimum ground clearance	5.9 in. (150mm)
Weight (unladen)	409 lbs. (185 kg)

Carburetor:

Type	BS38 x 2
Manufacturer	Mikuni
Main jet	#130
Jet needle	4JN19—4th
Pilot fuel jet	42.5
Starter jet	0.6
Needle jet	Z-6
Float level	25mm
Air screw	1 turn-out
	(continued)

SPECIFICATIONS — XS1 AND XS1B (continued)

Engine:

Type	Twin cylinder air-cooled 4 stroke wet sump OHC
Lubrication system	Pressure lubricated, wet sump
Bore and stroke	2.953 x 2.913 in. (75 x 74mm)
Displacement	39.8 cu. in. (653cc)
Compression ratio	8.7:1
Compression pressure	145 lbs./in.^{2}
Maximum power	53 BHP/7,000 rpm
Maximum torque	40.1 ft.-lbs./6,000 rpm
Cylinder description	Twin parallel cylinders, aluminum with cast iron sleeves
Camshaft timing	Intake BTDC 47° (Open) ABDC 67° (Close)
	Exhaust BBDC 60° (Open) ATDC 41° (Close)
Valve clearance (cold)	Intake 0.002-0.004 in. (0.05-0.10mm)
	Exhaust 0.006-0.008 in. (0.15-0.20mm)
Sump capacity	3.2 qt. (3.0 L)
Ignition timing (fully retarded)	13° BTDC
Piston clearance	0.002—0.0022″
Starting system	Kickstarter

Performance:

Maximum speed	115 mph
Fuel consumption (on paved level road)	82.5 mpg at 37 mph
Climbing ability	26 degrees
Minimum turning radius	98.4 in. (2,500mm)
Braking distance	46 ft. at 31 mph

Air Filter: Dry, paper filter

Clutch:

Type	Wet, multi-disc (6 friction + 5 metal plates)

Primary Drive:

Type:	Spur gear (straight cut)
Reduction ratio (gear and total)	72/27 (2.666)

Transmission:

Type	Constant mesh, five-speed, wide-ratio
1st	32/13 = 2.461 (5.185)
2nd	27/17 = 1.588 (4.235) Internal engine ratio
3rd	26/20 = 1.300 (3.466) (Pri. x Trans.)
4th	23/21 = 1.095 (2.920) Multiply by drive chain ratio
5th	22/23 = 0.956 (2.550) for overall gearing

Secondary Reduction System:

Type	Single row chain

Secondary Reduction Ratio: 34/17 = 2.000

Alternator:

Model	LD 115
Manufacturer	Hitachi **(continued)**

SPECIFICATIONS — XS1 AND XS1B (continued)

Rectifier:

Model	SD6D-9
Manufacturer	Hitachi

Chassis:

Frame type	Tubular steel double cradle type
Fuel tank capacity	3.3 U.S. gals. (12.5 L)
Suspension system, rear	Swing arm
Fork travel	5.12 in. (130mm)
Fork oil quantity (each)	7.5 oz. (223cc)
Caster	63°
Trail	3.9 in. (101mm)
Front rim size	1.85B x 19
Spoke diameter, length & number	Inner 3.5 x 160.5mm. Outer 3.5 x 160mm
Front tire	
Size	3.50 x 19 4PR
Inflation pressure	23-25-lbs./in.^{2}
Rear rim size	2.15B x 18
Spoke diameter, length & number	Inner 4 x 152.0mm. Outer 4 x 151.5mm
Rear tire	
Size	4.00 x 18 4PR
Inflation pressure	28-30 lbs./in.^{2}
Front brake type	Internal expansion, double leading shoe
Rear brake type	Internal expansion, single leading shoe
Diameter & width	7.1 in. x 1.18 in. (180mm x 30mm)

Regulator:

Model	TLIZ - 49
Manufacturer	HItachi
No load voltage rate	14.5 volts/2,000 rpm

Ignition System:

Type		Battery ignition
Ignition timing		13° BTDC (fully retarded)
Breaker point gap		0.012-0.016 in. (0.30-0.40mm)
Spark plug	Manufacturer	NGK
	Heat range	B-8ES
Ignition coil	Manufacturer	Hitachi
	Voltage output	10 kV @ 4,000 rpm

Battery:

Model	(12N12-4A-1) x 1
Manufacturer	G.S.
Capacity	12V 12A.H.
Dimensions	5.36 x 2.36 x 5.16" (134mm x 59mm x 129mm)

Lighting System:

Headlight	12V 50W/40W
Taillight	12V/8W
Stoplight	12V/27W
Neutral light	12V/3W
Flasher indicator light	12V/3W
Flasher light	12V/27W
High beam indicator	12V/2W
Speedometer light	12V/3W
Tachometer light	12V/3W

9

SPECIFICATIONS — XS2, TX650, AND TX650A

Dimensions:

Overall length	85.6 in. (2,175mm)
Overall width	35.6 in. (905mm)
Overall height	45.9 in. (1,165mm)
Wheelbase	55.5 in. (1,410mm)
Minimum ground clearance	5.9 in. (150mm)
Weight (unladen)	427 lbs. (194 kg)

Performance:

Maximum speed	115 mph
Fuel consumption (on paved level road)	82.5 mpg at 37 mph
Climbing ability	26 degrees
Minimum turning radius	98.4 in. (2,500mm)
Braking distance	46 ft. at 31 mph

Engine:

Type	Twin cylinder air-cooled 4 stroke wet sump OHC
Lubrication system	Pressure lubricated, wet sump
Bore and stroke	2.953 x 2.913 in. (75 x 74mm)
Displacement	39.8 cu. in. (653cc)
Compression ratio	8.7 : 1
Compression pressure	145 lbs./in.^{2}
Maximum power	53 BHP/7,000 rpm
Maximum torque	40.1 ft.-lbs. /6,000 rpm
Cylinder description	Twin parallel cylinders, aluminum with cast iron sleeves
Camshaft timing	Intake BTDC 47° (Open) ABDC 67° (Close)
	Exhaust BBDC 60° (Open) ATDC 41° (Close)
Valve clearance (cold)	Intake 0.002-0.004 in. (0.05-0.10mm)
	Exhaust 0.006-0.008 in. (0.15-0.20mm)
Sump capacity	2.6 qt. (2.5 L)
Ignition timinig (fully retarded)	13° BTDC
Piston clearance	0.002-0.0022"
Starting system	Kick and electric starter

Carburetor:

Type	BS38 x 2
Manufacturer	Mikuni
Main jet	#130 (TX650A : 127.5)
Jet needle	4JN19—4th (TX650A : 4N8-4)
Pilot fuel jet	42.5 (TX650A : 45)
Starter jet	0.7
Needle jet	Z-6
Float level	24mm
Air screw	¾ turn out

Air Filter: Dry, paper filter (TX650A : oiled foam)

(continued)

SPECIFICATIONS — XS2, TX650, AND TX650A (continued)

Clutch:	
Type	Wet, multi-disc (6 friction + 5 metal plates)
Primary Drive:	
Type	Spur gear (straight cut)
Reduction ratio (gear and total)	72/27 (2.666)
Transmission:	
Type	Constant mesh, five-speed, wide-ratio
1st	32/13 = 2.461 (5.185)
2nd	27/17 = 1.588 (4.235)
3rd	26/20 = 1.300 (3.466)
4th	23/21 = 1.095 (2.920)
5th	22/23 = 0.956 (2.550)

Internal engine ratio
  (Pri. x Trans.)
Multiply by drive chain ratio
for overall gearing

Secondary Reduction System:	
Type	Chain
Secondary Reduction Ratio:	34/17 = 2.000
Chassis:	
Frame type	Tubular steel double cradle type
Fuel tank capacity	3.3 U.S. gals. (12.5 L) XS2
	3.9 U.S. gals. (14.0 L) TX650
Suspension system, rear	Swing arm
Fork travel	5.12 in. (130mm)
Fork oil quantity (each)	4.25 oz. (136cc)
Caster	63°
Trail	3.9 in. (101mm)
Front rim size	1.85B x 19
Spoke diameter, length	Inner 3.5 x 160.5mm. Outer 3.5 x 160mm
Front tire	
Size	3.50 x 19 4PR
Inflation pressure	23-25 lbs./in.^{2}
Rear rim size	2.15B x 18
Spoke diameter, length	Inner 4 x 152.0mm. Outer 4 x 151.5mm
Rear tire	
Size	4.00 x 18 4PR
Inflation pressure	28-30 lbs./in.^{2}
Front brake type	Hydraulic disc brake (fixed type)
Rear brake type	Internal expansion, single leading shoe
Diameter & width	7.1 in. x 1.18 in. (180mm x 30mm)
Alternator:	
Model	LD 115
Manufacturer	Hitachi
Rectifier:	
Model	SD6D-9
Manufacturer	Hitachi

9

(continued)

SPECIFICATIONS — XS2, TX650, AND TX650A (continued)

Regulator:		
Model		TLIZ - 49
Manufacturer		Hitachi
No load voltage rate		14.5 volts/2,000 rpm
Ignition System:		
Type		Battery ignition
Ignition timing		13° BTDC (fully retarded)
Breaker point gap		0.012-0.016 in. (0.30-0.40mm)
Spark plug	Manufacturer	NGK
	Heat range	B-8ES
Ignition coil	Manufacturer	Hitachi
	Voltage output	10 kV @ 4,000 rpm
Battery:		
Model		(12N12-4A-1) x 1
Manufacturer		G.S.
Capacity		12V 12A.H.
Dimensions		5.36 x 2.36 x 5.16″ (134mm x 59mm x 129mm)
Lighting System:		
Headlight		12V 50W/40W
Taillight		12V/8W
Stoplight		12V/27W
Neutral light		12V/3W
Flasher indicator light		12V/3W
Flasher light		12V/27W
High beam indicator		12V/2W
Speedometer light		12V/3W
Tachometer light		12V/3W

SPECIFICATIONS—XS650 (1975-EARLY 1978)

Engine:

Type	Twin cylinder air-cooled 4-stroke wet sump OHC
Lubrication system	Pressure lubricated, wet sump
Bore and stroke	2.953 x 2.913 in. (75 x 74mm)
Displacement	39.8 cu. in. (653cc)
Compression ratio	8.4 : 1
Compression pressure	138 lbs./in.^{2}
Maximum power	Not given (approx. 50 @ 7,000 rpm)
Maximum torque	40.1 ft.-lb./6,000 rpm
Camshaft timing	Intake BDTC 36° (Open) ABDC 68° (Close)
	Exhaust BBDC 68° (Open) ATDC 36° (Close)
Valve clearance (cold)	Intake 0.002-0.004 in. (0.05-0.10mm)
	Exhaust 0.006-0.008 in. (0.15-0.20mm)
Sump capacity	2.6 qt. (2.5 liter)
Ignition timing (fully retarded)	15° BTDC ± 2°
Piston clearance	0.002-0.0022 in.
Starting system	Kick and electric starter

Carburetor:

Type	BS38 x 2
Manufacturer	Mikuni
Main jet	122.5
Jet needle	4M1-3
Pilot fuel jet	45.0
Starter jet	0.5
Needle jet	Z-8
Float level	25mm
Air screw	1½ turns out

Air Filter:

Type	Dry foam

Clutch:

Type	Wet, multi-disc (6 friction + 5 metal plates)

Primary Drive:

Type	Spur gear (straight cut)
Reduction ratio (gear and total)	72/27 (2.666)

Transmission:

Type	Constant mesh, five-speed, wide-ratio		
1st	32/13 = 2.461	(5.185)	
2nd	27/17 = 1.588	(4.235)	Internal engine ratio
3rd	26/20 = 1.300	(3.466)	(Pri. x Trans.)
4th	23/21 = 1.095	(2.920)	Multiply by drive chain ratio
5th	22/23 = 0.956	(2.550)	for overall gearing

Secondary Reduction Ratio: 34/17 = 2.000

Chassis:

Frame type	Tubular steel double cradle type
Fuel tank capacity	4.0 U.S. gals. (14.2 liter)
Suspension system, rear	Swing arm

(continued)

9

SPECIFICATIONS—XS650 (1975-EARLY 1978) (Continued)

Chassis: (continued)

Fork travel	**5.12 in. (130 mm)**
Fork oil quantity (each)	**5.4 oz. (160 cc)**
Caster	**63°**
Trail	3.9 in. (101mm)
Front tire	
Size	3.50 x 19 4PR
Inflation pressure	23-25 lb./in.²
Rear tire	
Size	4.00 18 4PR
Inflation pressure	28-30 lb./in.²
Front brake type	Hydraulic disc brake (fixed type)
Rear brake type	Internal expansion, single leading shoe
Diameter & width	7.1 x 1.18 in. (180 x 30mm)

Alternator:

Model	LD 115
Manufacturer	Hitachi

Rectifier:

Model	SD6D-9
Manufacturer	Hitachi

Regulator:

Model	TLIZ - 49
Manufacturer	Hitachi
No load voltage rate	14.5 volts/2,000 rpm

Ignition System:

Type		Battery ignition
Ignition timing		15° BTDC (fully retarded)
Breaker point gap		0.012-0.018 in. (0.30-0.45mm)
Spark plug	Manufacturer	NGK
	Heat range	BP-7ES
Ignition coil	Manufacturer	Hitachi
	Voltage output	10 kV @ 4,000 rpm

Battery:

Model	12N12-4A-1 (through 1973)—YB14L-A2 (1974-on)
Manufacturer	G.S.
Capacity	12V 12 Ah
Dimensions	5.36 x 2.36 x 5.16 in. (134 x 59 x 129mm)

Lighting System:

Headlight	12V 50W/40W
Taillight	12V/8W
Stoplight	12V/27W
Neutral light	12V/3W
Flasher indicator light	12V/3W
Flasher light	12V/27W
High beam indicator	12V/2W
Speedometer light	12V/3W
Tachometer light	12V/3W

SPECIFICATIONS—1978 (LATE) XS650E, SE

General:

Engine number starts	E:	2F0-006501
	SE:	2F0-114241
Engine type		4-stroke twin, SOHC, 2 valves/cyl
Lubrication system		Trochoid pump, wet sump
Clutch		Wet, 7 friction, 6 discs
Starting system		Kick and electric starter
Ignition system		Battery, point
Charging system		Alternator, rectifier, regulator
Carburetion		2 constant vacuum slide/needle
Air filter		Dry foam
Dry weight	E:	467 lb. (212kg)
	SE:	463 lb. (210kg)

Engine:

Bore X Stroke		2.95 x 2.91 (75 x 74mm)
Displacement		39.8 cu. in. (653cc)
Compression ratio		8.5:1
Valve timing	IN:	Open 36° BTDC Close 68° ATDC
	EX:	Open 68° BBDC Close 36° ATDC
Valve clearance (cold)	IN:	0.004 in. (0.10mm)
	EX:	0.006 in. (0.15mm)
Piston clearance		0.0020-0.0022 in. (0.050-0.055mm)

Carburetor:

Type	2 Mikuni BS38
I.D. mark	2F0-00
Main jet	#135
Needle jet	Z-2
Needle	502-3rd
Throttle cutaway	#120
Pilot jet	#27.5
Pilot screw	Preset
Float level	0.94 in. (24mm)
Idle speed	1,200 rpm

Transmission:

Primary drive	Straight cut gears
Primary drive ratio	72/27 (2.666)
Transmission gears	Constant mesh, 5-speed
1st ratio	32/13 (2.461)
2nd ratio	27/17 (1.588)
3rd ratio	26/20 (1.300)
4th ratio	23/21 (1.095)
5th ratio	22/23 (0.956)
Secondary drive ratio	34/17 (2.0)
Drive chain	50HDS 103 links

(continued)

9

SPECIFICATIONS—1978 (LATE) XS650E, SE (continued)

Chassis:

Type	**Double cradle**
Caster	**27°**
Trail	**4.53 in. (115mm)**
Front suspension	**Telescopic fork, oil dampened**
Travel	**5.91 in. (150mm)**
Oil quantity (each)	**5.7 oz. (169cc) SAE10**
Oil level	**17.9 in. (454mm) without spring**
Rear suspension	Swing arm
Shock travel	3.15 in. (80mm)
Wheel type	E: Wire spoked
	SE: Cast aluminum
Wheel size	E: Front 1.85-19 Rear 2.15-18
	SE: Front 1.85-19 Rear MT3.00-16
Tire type	Inner tube
Front tire	E: 3.50H19-4PR
	SE: 3.50S19-4PR
Rear tire	E: 4.00H18-4PR
	SE: 130/90S16-4PR
Front brake	Hydraulic disc, 11.7 in. (298mm)
Rear brake	E: Single leading shoe, 7.09 x 1.18 in. (180 x 30mm)
	SE: Hydraulic disc, 10.5 in. (267mm)
Fuel tank capacity	E: 4.0 gal. (15 liters)
	SE: 2.9 gal. (11.0 liters)

Electrical:

Ignition system	Battery, point
Ignition timing	15° BTDC @ 1,200 rpm
Advance	41.5° BTDC @ 3,300 rpm
Spark plug type	BP7ES (NGK); N7Y (Champion)
Spark plug gap	0.028-0.032 in. (0.7-0.8mm)
Breaker point gap	0.012-0.016 in. (0.3-0.4mm)
Condensers	0.22 microfarad
Charging system	Alternator, rectifier, regulator
Alternator output	14V, 11A @ 2,000 rpm
Regulator	14.5 ±0.5V
Battery	YUASA YB14L-A2
Capacity	12V, 14AH
Lighting	
Headlight	Sealed beam 50/40W
Tail/brakelights	8/27W
Turn signals	27W
Meters & indicators	3.4W
Fuse	20A main

SPECIFICATIONS—1979 XS650-2F, SF

General:

Engine number starts	2F: 2F0-250101
	SF: 2F0-150101
Engine type	4-stroke twin, SOHC, 2 valves/cyl
Lubrication system	Trochoid pump, wet sump
Clutch	Wet, 7 friction, 6 discs
Starting system	Kick and electric starter
Ignition system	Battery, point
Charging system	Alternator, rectifier, regulator
Carburetion	2 constant vacuum slide/needle
Air filter	Dry foam
Dry weight	2F: 452 lb. (205kg)
	SF: 463 lb. (210kg)

Engine:

Bore X Stroke	2.95 x 2.91 (75 x 74mm)
Displacement	39.8 cu. in. (653cc)
Compression ratio	8.5:1
Valve timing	IN: Open 36° BTDC Close 68° ATDC
	EX: Open 68° BBDC Close 36° ATDC
Valve clearance (cold)	IN: 0.0024 in. (0.06mm)
	EX: 0.006 in. (0.15mm)
Piston clearance	0.0020-0.0022 in. (0.050-0.055mm)

Carburetor:

Type	2 Mikuni BS38
I.D. mark	2F0-00
Main jet	#135
Needle jet	Z-2
Needle	502-3rd
Throttle cutaway	#120
Pilot jet	#27.5
Pilot screw	Preset
Float level	0.94 in. (24mm)
Idle speed	1,200 rpm

Transmission:

Primary drive	Straight cut gears
Primary drive ratio	72/27 (2.666)
Transmission gears	Constant mesh, 5-speed
1st ratio	32/13 (2.461)
2nd ratio	27/17 (1.588)
3rd ratio	26/20 (1.300)
4th ratio	23/21 (1.095)
5th ratio	22/23 (0.956)
Secondary drive ratio	34/17 (2.0)
Drive chain	50HDS 103 links

(continued)

9

SPECIFICATIONS—1979 XS650-2F, SF (continued)

Chassis:

Type	**Double cradle**
Caster	**27°**
Trail	**4.53 in. (115mm)**
Front suspension	**Telescopic fork, oil dampened**
Travel	**5.91 in. (150mm)**
Oil quantity (each)	**5.7 oz. (169cc) SAE10**
Oil level	**17.9 in. (454mm) without spring**
Rear suspension	Swing arm
Shock travel	3.15 in. (80mm)
Wheel type	2F: Wire spoked
	SF: Cast aluminum
Wheel size	2F: Front, 1.85-19 Rear, 2.75-16
	SF: Front, 1.85-19 Rear, MT3.00-16
Tire type	2F: Inner tube
	SF: Tubeless
Front tire	3.50S19-4PR
Rear tire	130/90S16-4PR
Front brake	Hydraulic disc, 11.7 in. (298mm)
Rear brake	2F: Single leading shoe, 7.09 x 1.18 in. (180 x 30mm)
	SF: Hydraulic disc, 10.5 in. (267mm)
Fuel tank capacity	2.9 gal. (11 liters)

Electrical:

Ignition system	Battery, point
Ignition timing	15° BTDC @ 1,200 rpm
Advance	40° BTDC @ 3,000 rpm
Spark plug type	BP7ES (NGK); N7Y (Champion)
Spark plug gap	0.028-0.032 in. (0.7-0.8mm)
Breaker point gap	0.012-0.016 in. (0.3-0.4mm)
Condensers	0.22 microfarad
Charging system	Alternator, rectifier, regulator
Alternator output	14V, 11A @ 2,000 rpm
Regulator	14.5 ±0.5V
Battery	YUASA YB14L-A2
Capacity	12V, 14AH
Lighting	
Headlight	Sealed beam 50/40W
Tail/brakelights	8/27W
Turn signals	27W
Meters & indicators	3.4W
Fuse	20A main

SPECIFICATIONS—1980 XS650G, SG

General:

Engine number starts	G:	3G0-000101
	SG:	2F0-200101
Engine type		4-stroke twin, SOHC, 2 valves/cyl
Lubrication system		Trochoid pump, wet sump
Clutch		Wet, 7 friction, 6 discs
Starting system		Kick and electric starter
Ignition system		Transistorized
Charging system		Alternator, rectifier/regulator
Carburetion		2 constant vacuum slide/needle
Air filter		Dry foam
Dry weight	G:	452 lb. (205kg)
	SG:	463 lb. (210kg)

Engine:

Bore X Stroke		2.95 x 2.91 (75 x 74mm)
Displacement		39.8 cu. in. (653cc)
Compression ratio		8.7:1
Valve timing	IN:	Open 35° BTDC Close 67° ATDC
	EX:	Open 67° BBDC Close 35° ATDC
Valve clearance (cold)	IN:	0.0024 in. (0.06mm)
	EX:	0.006 in. (0.15mm)
Piston clearance		0.0020-0.0022 in. (0.050-0.055mm)

Carburetor:

Type	2 Mikuni BS34
I.D. mark	3G1-00
Main jet	#132.5
Needle jet	Y-0
Needle	5HX12
Throttle cutaway	#135
Pilot jet	#42.5
Pilot screw	Not equipped
Float level	1.08 in. (27.3mm)
Idle speed	1,200 rpm

Transmission:

Primary drive	Straight cut gears
Primary drive ratio	72/27 (2.666)
Transmission gears	Constant mesh, 5-speed
1st ratio	32/13 (2.461)
2nd ratio	27/17 (1.588)
3rd ratio	26/20 (1.300)
4th ratio	23/21 (1.095)
5th ratio	22/23 (0.956)
Secondary drive ratio	34/17 (2.0)
Drive chain	50HDS 103 links

9

(continued)

SPECIFICATIONS—1980 XS650G, SG (continued)

Chassis:

Type	**Double cradle**
Caster	**27°**
Trail	**4.53 in. (115mm)**
Front suspension	**Telescopic fork, oil dampened**
Travel	**5.91 in. (150mm)**
Oil quantity (each)	**5.7 oz. (169cc) SAE10**
Oil level	**17.9 in. (454mm) without spring**
Rear suspension	Swing arm
Shock travel	3.15 in. (80mm)
Wheel type	G: Wire spoked
	SG: Cast aluminum
Wheel size	G: Front 1.85-19 Rear, 2.75-16
	SG: Front MT1.85-19 Rear, MT3.00-16
Tire type	G: Inner tube
	SG: Tubeless
Front tire	3.50S19-4PR
Rear tire	130/90S16-4PR
Front brake	Hydraulic disc, 11.7 in. (298mm)
Rear brake	G: Single leading shoe, 7.09 x 1.18 in. (180 x 30mm)
	SG: Hydraulic disc, 10.5 in. (267mm)
Fuel tank capacity	3.04 gal. (11.5 liters)

Electrical:

Ignition system	Transistorized
Ignition timing	15° BTDC @ 1,200 rpm
Advance	40° BTDC @ 3,200 rpm
Spark plug type	BP7ES (NGK); N7Y (Champion)
Spark plug gap	0.028-0.032 in. (0.7-0.8mm)
Charging system	Alternator, rectifier, regulator
Alternator output	14V, 16A @ 5,000 rpm
Regulator/rectifier	14.5 ±0.5V
Battery	YUASA YB14L-A2
Capacity	12V, 14AH
Lighting	
Headlight	Sealed beam 50/40W
Tail/brakelights	8/27W
Turn signals	27W
Meters & indicators	3.4W
License lights	SG: 3.8W
Fuses	
Main	20A
Head light	10A
Signals	10A
Ignition	10A

SPECIFICATIONS—1981 XS650H, SH

General:

Engine number starts	H: 4N9-000101
	SH: 4M4-000101
Engine type	4-stroke twin, SOHC, 2 valves/cyl
Lubrication system	Trochoid pump, wet sump
Clutch	Wet, 7 friction, 6 metal
Starting system	Kick and electric starter with starting circuit cut-off system
Ignition system	Transistorized
Charging system	Alternator, rectifier/regulator
Carburetion	2 constant vacuum slide/needle
Air filter	Dry foam
Dry weight	H: 452 lb. (205 kg)
	SH: 459 lb. (208 kg)

Engine:

Bore x stroke	2.95 x 2.91 in. (75 x 74 mm)
Displacement	39.8 cu. in. (653 cc)
Compression ratio	8.7:1
Valve timing	IN: Open 35° BTDC
	Close 69° ABDC
	EX: Open 67° BBDC
	Close 37° ATDC
Valve clearance (cold)	IN: 0.0024 in. (0.06 mm)
	EX: 0.006 in. (0.15 mm)
Piston clearance	0.0020-0.0022 in. (0.050-0.055 mm)

Carburetor:

Type	2 Mikuni BS34
I.D. mark	3G1-00
Main jet	No. 132.5
Needle jet	Y-0
Needle	5HX12
Throttle cutaway	No. 135
Pilot jet	No. 42.5
Pilot screw	Preset
Float level	1.08 in. (27.3 mm)
Idle speed	1,200 rpm

Transmission:

Primary drive	Straight cut gears
Primary drive ratio	72/27 (2.666)
Transmission gears	Constant mesh, 5-speed
1st ratio	32/13 (2.461)
2nd ratio	27/17 (1.588)
3rd ratio	26/20 (1.300)
4th ratio	23/21 (1.095)
5th ratio	22/23 (0.956)
Secondary drive ratio	34/17 (2.000)
Drive chain	50HDS, 104 links

Chassis:

Type	Double cradle
Caster	27°

9

(continued)

SPECIFICATIONS—1981 XS650H, SH (Continued)

Trail	4.53 in. (115 mm)
Front suspension	Telescopic fork, oil damped
Travel	5.91 in. (150 mm)
Oil quantity (each)	5.72 oz. (169 cc) SAE 10
Oil level	17.9 in. (454 mm) without spring
Rear suspension	Swingarm
Shock travel	3.15 in. (80 mm)
Wheel type	H: Wire spoked
	SH: Cast aluminum
Wheel size	H: Front 1.85 x 19
	Rear 3.00 x 16
	SH: Front 1.85 x 19
	Rear 2.75 x 16
Tire type	H: Inner tube
	SH: Tubeless
Front tire	3.50S19-4PR
Rear tire	130/90-16 67S
Front brake	Hydraulic disc, 11.7 in.
	(298 mm)
Rear brake	Leading shoe,
	7.09 x 1.18 in. (180 x 30 mm)
Fuel tank capacity	3.04 gal. (11.5 liters)
Reserve capacity	0.61 gal. (2.3 liters)
Fuel type	Regular

Electrical:	
Ignition system	Transistorized
Ignition timing	15° BTDC @ 1,200 rpm
Advance	40° BTDC @ 3,200 rpm
Spark plug type	BP7ES (NGK); N7Y (Champion)
Spark plug gap	0.027-0.031 in. (0.7-0.8 mm)
Charging system	Alternator, rectifier, regulator
Alternator output	14V, 16A @ 5,000 rpm
Regulator/rectifier setting	14.5 +/- 0.5V
Battery	YUASA YB14L-A2
Capacity	12V, 14AH
Lighting	
Headlight	Sealed beam
Tail/brakelights	8W/27W
Turn signals	27W
Meters & indicators	3.4W
License light	3.8W
Fuses	
Main	20A
Headlight	10A
Signal	10A
Ignition	10A

LATE 1978 AND LATER SERVICE INFORMATION

10

The following supplement provides additional information for servicing the late 1978-1981 emission controlled models. Other service procedures remain the same as described in the basic book, Chapters One through Eight.

The chapter headings in this supplement correspond to those in the main portion of this book. If a chapter is not referenced in this supplement, there are no changes affecting that chapter.

If your bike is covered by this supplement, carefully read the supplement and then read the appropriate chapter in the basic book before beginning any work.

Emission Controlled Motorcycles

If your motorcycle is emission controlled, we urge you to follow all procedures specifically designated for your bike. If you do not follow the maintenance schedule in this manual, if you do not perform a tune-up according to these procedures or if you alter engine parts or change their settings from the standard factory specifications (ignition timing, carburetor air screw, slide needle, exhaust system, etc.), your bike may not comply with federal emissions standards.

In addition, since most emission controlled bikes are carburetted on the lean side, any changes to emission-related parts (such as exhaust system modifications) could cause the engine to run so lean that overheating and engine damage could result.

CHAPTER TWO

PERIODIC SERVICE AND GENERAL MAINTENANCE

See the tables in the Appendix for general specifications for the late 1978 and later models.

PERIODIC MAINTENANCE AND LUBRICATION

Refer to **Table 1** for suggested lubrication intervals and to **Table 2** for suggested emission-related maintenance. Use these tables as a minimum schedule only. If you ride in dusty areas, at high speeds or make a lot of short 5- to 10-minute rides, service the items more often.

Perform the maintenance at each *time* or *mileage* interval, whichever comes first.

NOTE
If you have a brand new motorcycle, we recommend that you take the motorcycle to your dealer for the initial break-in maintenance at 600 miles (1 month) and at 3,000 miles (7 months).

ENGINE OIL LEVEL MEASUREMENT

All 1981 models are now equipped with an oil level inspection window located on the right side crankcase cover (**Figure 1**) in addition to the engine oil dipstick. The dipstick is used as with 1980 and earlier models. To check the oil level using the oil level inspection window, perform the following:

1. Warm up engine and set bike on centerstand.

2. Turn the engine off and wait a few minutes to allow the oil to settle in the bottom crankcase.

3. Check the oil level through the window (**Figure 1**).

4. If you prefer to check the oil level using the dipstick, unscrew the dipstick and wipe it clean. Place the cap on the case threads. Then remove the dipstick and read the oil level (**Figure 2**).

1. Level window
2. Maximum level
3. Minimum level

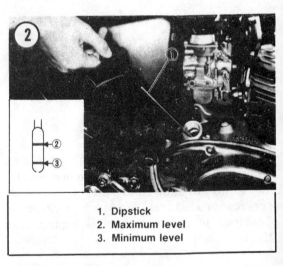

1. Dipstick
2. Maximum level
3. Minimum level

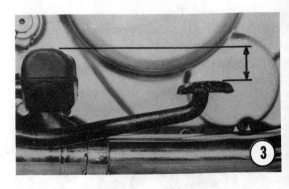

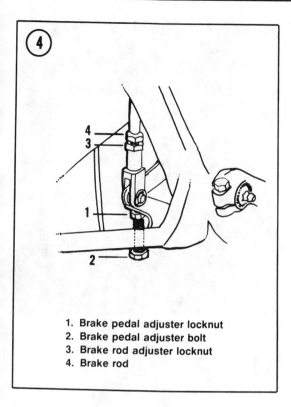

1. Brake pedal adjuster locknut
2. Brake pedal adjuster bolt
3. Brake rod adjuster locknut
4. Brake rod

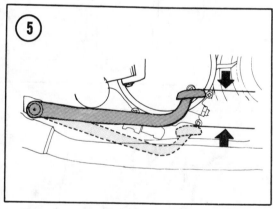

5. In Steps 3 and 4, the oil level should be between the maximum and minimum markings. If not, add a sufficient quantity of oil (Chapter Two, main book) to raise the level within specifications.

BRAKES

Rear Disc Brake Adjustment (1979-1980 Models Only)

The rear disc brake linkage should be adjusted every 2,500 miles (4,000 km), as follows:

1. The brake pedal resting height should be 7/16-3/4 in. (12-18 mm) below the upper surface of the right footrest as shown in **Figure 3**. If so, proceed to Step 4; if not, continue with Step 2.

2. Referring to **Figure 4**, loosen the brake pedal adjuster locknut (1), then turn the brake pedal adjuster bolt (2) clockwise or counterclockwise to adjust the brake pedal height until the top of the brake pedal is within the specifications recommended in Step 1. When height is correct, tighten the brake pedal adjuster locknut (1, **Figure 4**).

3. Referring to **Figure 4**, loosen the brake rod adjuster locknut (3) and screw the brake rod (4) downward until there is some free play between the brake rod and the master cylinder. Turn the brake rod in until it lightly touches the master cylinder. Then turn it out approximately 1 1/2 turns for proper free play.

4. Tighten the brake rod adjuster locknut (3, **Figure 4**).

CAUTION
The pinhole mark on the brake rod must not show above the locknut. If it does, the brake pads are excessively worn and should be replaced.

5. The rear brake pedal free play must be maintained at 1/2-5/8 in. (13-15 mm) to prevent premature rear wheel brake wear and overheating. Free play is the distance from the point where the brake pedal begins to move to the point where the brake begins to be applied. Refer to **Figure 5** for the following free play adjustment procedure:

   a. Loosen the adjuster locknut at the pushrod.

   b. Turn the adjuster in or out as required to bring the free play within the 1/2-5/8 in. (13-15 mm) travel distance.

   c. Tighten the locknut and check to be sure that the free play is correct.

Front Brake Lever Adjustment

The front disc brake piston moves forward in the caliper as the brake pad wears out. This action provides automatic adjustment between the brake pad and the brake disc. However, it is necessary to adjust the distance

10

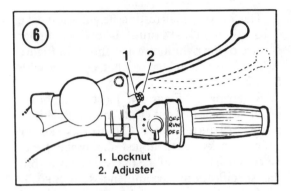

1. Locknut
2. Adjuster

that the brake lever can travel. Refer to **Figure 6** for the following procedure:

1. Loosen the brake lever adjusting screw locknut.

2. Turn the adjusting screw in or out and adjust the handbrake lever free play to 3/16-5/16 in. (5-8 mm). Tighten the locknut and check to see that the free play is correct.

Brake Pad Wear Inspection

The disc brake calipers are provided with wear indicators. Open the inspection window (**Figure 7**) every 2,500 miles (4,000 km) and examine the brake pads with a flashlight. If either pad is worn to the red line (**Figure 8**, pads shown removed for clarity), replace both pads. Refer to Chapter Eight of basic book, *Brakes*, for procedure.

If it becomes necessary to remove the brake pads for inspection, their thickness can be measured with a vernier caliper. New brake pad thickness is 0.43 in. (11 mm); wear limit thickness is 0.24 in. (6 mm).

CAM CHAIN ADJUSTMENT

1. Remove the tension adjuster cap (**Figure 9**).

2. Turn the engine kill switch to OFF and crank the engine slowly with the kickstarter. As the engine turns, watch the end of the pushrod to see that it stays flush with the end of the adjuster (**Figure 10**).

3. If the pushrod is flush with the adjuster, no adjustment is needed. Install the cap. If the pushrod is not flush with the end of the adjuster, adjust as follows.

4. *1979 and later models:* Loosen the adjuster locknut (**Figure 11**).

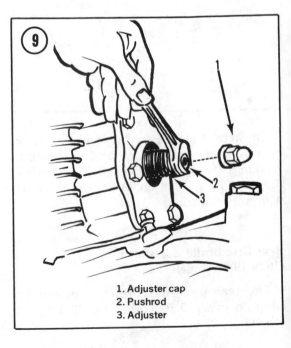

1. Adjuster cap
2. Pushrod
3. Adjuster

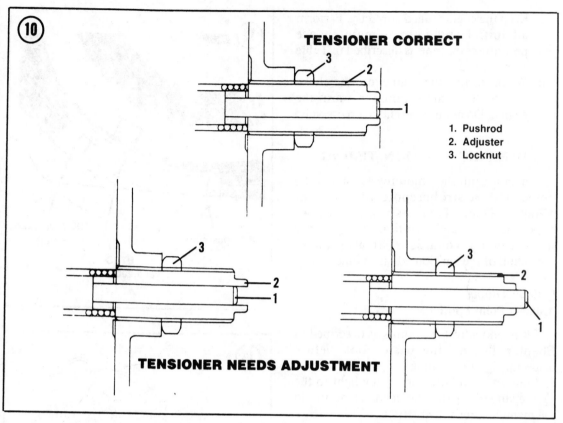

⑩

TENSIONER CORRECT

1. Pushrod
2. Adjuster
3. Locknut

TENSIONER NEEDS ADJUSTMENT

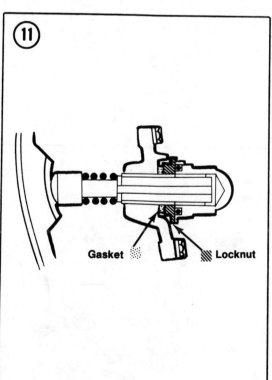

⑪

Gasket   Locknut

5. Turn the threaded adjuster in or out until the end of the pushrod is even with the end of the adjuster as the engine turns (**Figure 10**). Tighten the locknut on 1979 and later models.
6. Install the tension adjuster cap and tighten.

NOTE
On late 1978 models, the tension adjuster cap serves as a locknut for the adjuster.

EMISSION CONTROL

Exhaust Pipe Discoloration

Because of the leaner carburetor settings required on emission-controlled motorcyles, the possibility of having the exhaust pipes discolor increases. When performing service work to your motorcycle, consider the following precautions:

    a. When adjusting the engine at idle, make sure to place a fan in front of the engine to allow air to flow over the engine.
    b. Do not run the engine at idle for long periods of time.

10

c. Keep the engine tuned correctly. Perform all initial and normal maintenance procedures on time as described in **Table 1** or **Table 2**.

d. When starting the engine, use the choke only for the time required to warm the engine. Do not use the choke excessively.

DYNAMIC IGNITION TIMING

Emission controlled motorcycles should be timed with a stroboscopic timing light (Chapter One). This instrument allows inspection of dynamic ignition timing, under actual running conditions. It also allows inspection of the ignition advance function.

Ignition Timing
(Contact Point Ignition)

1. Clean and adjust the points as described in Chapter Two of the basic book before inspecting ignition timing.

2. Connect a stroboscopic timing light to the *right* cylinder's spark plug lead, according to the manufacturer's instructions.

3. Place a fan in front of the engine. Start the engine and check the idle speed with a tachometer. It should be 1,200 rpm. Adjust if necessary as described in this supplement under *Idle Speed.*

4. Point the light at the stator timing and rotor index marks. The light should flash and freeze the rotor mark as it lines up with the "F" mark (**Figure 12**).

5. If adjustment is required, loosen the 2 large point baseplate lock screws (**Figure 13**) and turn the baseplate until the rotor mark and "F" mark align. Tighten the 2 screws.

6. Switch the timing light lead to the *left* plug lead and check that the rotor mark again aligns with the "F" mark as in Step 4.

7. If not, loosen the 2 smaller screws for the left points (**Figure 14**) and move the left point set as required to align the marks. Tighten the screws.

8. Recheck timing for the *right* cylinder and then again for the *left* cylinder. Timing is now set at idle.

9. To check the ignition advance operation, gradually increase the engine speed to 3,000 rpm. The rotor mark should now align with the

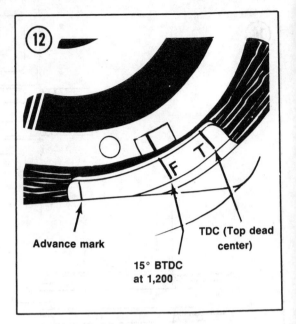

Advance mark

15° BTDC
at 1,200

TDC (Top dead center)

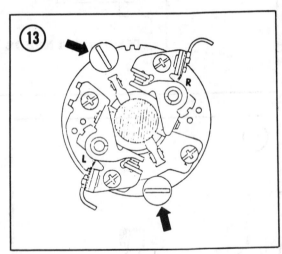

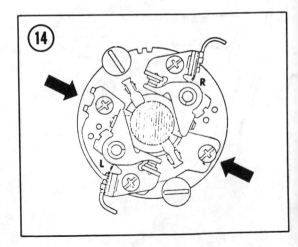

Table 1 LUBRICATION INTERVALS

INITIAL MAINTENANCE

Every 300 miles (500 km)
- Check drive chain tension and lubricate

First 600 miles (1,000 km) or 1 month
- Change engine oil
- Inspect brake system, adjust free play
- Adjust clutch free play
- Lube control and meter cables

First 3,000 miles (5,000 km) or 7 months
- All items above, plus the following:
- Clean oil filter
- Clean air filter
- Lube brake and shift pedal shafts
- Lube center and kickstand and kickstarter pivots
- Inspect wheel bearings for looseness
- Inspect steering bearings for looseness
- Inspect battery's specific gravity, inspect vent tube

NORMAL MAINTENANCE

Every 300 miles (500 km)
- Check drive chain tension and lubricate

Every 2,500 miles (4,000 km) or 6 months
- Change engine oil
- Inspect brake system, adjust free play, replace pads if necessary
- Adjust clutch free play
- Lube control and meter cables
- Lube swing arm pivot
- Lube brake and shift pedal shafts
- Lube center and kickstand and kickstarter pivots
- Inspect wheel bearings for looseness
- Inspect steering bearings for looseness
- Inspect battery's specific gravity, inspect vent tube

Every 5,000 miles (8,000 km) or 12 months
- All items above, plus the following:
- Clean oil filter
- Clean air filter
- Replace generator brushes

Every 10,000 miles (16,000 km) or 24 months
- All items above, plus the following:
- Change fork oil
- Repack wheel bearings
- Repack steering bearings

10

Table 2   EMISSION-RELATED MAINTENANCE

INITIAL MAINTENANCE
First 600 miles (1,000 km) or 1 month • Check/adjust cam chain tension • Check/adjust valve clearance • 1978-1979: Check/adjust/replace breaker points if necessary • 1978-1979: Check/adjust ignition timing • Check exhaust for leakage; replace gaskets if necessary • Synchronize carburetors • Check/adjust throttle cable free play and idle speed First 3,000 miles (5,000 km) or 7 months • All items above, plus the following: • Check/adjust/replace spark plugs if necessary • Check crankcase ventilation hose for cracks; replace if necessary • Check fuel hose for cracks or damage; replace if necessary
NORMAL MAINTENANCE
Every 2,500 miles (4,000 km) or 6 months • 1978-1979: Check/adjust/replace breaker points if necessary • 1978-1979: Check/adjust ignition timing • Check exhaust for leakage; replace gaskets if necessary • Synchronize carburetors • Check/adjust throttle cable free play and idle speed Every 5,000 miles (8,000 km) or 12 months • All items above, plus the following: • Check/adjust cam chain tension • Check/adjust valve clearance • Check/adjust/replace spark plugs if necessary • Check crankcase ventilation hose for cracks; replace if necessary • Check fuel hose for cracks or damage; replace if necessary Every 7,500 miles (12,000 km) or 18 months • All items above, plus the following: • Replace spark plugs

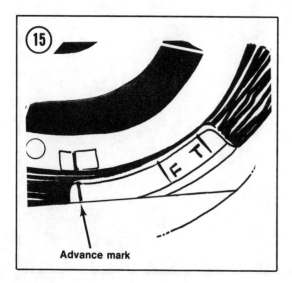

Advance mark

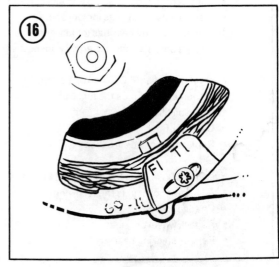

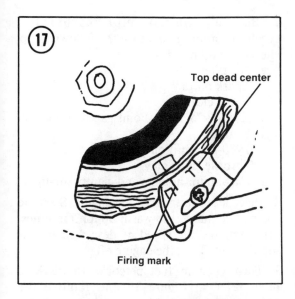

Top dead center

Firing mark

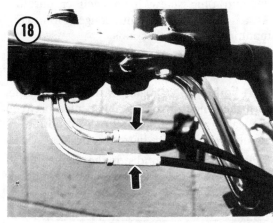

1. Connect a stroboscopic timing light to the *left* cylinder's spark plug lead, according to the manufacturer's instructions.

2. Place a fan in front of the engine. Start the engine and check the idle speed with a tachometer. It should be 1,200 rpm. Adjust if necessary as described in this supplement under *Idle Speed*.

3. Point the light at the stator timing and rotor index marks. The light should flash and freeze the rotor mark as it lines up with the timing mark. See **Figure 16** (1980) or **Figure 17** (1981).

4. Gradually increase engine speed to 3,200 rpm. The rotor mark should smoothly advance to a maximum position and stay there.

5. If the marks do not align, the rotor's Woodruff key may be damaged, the pickup coil assembly may be faulty, the transistorized ignitor unit may be faulty or someone may have tampered with the ignition system. Refer to the Chapter Six information in this supplement to inspect the timing marks and to install new parts.

SPARK PLUGS

On 1980 and later XS650's, new spark plugs should be installed every 7,500 miles (12,000 km) or 18 months, whichever comes first. This is necessary to meet 1980 emissions specifications and it should be done even if the old plugs look serviceable.

advance timing mark (**Figure 15**). If it does not, disassemble and inspect the ignition advance mechanism as described under *Cylinder Head Cover* in Chapter Four of the basic book.

Ignition Timing (Transistorized Ignition)

The 1980 and later XS650's use a transistorized ignition system. The ignition timing cannot be altered after initial assembly. On 1980 models, the pickup coil assembly is permanently mounted on the stator with special TORX fasteners and epoxy on the screw threads. On 1981 models, regular screws are used to secure the pickup coil on the stator.

Although ignition timing is no longer part of scheduled maintenance, it should be inspected when trouble is suspected.

CARBURETOR

Cable Free Play

Always check the throttle cables before you make any carburetor adjustments. Too much free play causes delayed throttle response; too little free play will cause unstable idling.

1. Check free play at the throttle grip flange. It should be about 3/16-5/16 in. (5-8 mm).

2. Adjust free play by loosening the locknuts and turning the adjusters as required (**Figure 18**).

3. Tighten the locknuts.

Idle Mixture Adjustment

The idle mixture on late 1978 and 1979 emission-controlled motorcycles is set at the factory. Do not try to alter the idle mixture

10

adjustment in any way. All 1980 and later models have no idle mixture adjustment method.

Idle Speed

Proper idle speed setting is necessary to prevent stalling and to provide adequate engine compression braking. A portable tachometer is required for this procedure. Your bike's tachometer is not accurate enough at low rpm.

1. Set the bike on the centerstand.
2. Place a fan in front of the engine. Start the engine and let it warm up (about 5 minutes).
3. Check the idle speed on the tachometer. It should be 1,200 rpm. If not, turn the idle speed adjust screw in or out as required to obtain the correct idle speed (**Figure 19**).
4. Rev the engine a couple of times to see if it settles down to the set speed. Readjust, if necessary.

Synchronization

Carburetor synchronization makes sure that one cylinder does not try to run faster than the other—cutting power and gas mileage. Accurate synchronization of the carburetors requires a set of vacuum gauges (described in Chapter One) to measure intake vacuum of both cylinders at the same time.

1. Before you attempt carburetor synchronization, make sure the following are checked or adjusted.
  a. Air filter
  b. Spark plugs
  c. Valve clearance
  d. *Late 1978-1979:* Point gap and ignition timing
  e. *1980-on:* Ignition timing
  f. Throttle cable play
  g. Carburetor holders and clamps air-tight

2. Place a fan in front of the engine. Start the engine and allow it to warm up for 5 minutes. Then set the idle speed as described in this supplement. Turn the engine off.

3. Turn vacuum fuel petcocks to PRIME. Then refer to **Figure 19** and remove the vacuum plug screw from each carburetor. Attach a set of vacuum gauges, following manufacturer's instructions.

4. Start the engine and check the gauge readings. Both cylinders should read the same.

5. If both cylinder readings are not the same, turn the synchronizing screw located between the carburetors (**Figure 20**) as required to equalize the vacuum in both cylinders.

6. Reset idle speed and stop the engine. Install the vacuum plug screws, making sure that their sealing gaskets are in good condition.

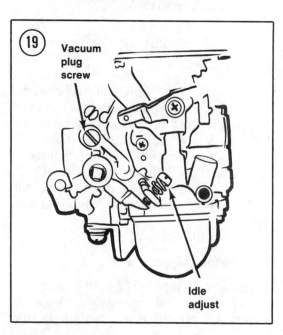

(19) Vacuum plug screw / Idle adjust

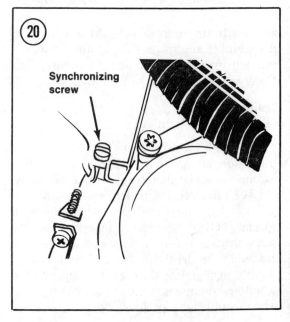

(20) Synchronizing screw

CHAPTER THREE

TROUBLESHOOTING

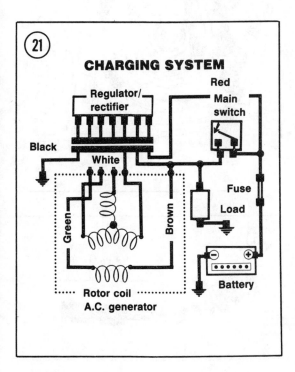

CHARGING SYSTEM

Refer to the schematic diagram of the charging circuit (**Figure 21**). Whenever charging system trouble is suspected, clean the battery terminals and check the battery's specific gravity. See *Battery Inspection and Service*, Chapter Six of main book. Battery voltage should be above 12 volts. If not, remove and charge the battery.

> *CAUTION*
> *Do not disconnect the battery terminals when the engine is running. A resultant high voltage surge will damage the solid state regulator/rectifier.*

Initial Inspection

1. Start the engine and let it reach normal operating temperature.
2. Remove the headlight fuse (10A) to keep the headlight off (**Figure 22**).
3. Connect a DC voltmeter across the battery terminals (**Figure 23**).
4. Bring the engine speed from idle to approximately 2,000 rpm, observing the battery voltage. It should be approximately 14.2-14.8 volts. Interpret results as follows:
   a. If voltmeter reads more than 14.8 volts, the regulator/rectifier is faulty and should be replaced.

10

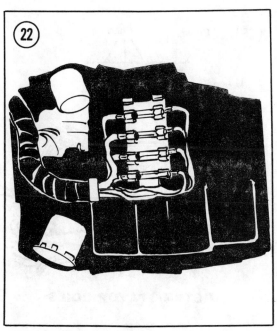

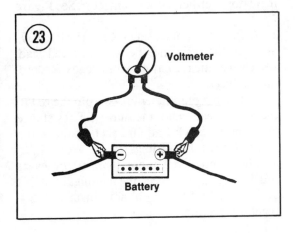

b. If voltmeter reads less than 14.2 volts, inspect the alternator and the regulator/rectifier.

Brush Inspection and Replacement

1. Rotor brush inspection: Remove the brushes (**Figure 24**) and measure the brush length (**Figure 25**). If a brush has worn to less than 1/4 in. (7 mm), install new brushes. See Chapter Six, main book.

2. Rotor brush spring inspection: With the brush installed, check to see that the brush spring presses the brush firmly against the rotor. If not, install a new brush and spring.

3. Stator coil inspection: With the engine off, disconnect the 8-pole alternator wiring connector (**Figure 26**). Using an ohmmeter set to the R x 1 scale, measure the resistance between each pair of white leads going to the alternator. The resistance should be 0.4-1.0 ohms. Set the ohmmeter on its highest scale and measure the resistance between each white lead and the stator housing (ground). The readings should be infinite. If either reading is incorrect, install a new stator.

4. Rotor coil inspection: Measure the resistance between the green and brown leads going to the alternator. The resistance should be 5-7 ohms. Set the ohmmeter on its highest scale and measure the resistance between the rotor leads and the rotor core (ground). The readings should be infinite. If either reading is incorrect, install a new rotor.

Regulator/Rectifier Inspection

1. With the engine off, disconnect the 8-pole regulator/rectifier wiring connector. See **Figure 27**.

2. With an ohmmeter set at R x 10 or R x 100, measure the resistance between the red lead and each of the regulator's white leads. Record the readings.

3. Switch the ohmmeter probe from the red to the black lead, and measure the resistance between the black lead and each of the white leads. Record the readings.

4. There should be more than 10 times as much resistance between the readings in Step 2 and those in Step 3. If not, install a new regulator/rectifier.

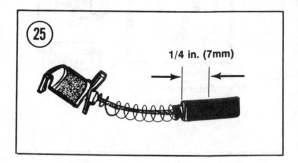

1/4 in. (7mm)

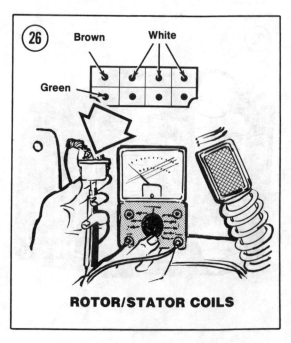

Brown   White

Green

ROTOR/STATOR COILS

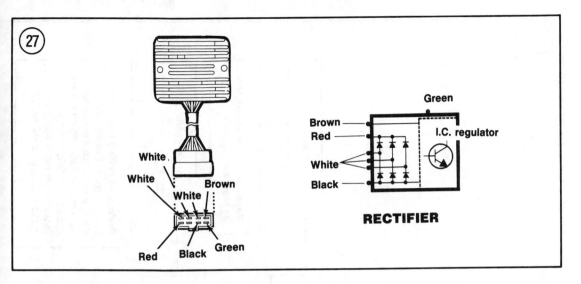

RECTIFIER

IGNITION SYSTEM TROUBLESHOOTING (1980-ON)

Basic ignition system and spark plug troubleshooting information can be found in Chapter Three of the main book. The following procedures, together with the troubleshooting procedures included in Chapter Three, can help you to determine the system or component which is operating incorrectly. If the ignition system is operating incorrectly, test procedures unique to the Yamaha electronic ignition system are found in this section and can be used to troubleshoot and locate the problem source. An ohmmeter (described in Chapter One) is required to perform the test procedures.

Before starting actual troubleshooting, read the entire test procedure (**Figure 28**). When required, the diagnostic chart will refer you back to a test procedure found in this section.

Pickup Coil Inspection

1. With the engine OFF, disconnect the 3-pole pickup coil connector.
2A. *1980-1981*: Using an ohmmeter set on R×100, perform the following tests:
  a. Measure the resistance between the black/white lead and the white/red lead.
  b. Measure the resistance between the black/white lead and the white/green lead.

  c. Both coils should measure 550-850 ohms.
2B. *1982:* Using an ohmmeter set on R×100, perform the following tests:
  a. Measure the resistance between the grey and black lead.
  b. Measure the resistance between the orange and black lead.
  c. Both coils should measure 630-770 ohms.

3. If either coil tests incorrectly in Step 2A or Step 2B, install a new stator/pickup coil assembly as described in the Chapter Six section of this supplement.

Ignition Coil Inspection

A single ignition coil is used for both cylinders. The ignition coil can be inspected for resistance of the primary and secondary windings. Refer to **Figure 29** when performing the following test procedures. Disconnect coil wires before testing.
1. Measure the coil primary resistance, using an ohmmeter, at the coil primary plug terminal between the orange and red/white wires. Primary winding resistance should be 2.25-2.75 ohms.
2. Measure the coil secondary resistance between both primary leads. The secondary winding resistance should be 10,500-15,500 ohms. Install a new coil if the resistance is incorrect.

10

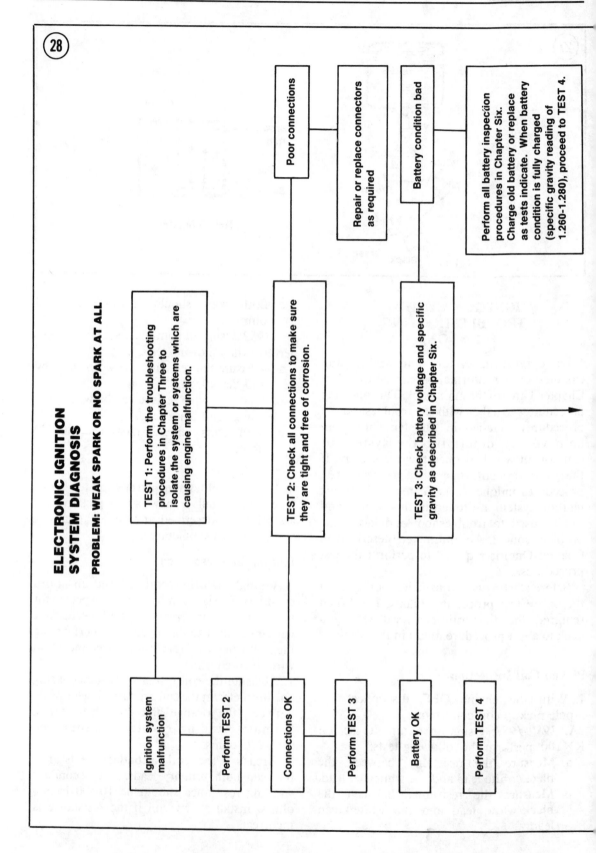

(28)

ELECTRONIC IGNITION SYSTEM DIAGNOSIS

PROBLEM: WEAK SPARK OR NO SPARK AT ALL

TEST 1: Perform the troubleshooting procedures in Chapter Three to isolate the system or systems which are causing engine malfunction.

Ignition system malfunction

Perform TEST 2

TEST 2: Check all connections to make sure they are tight and free of corrosion.

Connections OK

Perform TEST 3

Poor connections

Repair or replace connectors as required

TEST 3: Check battery voltage and specific gravity as described in Chapter Six.

Battery OK

Perform TEST 4

Battery condition bad

Perform all battery inspection procedures in Chapter Six. Charge old battery or replace as tests indicate. When battery condition is fully charged (specific gravity reading of 1.260-1.280), proceed to TEST 4.

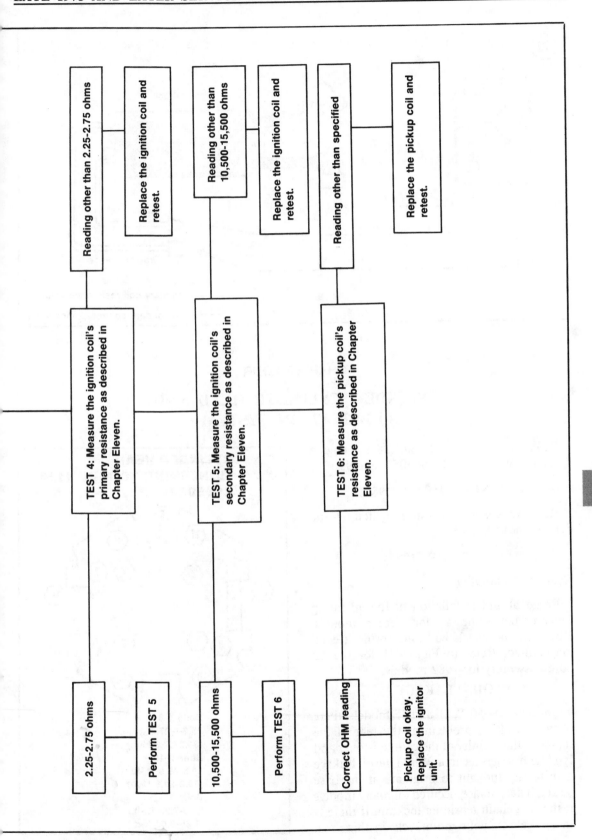

TEST 4: Measure the ignition coil's primary resistance as described in Chapter Eleven.

2.25-2.75 ohms → Perform TEST 5

Reading other than 2.25-2.75 ohms → Replace the ignition coil and retest.

TEST 5: Measure the ignition coil's secondary resistance as described in Chapter Eleven.

10,500-15,500 ohms → Perform TEST 6

Reading other than 10,500-15,500 ohms → Replace the ignition coil and retest.

TEST 6: Measure the pickup coil's resistance as described in Chapter Eleven.

Correct OHM reading → Pickup coil okay. Replace the ignitor unit.

Reading other than specified → Replace the pickup coil and retest.

10

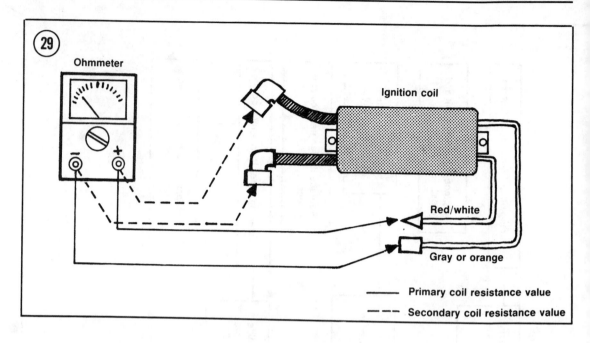

CHAPTER FOUR

CYLINDER, CYLINDER HEAD AND LUBRICATION SYSTEM

Refer to **Table 3** and **Table 4** for engine specifications for 1982 XS650SJ models.

CYLINDER HEAD (1982)

Refer to **Figure 30** when tightening the cylinder head bolts.

OIL PUMP (1982)

Removal/Installation

Removal and installation of the oil pump remains the same as for earlier models. However, the check ball and spring are no longer used. Refer to **Figure 31** for the oil pump assembly for 1982 models.

OIL LEAKAGE

On some XS650, S, SF and 2F models, there is an oil leakage problem at the rear of the engine in the vicinity of the cam tensioner and cylinder base gasket area. While the oil leakage is primarily thought to originate at the base gasket, it has, in fact, occured on many models at the cam chain tensioner locknut. If there is an oil leak on your motorcycle in this area,

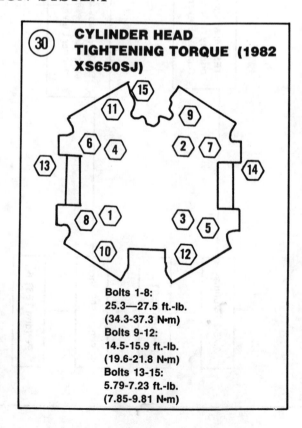

CYLINDER HEAD TIGHTENING TORQUE (1982 XS650SJ)

Bolts 1-8:
25.3—27.5 ft.-lb.
(34.3-37.3 N•m)
Bolts 9-12:
14.5-15.9 ft.-lb.
(19.6-21.8 N•m)
Bolts 13-15:
5.79-7.23 ft.-lb.
(7.85-9.81 N•m)

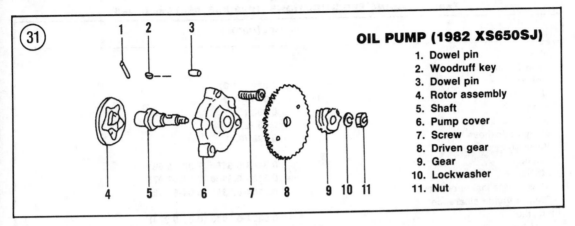

OIL PUMP (1982 XS650SJ)

1. Dowel pin
2. Woodruff key
3. Dowel pin
4. Rotor assembly
5. Shaft
6. Pump cover
7. Screw
8. Driven gear
9. Gear
10. Lockwasher
11. Nut

perform the following procedure to trace the exact leakage point.

1. Clean the affected area thoroughly with a commercial degreaser such as Yamaha Mud and Grease Release. Follow the manufacturer's directions on cleaning and rinsing to obtain a clean and dry surface.

2. Using a powder-based anti-perspirant, spray the area around the cam chain tensioner and cylinder housings.

3. Start the engine and observe the powdered area. Any darkening of the powder will indicate the point of oil leakage. If the leakage is minor, it may be necessary to ride the motorcycle for several miles until the leakage increases and darkens the powder sufficiently for detection.

4. If the leakage is at the cam chain tensioner, remove the chain cam tensioner cap, nut, O-ring and copper gasket (**Figure 11**). Replace the copper gasket and reinstall the parts. If the base gasket is leaking, refer to engine disassembly procedures in Chapter Four of the basic book.

Table 3 ENGINE SPECIFICATIONS (1982 XS650SJ)

	in. (mm)
Cylinder head	
Warp limit	0.0012 (0.03)
Head gasket thickness (new)	0.047 (1.2)
Cylinder	
Bore	2.95 (75)
Taper limit	0.002 (0.05)
Camshaft	
Outside diameter	
A	0.9435-0.9440 (23.965-23.977)
B	0.9830-0.9835 (24.968-24.981)
Bearing clearance	0.0008-0.0021 (0.020-0.054)
Camshaft	
Lobe height wear limit	
Intake	1.569 (39.84)
Exhaust	1.570 (39.88)
Lobe base diameter	
Intake	1.263 (32.09)
Exhaust	1.266 (32.15)
Rocker arm	
Rocker arm inside diameter	0.5910-0.5917 (15.000-15.018)
Rocker arm shaft outside diameter	0.5904-0.5906 (14.996-15.001)
Rocker arm-to-shaft clearance	0.00035-0.00130 (0.009-0.033)

(continued)

10

Table 3 ENGINE SPECIFICATIONS (1982 XS650SJ) (continued)

	in. (mm)
Valves	
Head diameter	
Intake	1.614 (41.0)
Exhaust	1.378 (35.0)
Face width	0.083 (2.1)
Seat width limit	0.08 (2.0)
Margin thickness limit	0.028 (0.7)
Valve stem diameter	
Intake	0.3144-0.3150 (7.986-8.001
Exhaust	0.3134-0.3140 (7.960-7.975
Valve guide inside diameter	0.3154-0.3157 (8.01-8.018)
Stem-to-guide clearance	
Intake	0.0004-0.0013 (0.01-0.034)
Exhaust	0.0014-0.0023 (0.035-0.059)
Valve stem runout	0.0012 (0.03)
Valve springs	
Free length	
Intake	1.654 (42.0)
Exhaust	1.675 (42.55)
Piston	
Diameter	2.95 (75.0)
Piston clearance	0.0020-0.0022 (0.050-0.055)
Piston rings	
End gap	
1st and 2nd	0.0079-0.0157 (0.2-0.4)
Oil control	0.0118-0.0351 (0.3-0.9)
Side clearance	
1st	0.0016-0.0031 (0.04-0.08)
2nd	0.0012-0.0028 (0.03-0.07)
Crankshaft	
Runout	0.002 (0.05)
Connecting rod side clearance	0.0059-0.0157 (0.15-0.4)
General:	
Engine number starts	5V4-000101
Engine type	4-stroke twin, SOHC, 2 valves/cylinder
Lubrication system	Trochoid pump, wet sump
Clutch	Wet, 7 friction, 6 metal
Starting system	Kick and electric starter with cut-off system
Ignition system	Transistorized
Charging system	Alternator, rectifier/regulator
Carburetion	2 constant vacuum slide/needle
Air filter	Dry foam
Dry weight	467 lb. (212 kg)
Fuel type	Regular
Fuel tank capacity	3.0 gal. (11.5 liters)
Reserve capacity	0.6 gal. (2.3 liters)
Engine:	
Bore×stroke	2.95×2.91 in. (75×74 mm)
Displacement	39.8 cu. in. (653 cc)
Compression ratio	8.7:1
Valve timing	Not specified
Valve clearance (cold)	IN: 0.0024 in. (0.06 mm)
	EX: 0.0059 in. (0.15 mm)
Piston clearance	0.0020-0.0022 in.
	(0.050-0.055 mm)

(continued)

Table 3 ENGINE SPECIFICATIONS (1982 XS650SJ) (continued)

	in. (mm)
Carburetor:	
Type	2 Mikuni BS34III
I.D. mark	5V4-00
Main jet	132.5
Main air jet	85
Jet needle	5HX12
Pilot jet	42.5
Pilot air jet	135
Pilot screw	Preset
Starter jet	30
Fuel level	0.12 +/1 0.04 in.
	(1.0 +/1 1.0 mm)
Float height	0.87 ±0.04 in.
	(22.0 ±1.0 mm)
Idle speed	1,200 rpm
Transmission:	
Primary drive	Gear
Primary drive ratio	72/27 (2.666)
Transmission gears	Constant mesh, 5-speed
1st ratio	32/13 (2.461)
2nd ratio	27/17 (1.588)
3rd ratio	26/20 (1.300)
4th ratio	23/21 (1.095)
5th ratio	22/23 (0.956)
Secondary drive ratio	34/17 (2.000)
Drive chain	50 HDS, 104 links
Chassis:	
Type	Double cradle
Caster	27°
Trail	4.52 in. (115 mm)
Front suspension	Telescopic fork, oil damped
Travel	5.91 in. (150 mm)
Oil quantity (each)	5.72 oz. (169 cc)
Oil type	SAE 10 wt.
Oil level	Not specified
Rear suspension	Swingarm
Shock travel	3.15 in. (80 mm)
Wheel type	Spoked
Wheel size	Front: 1.85×19
	Rear: 2.75×16
Tire type	Inner tube
Front tire	Front: 3.50S 19-4PR
	Rear: 130/90-16 67S
Front brake	Hydraulic disc
Rear brake	Leading shoe
Electrical:	
Ignition system	
Ignition system	Transistorized
Ignition timing	Fixed
Spark plug type	NGK BP7ES; Chanmpion N7Y
Spark plug gap	0.027-0.031 in. (0.7-0.8 mm)

10

(continued)

Table 3 ENGINE SPECIFICATIONS (1982 XS650SJ) (continued)

	in. (mm)
Electrical: (cont.)	
Charging system	Alternator, rectifier/regulator
Alternator output	14V, 16A @ 5,000 rpm
Regulator/rectifier setting	14.5 ±0.5 V
Battery	
Capacity	12V-14AH
Lighting	
Headlight	50-40W (sealed beam)
Tail/brake light	8W/27W
Turn light	27W
Meter light	3.4W
License light	3.8W
Indicator light	3.4W
Fuses	
Main	20A
Headlight	10A
Signal	10A
Ignition	10A

Table 4 ENGINE TIGHTENING TORQUES (1982 XS650SJ)

	ft.-lb.	N·m
Cylinder head		
6 mm screw	6.5	8.8
8 mm bolt	15	21
10 mm nut	27	36
Cylinder head cover side		
6 mm	6.5	8.8
8 mm	9.5	12.7
Cam chain tensioner cap	15	21
Oil pump cover	7.2	9.8
Strainer cover	7.2	9.8
Drain plug	30.5	41.2
Oil delivery pipe	15	21
Exhaust pipe	9.5	12.7
Crankcase	15	21
Kickstarter crank boss	14.5	20
Clutch boss	58	78.5
Upper engine mount nut		
8 mm	13	17.7
10 mm	21.5	29.4
Front engine mount nut (10 mm)	33.5	45.1
Rear engine mount (10 mm)	29.5	40.2
Rear lower engine mount (10 mm)	33.5	45.1

CHAPTER FIVE

CLUTCH, TRANSMISSION AND CRANKCASE

KICKSTARTER (1982)

Procedures used to service the kickstarter are the same as for 1981 and earlier models. However, the kickstarter on 1982 models uses more shims and a circlip. See **Figure 32**.

SHIFT MECHANISM (1982)

Refer to **Figure 33** when servicing the shifting mechanism on 1982 models. Service procedures remain the same.

DRIVE AXLE

Oil Seal Replacement

Yamaha has redesigned the drive axle oil seal allowing the seal to be replaced without removing and disassembling the engine. The new seal has a lip which allows the seal to be driven into the case housing with a drift or other suitable driver. The new and old seals are shown in **Figure 34**. The new seal can be installed in all 650 models.

The transmission drive axle oil seal can be replaced on all 650 models by performing the following procedure:

1. Place the motorcycle on the centerstand.

2. Remove the following from the left side of the motorcycle:
   a. Shift lever
   b. Footpeg
   c. Side cover

3. Pry back the front sprocket lockwasher (**Figure 35**) using a drift punch. Then have an assistant depress the rear brake pedal to lock the rear wheel. Loosen the front sprocket nut.

10

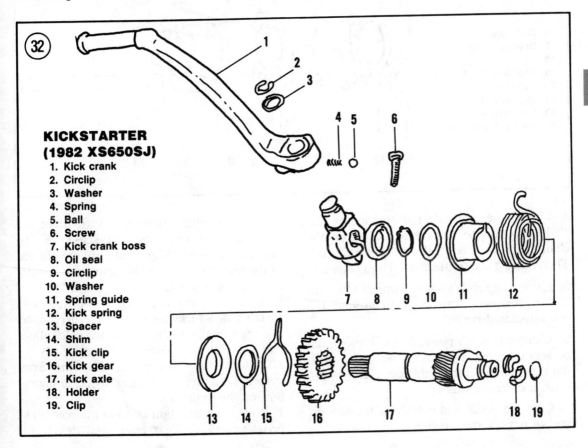

KICKSTARTER (1982 XS650SJ)
1. Kick crank
2. Circlip
3. Washer
4. Spring
5. Ball
6. Screw
7. Kick crank boss
8. Oil seal
9. Circlip
10. Washer
11. Spring guide
12. Kick spring
13. Spacer
14. Shim
15. Kick clip
16. Kick gear
17. Kick axle
18. Holder
19. Clip

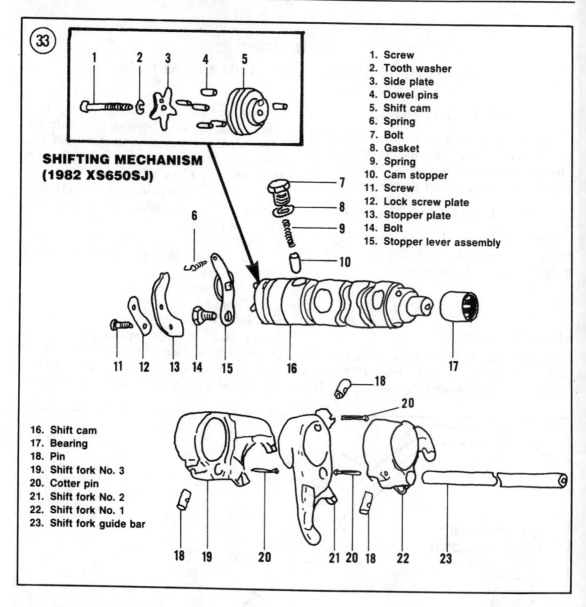

SHIFTING MECHANISM (1982 XS650SJ)

1. Screw
2. Tooth washer
3. Side plate
4. Dowel pins
5. Shift cam
6. Spring
7. Bolt
8. Gasket
9. Spring
10. Cam stopper
11. Screw
12. Lock screw plate
13. Stopper plate
14. Bolt
15. Stopper lever assembly

16. Shift cam
17. Bearing
18. Pin
19. Shift fork No. 3
20. Cotter pin
21. Shift fork No. 2
22. Shift fork No. 1
23. Shift fork guide bar

4. Loosen the rear axle nut and loosen the chain adjusters to remove tension from the chain. Pull the chain off the front sprocket. Then remove the front sprocket and collar.

5. Using a degreaser such as Yamaha Mud and Grease Release, clean the area around the transmission drive axle.

6. Using a suitable pointed tool, remove the oil seal from the crankcase. Make sure not to damage the side of the crankcase as this would cause a severe oil leak.

7. Coat the inside and outside of the new oil seal with molybdenum grease.

8. Using a 60mm diameter drift, drive the new oil seal into the crankcase in the direction shown in **Figure 34** until the outside of the seal is flush with the crankcase. *Do not drive the seal too far into the crankcase.*

9. Install the sprocket collar and sprocket. Install a new lockwasher onto the drive axle, making sure the washer fits on the axle splines correctly. Install the drive axle nut loosely.

10. Place the drive chain over the front sprocket and turn the chain adjusters to slightly tension the chain.

11. Have an assistant depress the rear brake pedal to lock the rear wheel and tighten the

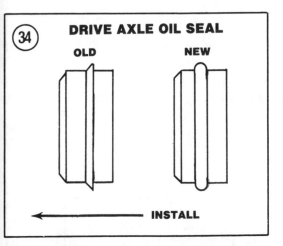

DRIVE AXLE OIL SEAL

OLD   NEW

← INSTALL

sprocket nut to 72-87 ft.-lb. (10-12 mkg). Bend the locknut over the sprocket nut (**Figure 35**).

12. Complete chain adjustment as described in Chapter Two of the basic book.

13. Install the side cover, shift lever and footpeg.

STARTING SYSTEM (1981)

All 1981 models are equipped with a starting circuit cut-off switch (**Figure 36**). When the engine stop switch and the main switch are turned to ON, the engine can only be started if:

a. The transmission is in NEUTRAL.

b. The clutch lever is pulled in (transmission in gear).

If the above conditions are not met, the starting circuit cut-off switch will prevent the starter from operating.

STARTING SYSTEM (1982)

The starting system consists of the starter motor, starter solenoid, starter relay, starter circuit cutoff relay, starter cutout relay and the starter button.

The starting system is shown in **Figure 37**. When the starter button is pressed, it engages the solenoid switch that closes the circuit. The electricity flows from the battery to the starter motor.

CAUTION
Do not operate the starter for more than five seconds at a time. Let it rest approximately ten seconds, then use it again.

When the engine stop switch and the main switch are turned ON, the engine can only be started if:

a. The transmission is in NEUTRAL.

b. The clutch lever is pulled in (transmission in gear) and the sidestand is up.

If the above conditions are not met, the starting circuit cut-off relay will prevent the starter from operating.

Starting Circuit Cut-Off Relay Testing

1. Place the motorcycle on the centerstand.

2. Remove the seat.

3. Disconnect the starting circuit cut-off relay connector from the rear fender bracket. It contains 4 wires—1 sky blue, 1 black/yellow and 2 red/white.

4. Set the ohmmeter scale to read ohms×100. Measure the resistance between the terminals shown in **Figure 38**. It should read 100 ohms.

5. Connect a ohmmeter and 12 volt battery to the starting circuit cut-off relay as shown in **Figure 39**. Set the ohmmeter to read ohms×1. Interpret results as follows:

a. Battery connected: 0 ohms.

b. Battery disconnected: Infinity.

6. Set the ohmmeter scale to read ohms×1. Measure the resistance between the terminals shown in **Figure 40**. It should be 9.5 ohms.

7. If the starting circuit cut-off relay failed any of the test procedures in Steps 4-6, pull it out of its holder and insert a new one.

10

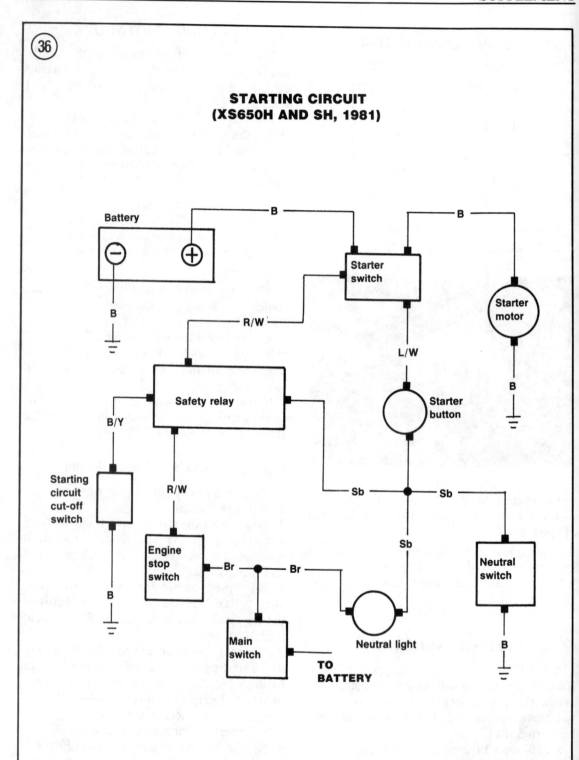

36

**STARTING CIRCUIT
(XS650H AND SH, 1981)**

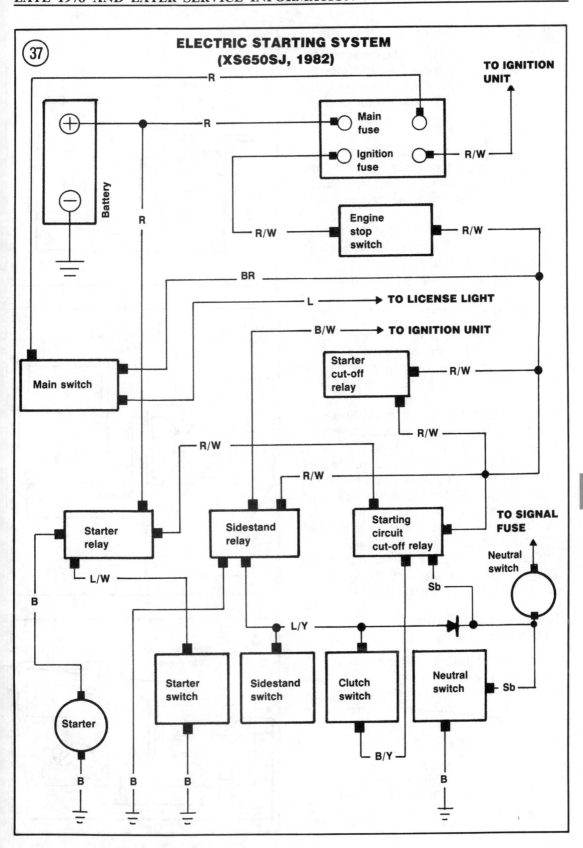

**ELECTRIC STARTING SYSTEM
(XS650SJ, 1982)**

37

Sidestand Switch Testing

1. Place the motorcycle on the centerstand.
2. Disconnect the sidestand switch from the rear fender bracket. Then disconnect the electrical connector. The connector contains four wires—black, red/white, blue/yellow and black/white.
3. Connect an ohmmeter to the blue/yellow and black connector contacts. With the sidestand up, the reading should be 0 ohms. With the sidestand down, the reading should be infinity.
4. If the sidestand switch failed the tests in Step 4, replace it. Remove the screws and switch. Install a new unit.
5. Install all parts previously removed.

Sidestand Relay Testing

1. Place the motorcycle on the centerstand.
2. Disconnect the starting circuit sidestand relay connector from the rear fender bracket. It contains 4 wires—1 black, 1 black/white, 1 red/white and 1 blue/yellow.
3. Set the ohmmeter scale to read ohms×10. Measure the resistance between the terminals shown in **Figure 41**. It should read 100 ohms.
4. Connect an ohmmeter and 12-volt battery to the starting circuit sidestand relay switch as shown in **Figure 42**. Set the ohmmeter to read ohms×1. Interpret results as follows:
   a. Battery connected: Infinite ohm reading.
   b. Battery disconnected: 0 ohm reading.
5. If the starting circuit sidestand relay failed any of the test procedures in Steps 4-6, pull it out of its holder and insert a new one.

Headlight/Starter Circuit Cut-Out Relay Testing

1. Place the motorcycle on the centerstand.
2. Remove the starting circuit cut-out relay connector from the rear fender bracket and disconnect the connector. It contains 6 wires—1 yellow, 1 black, 1 light blue, 1 red yellow and 2 red/white.

> *NOTE*
> *In Step 3, it is suggested to use a Yamaha Pocket Tester. The internal characteristics of other meters may give a higher or lower ohm reading.*

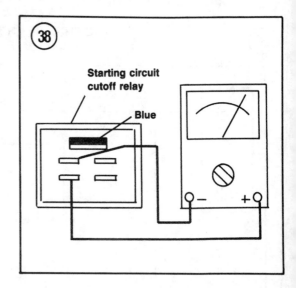

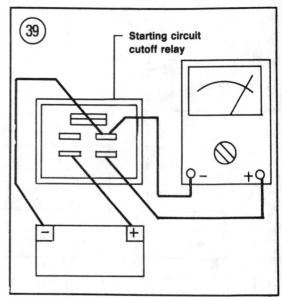

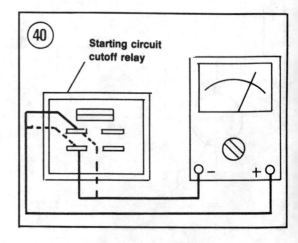

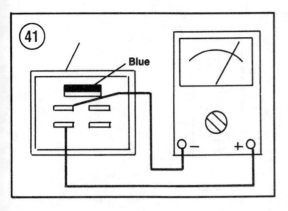

Blue

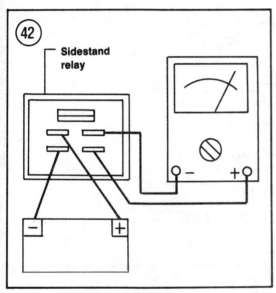

Sidestand
relay

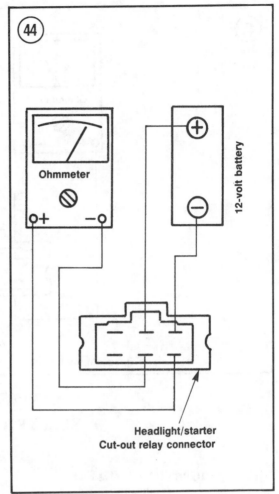

Ohmmeter

12-volt battery

Headlight/starter
Cut-out relay connector

10

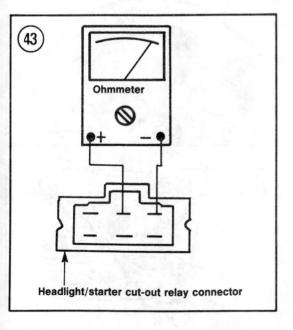

Ohmmeter

Headlight/starter cut-out relay connector

3. Set the ohmmeter scale to read ohms×1. Measure the resistance between the terminals shown in **Figure 43**. It should read 24 ohms.

4. Connect an ohmmeter and 12 volt battery to the starting circuit cut-out relay as shown in **Figure 44**. Set the ohmmeter to read ohms×1. Interpret results as follows:

   a. Battery disconnected: Infinity.

   b. Battery connected: 0 ohm reading.

5. Connect an ohmmeter and 12 volt battery to the starting circuit cut-out relay as shown in **Figure 45**. Set the ohmmeter to read ohms×1. Interpret results as follows:

   a. Battery disconnected: Infinity.

   b. Battery connected: 0 ohm reading.

6. If the starting circuit cut-out relay failed any of the test procedures in Steps 4-6, it must be replaced by pulling it out of its holder and inserting a new one.

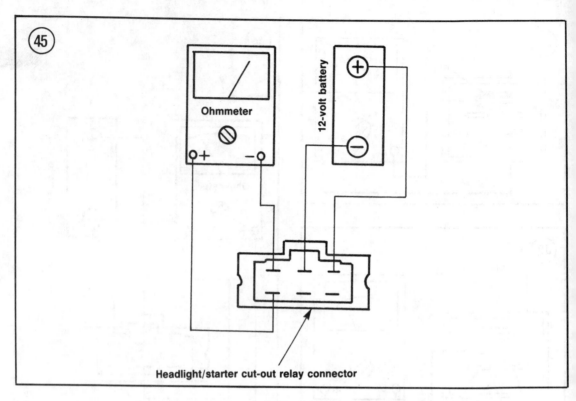

Headlight/starter cut-out relay connector

CHAPTER SIX

ELECTRICAL SYSTEM

IGNITION SYSTEM (1980-ON)

The 1980 and later XS650's use a transistorized ignition system. The transistorized ignition is very similar to a contact breaker point system, with these differences:

a. Mechanical contact points are replaced by magnetic triggering pickup coils.

b. An intermediate electronic switch, the battery-powered ignitor unit (TCI), receives the weak signals from the pickup coils and uses them to turn the ignition coil primary current on and off.

c. Ignition timing advance is controlled electronically.

d. Ignition timing is *not* adjustable.

e. Both spark plugs fire at the same time—once during the compression stroke and once during the exhaust stroke.

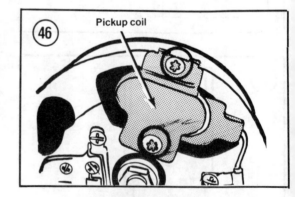

Pickup coil

NOTE

When both spark plugs fire at the same time, only one of the cylinders will be at TDC on the compression stroke. The other cylinder is on the exhaust stroke and the spark in that cylinder has no effect on it.

Precautions

Certain measures must be taken to protect the transistorized ignition system. Instantaneous damage to the semiconductors in the system will occur if the following precautions are not observed.

1. Never connect the battery backwards. If the battery polarity is wrong, damage will occur to the voltage regulator/rectifier, alternator and ignitor unit.

2. Do not disconnect the battery when the engine is running. A voltage surge will occur which will damage the voltage regulator/rectifier and possibly burn out the lights.

3. Do not substitute another type of ignition coil or battery.

4. Keep all connections between the various units clean and tight. Be sure that the wiring connectors are pushed together firmly.

5. Each unit is mounted with a rubber vibration isolator. Always be sure that the isolators are in place when replacing any units.

Troubleshooting

Problems with the transistorized ignition system are usually the production of a weak spark or no spark at all. Troubleshooting procedures are discussed in the Chapter Three section of this supplement.

PICKUP COIL ASSEMBLY (1980 MODELS)

On the 1980 models, the pickup coil assembly is permanemtly mounted on the stator with special Torx fasteners and epoxy on the screw threads. See **Figure 46**. Ignition timing cannot be altered without drilling out and extracting the special fasteners used to attach the pickup coil assembly to the stator.

If a pickup coil assembly is faulty, the complete stator assembly must be replaced. New pickup coil assemblies are not available separately.

Initial Adjustment

This procedure must be performed when you are installing a new stator/pickup coil assembly. The pickup coil assembly is not permanently fastened on replacement stators and the ignition timing must be calibrated to the specific motorcycle.

1. Install the new stator on the crankcase.

2. Position the pickup coil assembly with the upper bolt in the middle of the slot in the pickup coil plate (**Figure 46**). Tighten the bolts *slightly*.

NOTE

Yamaha uses special Torx bolts, which require a special driver and are designed so their heads snap off when tightened . You may prefer to install another type of bolt.

3. Remove the left cylinder spark plug. Then install a dial indicator as shown in **Figure 47** with the pointer touching the top of the piston. Using the kickstarter lever, turn the crankshaft and bring the left piston exactly to TDC (top dead center).

4. Loosen the timing plate screw at tne bottom of the stator and line up the timing plate's "T" mark with the index mark on the rotor. Tighten the timing plate screw. **Figure 48** shows the timing plate "F" and "T" marks.

5. Remove the dial indicator and install the left cylinder spark plug. Reconnect the spark plug cap.

6. Using a stroboscopic timing light, check the ignition timing as described in this supplement. If the rotor index mark does not

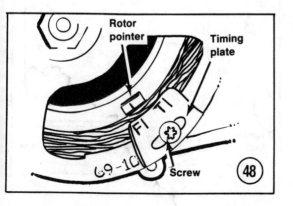

Rotor pointer   Timing plate

Screw   (48)

10

align with the "F" mark on the timing plate, loosen the pickup coil mounting screws and move the pickup coil as required to align the rotor index mark with the timing plate "F" mark. See **Figure 49**.

7. Tighten the pickup coil mounting bolts securely. Yamaha recommends using epoxy cement on the threads of the top bolt.

PICKUP COIL
(1981 MODELS)

The mounting of the pickup coil on 1981 models has been changed from that of 1980 models. The pickup coil is now secured to the stator housing by screws. If replacement of the pickup coil becomes necessary, simply remove the attaching screws and remove the pickup coil. Reverse to install. After installing a new pickup coil, perform the *Initial Adjustment* described in this supplement for 1980 models. Refer to **Figure 50** for 1981 model timing marks.

IGNITOR

The ignitor (**Figure 51**) is a transistorized "black box" that switches current to the ignition coil when signals are recieved from the pickup coils. The ignitor controls the ignition advance curve shape. In addition, the ignitor protects the ignition coil from burning out when the ignition switch is left ON while the engine is not running. The ignitor is a non-adjustable, non-repairable unit.

When ignition trouble is present and the pickup coils and other ignition components are good, substitute a known good ignitor and see if that solves the problem.

IGNITION COIL

A single ignition coil is used for both cylinders. The ignition coil can be tested as described in the Chapter Three section of this supplement.

CHARGING SYSTEM
(1980-ON)

A solid state combination voltage regulator/rectifier is used on 1980 and later

models. See the Chapter Three section of this supplement for troubleshooting procedures.

WIRING DIAGRAMS

Full color wiring diagrams covering late 1978 and later models are found at the end of this book.

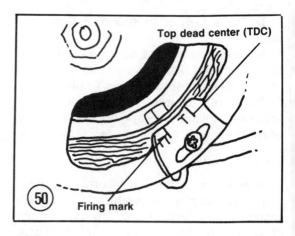

Top dead center (TDC)

Firing mark

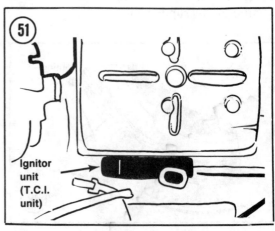

Ignitor unit (T.C.I. unit)

CHAPTER SEVEN

FUEL SYSTEM

PETCOCK (1980-ON)

There is only one vacuum-operated fuel petcock on 1980 and later models. It has a filter inside the fuel tank and a drain plug for cleaning. See **Figure 52**.

CARBURETOR
(1980-ON)

The carburetor on 1980 and later models has several design changes; however, its operation is the same as that of earlier models. Refer to **Figure 53**. Note the following major changes:

a. The starter plunger is horizontal rather than vertical.

b. The diaphragm valve/needle assembly is new and the jet needle has only one clip position.

c. The main jet and pilot jet both screw into the carburetor body, rather than into passages in the float bowl.

d. There is no idle mixture adjust screw.

CAUTION
Do not use caustic carburetor cleaning solutions to clean the carburetor. Emission-controlled carburetors have O-rings and other plastic or rubber parts inside that will be damaged by a caustic solution and will cause the carburetor to malfunction.

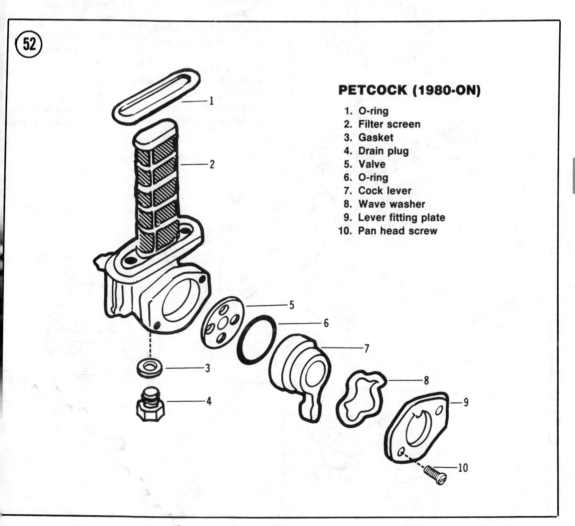

(52)

PETCOCK (1980-ON)

1. O-ring
2. Filter screen
3. Gasket
4. Drain plug
5. Valve
6. O-ring
7. Cock lever
8. Wave washer
9. Lever fitting plate
10. Pan head screw

10

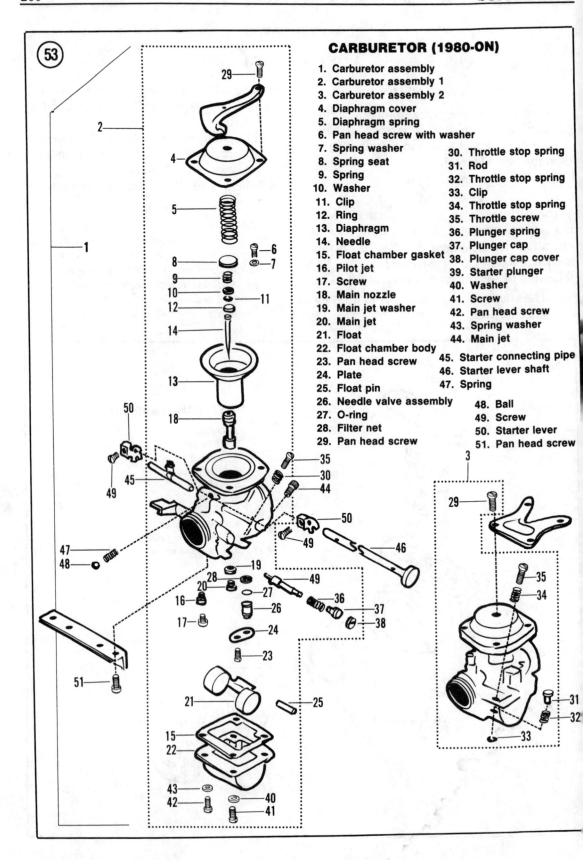

CARBURETOR (1980-ON)

1. Carburetor assembly
2. Carburetor assembly 1
3. Carburetor assembly 2
4. Diaphragm cover
5. Diaphragm spring
6. Pan head screw with washer
7. Spring washer
8. Spring seat
9. Spring
10. Washer
11. Clip
12. Ring
13. Diaphragm
14. Needle
15. Float chamber gasket
16. Pilot jet
17. Screw
18. Main nozzle
19. Main jet washer
20. Main jet
21. Float
22. Float chamber body
23. Pan head screw
24. Plate
25. Float pin
26. Needle valve assembly
27. O-ring
28. Filter net
29. Pan head screw
30. Throttle stop spring
31. Rod
32. Throttle stop spring
33. Clip
34. Throttle stop spring
35. Throttle screw
36. Plunger spring
37. Plunger cap
38. Plunger cap cover
39. Starter plunger
40. Washer
41. Screw
42. Pan head screw
43. Spring washer
44. Main jet
45. Starter connecting pipe
46. Starter lever shaft
47. Spring
48. Ball
49. Screw
50. Starter lever
51. Pan head screw

CHAPTER EIGHT

CHASSIS

Table 5 lists brake and chassis tightening torques for 1982 models.

FRONT FORK (1982)

Removal/Installation

1. If the fork assembly is going to be disassembled, perform the following:
   a. Have an assistant hold the front brake on, compress the front forks and hold them in that position.
   b. Using an Allen wrench, slightly loosen the Allen bolt at the base of the slider. If the bolt is loosened too much, fork oil may squirt out out the slider.
   c. Release the forks so they can return to their rest position.
2. Remove the front wheel.
3. Remove the brake caliper bolts and lift the caliper away from the fork tube. Secure the caliper with a Bunji cord or wire to prevent straining the brake hose.
4. Remove the fork tube rubber cap.
5. With a wrench, loosen but do not remove the fork cap bolts.
6. Remove the front fender.
7. Loosen the upper and lower fork tube pinch bolts.
8. Remove the fork tube. It may be necessary to slightly rotate the fork tube while pulling it down and out.
9. Installation is the reverse of these steps, noting the following.
10. Check the cap bolt O-ring. Replace if necessary.
11. Tighten the pinch bolts as follows:
    a. Upper: 7.23 ft.-lb. (9.8 N•m).
    b. Lower: 14.5 ft.-lb. (19.6 N•m).
12. Tighten the fork cap to 44.5 ft.-lb. (19.6 N•m).
13. Tighten the brake caliper bolts to 25.5 ft.-lb. (34.3 N•m).
14. Operate the front brake to make sure it is working correctly. If necessary, bleed the front brake as described under *Brake Bleeding* in this supplement.

Disassembly

Refer to **Figure 54** during the disassembly and assembly procedures.
1. Clamp the slider in a vise with soft jaws.
2. If not loosened during the fork removal sequence, loosen the Allen bolt (**Figure 55**) from the base of the slider.

NOTE
*This bolt has been secured with Loctite and is often difficult to remove because the damper rod will turn inside the slider. It sometimes can be removed with an air impact driver. It is easier to loosen when the fork tube is installed on the bike as described under **Front Fork Removal/Installation** in this supplement. If you are unable to remove it, take the fork tubes to a dealer and have the screws removed.*

3. Remove the Allen bolt (**Figure 55**) and gasket at the base of the slider.
4. Hold the upper fork tube in a vise with soft jaws and loosen the fork cap bolt (if it was not loosened during the removal sequence).

WARNING
Be careful when removing the fork cap bolt as the spring is under pressure. Protect your eyes accordingly.

5. Remove the fork cap bolt from the fork.
6. Remove the spring seat and fork spring.
7. Remove the fork from the vise, pour the fork oil out and discard it.
8. Pull the fork tube out of the slider.
9. Remove the taper spindle (**Figure 56**) from the end of the damper rod. Then turn the fork tube over and remove the damper rod (**Figure 57**).
10. Remove the rubber boot from the notch in the slider.

Inspection

1. Thoroughly clean all parts in solvent and dry them.

10

2. Check the damper rod and piston ring (**Figure 58**) for wear or damage.

3. Examine the oil seal for scoring, nicks or any signs of oil leakage. If necessary, replace the oil seals as follows:

   a. Carefully pry the retaining ring out of the groove in the slider.

   b. Remove the oil seal washer.

   c. Remove the oil seal by prying it out of the fork tube with a large screwdriver or tire iron. Make sure to pad the slider to prevent the tool from damaging it.

   d. Clean the oil seal mating area with solvent. Also check the area for nicks or other damage.

   e. Install the new oil seal by driving it squarely into the slider with a piece of pipe or large socket.

NOTE
Make sure the seal seats squarely and fully in the bore of the tube.

   f. Install the washer and the retaining ring. Make sure the retaining ring seats completely in the slider groove.

4. Check the upper fork tube exterior for scratches and straightness. If bent or scratched, it should be replaced.

5. Measure the uncompressed length of the fork spring. Replace the fork spring if it measures less than 24.0 in. (610 mm).

Assembly

1. Insert the damper rod into the fork tube (**Figure 57**) and install the taper spindle (**Figure 56**).

2. Install the fork tube into the slider.

3. Temporarily install the fork spring, spring seat and fork cap bolt. This will help tension the damper rod.

4. Clean the damper rod Allen bolt with contact cleaner and allow to dry thoroughly. Then apply Loctite 242 (blue) to the threads of the Allen bolt and install it and the copper washer. Tighten the bolt to 44.5 ft.-lb. (19.6 N•m).

5. Remove the fork cap bolt, spring seat and fork spring.

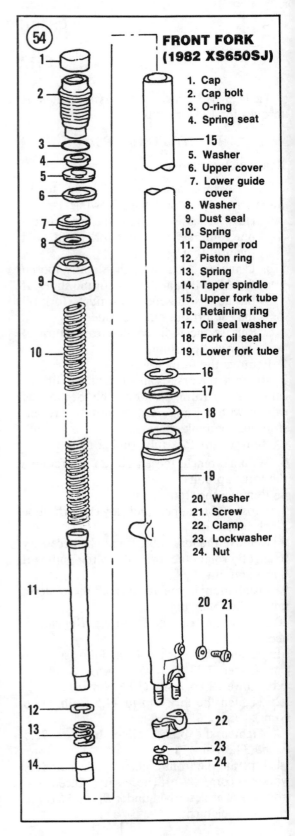

**FRONT FORK
(1982 XS650SJ)**

1. Cap
2. Cap bolt
3. O-ring
4. Spring seat
5. Washer
6. Upper cover
7. Lower guide cover
8. Washer
9. Dust seal
10. Spring
11. Damper rod
12. Piston ring
13. Spring
14. Taper spindle
15. Upper fork tube
16. Retaining ring
17. Oil seal washer
18. Fork oil seal
19. Lower fork tube
20. Washer
21. Screw
22. Clamp
23. Lockwasher
24. Nut

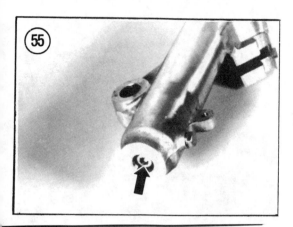

6. Reinstall the fork tube onto the motorcycle. Tighten the pinch bolts as described under *Fork Tube Removal/Installation.*

7. Fill the fork tube with 164-172 cc (5.54-5.82 oz.) of 10 wt. fork oil.

8. Install the fork spring, spring seat and fork cap bolt. Tighten the cap bolt to 44.5 ft.-lb. (19.6 N•m).

The 1978 XS650SE and later "S" models feature one-piece cast aluminum wheels. Rear disc brakes are also used on 1978-1980 "S" models. Tubeless tires are used on 1979 and later "S" models. Follow the appropriate procedure for your bike.

WHEEL AND SPOKE INSPECTION

Check the aluminum wheels for cracks, bends, or warping. If a wheel is damaged or cracked, replace it. Repair is not possible.

Wheel run-out tolerance is as follows: Vertical and lateral, 0.08 in. (2 mm).

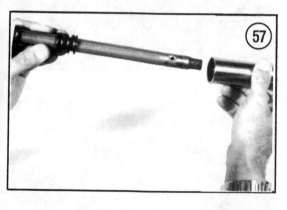

> *WARNING*
> *Do not install a tubeless tire on rims not originally equipped with tubeless tires. The tire bead may not seal properly. The tire could slip on the rim and sudden deflation may result.*

FRONT WHEEL

Removal

1. Support the motorcycle so that the front wheel is clear of the ground.

2. Loosen the axle clamp pinch nuts. See **Figure 59.**

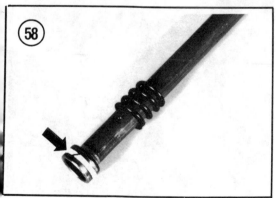

10

NOTE
It is not necessary to completely remove the axle clamp pinch nuts and clamp; just loosen them.

3. Disconnect the speedometer cable. See **Figure 60**.

4. Remove the cotter pin from the front axle nut and discard it. Then loosen the axle nut (**Figure 61**).

5. Pull the front axle out (**Figure 62**), then remove the front wheel (**Figure 63**).

Inspection

1. Remove any corrosion on the front axle with a piece of fine emery cloth.

2. Roll the front axle on a flat surface to check for bending. Replace the axle if any abnormality is found.

3. Check the rims for cracks or damage (refer to *Wheel and Spoke Inspection*).

4. If wheel bearings need servicing, perform this procedure at this time (refer to *Wheel Bearing* section in this supplement).

Installation

1. Lightly grease the lips of the front wheel oil seals and speedometer gear teeth with lightweight lithium base lubricant.

2. Position the front wheel as shown in **Figure 63**, then slide the front axle through the front axle clamp and front wheel bearing.

NOTE
Be sure that the boss on the outer fork tube is engaged with the locating slot on the speedometer gear housing.

3. Install the front axle nut and torque to 76.0 ft.-lb. (10.5 mkg). Install a new cotter pin (**Figure 61**).

4. Tighten the front axle clamp nut completely, then the rear one to 10.0 ft.-lb. (1.4 mkg). See **Figure 64**.

5. Connect the speedometer cable (**Figure 60**).

6. Remove the support from beneath the front of the motorcycle.

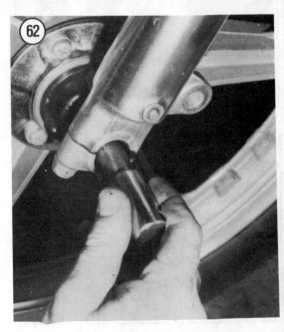

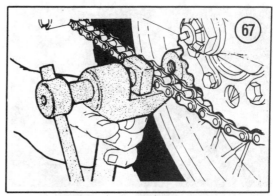

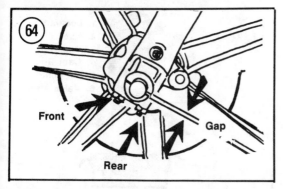

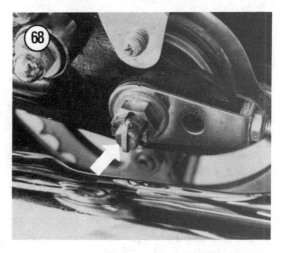

REAR WHEEL

Removal

1. Support the motorcycle on its centerstand.
2. Remove the cotter pin from the rear brake torque strut retaining nut and discard it, then remove the nut (**Figure 65**).
3. Loosen the chain tensioner locknuts and adjusting bolts on each side as shown in **Figure 66**.
4. Remove the master link with a chain removal tool. Remove the drive chain (**Figure 67**).
5. Remove the cotter pin from the rear axle nut and discard it, then remove the rear axle nut (**Figure 68**).
6. Slide the rear axle out, then roll the rear wheel back and out of the chassis (**Figure 69**).

Inspection

Perform all steps under *Front Wheel, Inspection*.

10

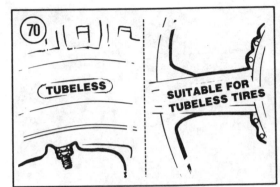

Installation

1. Roll the rear wheel into position and install the rear axle (**Figure 69**).
2. Install the rear axle nut and tighten to 108.5 ft.-lb. (15.0 mkg), then install a new cotter pin (**Figure 68**).
3. Install the drive chain and a new master link.
4. Install the rear brake torque strut retaining nut and a new cotter pin (**Figure 65**).
5. Adjust the drive chain (refer to Chapter Three, *Drive Chain* section, in the basic book), front brake (refer to *Front Brake Adjustment*, this supplement) and rear brake (refer to *Rear Brake Adjustment*, this supplement).

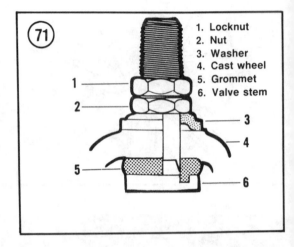

1. Locknut
2. Nut
3. Washer
4. Cast wheel
5. Grommet
6. Valve stem

TUBELESS TIRES
(1979 ON)

Tubeless tires are used on cast wheels from 1979 on. They are designated by the word "TUBELESS" cast into the tire sidewall (**Figure 70**) and are designed to be used only with tubeless rims that are dimensionally different from tube-type rims. These rims have "SUITABLE FOR TUBELESS TIRES" stamped on them.

> *WARNING*
> *Do not install a tubeless tire on rims not originally designed for tubeless tires. The tire bead may not seal properly. The tire could slip on the rim and sudden deflation may result.*

TUBELESS TIRE REPAIR

When a tubeless tire is flat, your best recourse is to take it to a motorcycle dealer for repair. Punctured tubeless tires should be removed from the rim to inspect the inside of the tire and to apply a combination plug/patch from the inside. Don't rely on a plug or cord repair applied from outside the tire. They might be okay on a car, but they're too dangerous on a motorcycle.

After repairing a tubeless tire, don't exceed 50 mph (80 kph) for the first 24 hours. Never race on a repaired tubeless tire. The patch could work loose from tire flexing and heat.

Tubeless Tire
Removal/Installation

> *CAUTION*
> *The inner rim and tire bead area are sealing surfaces on a tubeless tire. Do not scratch the inside of the rim or damage the tire bead.*

Tubeless tire removal and installation is similar to that of tube-type tires, with these additional requirements:

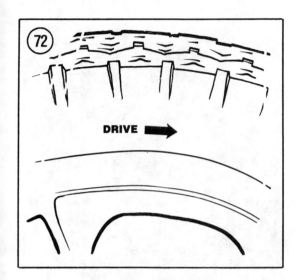

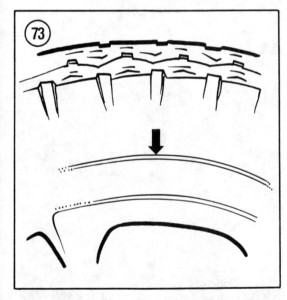

a. Install a new valve stem whenever you have the tire off the rim (**Figure 71**). Rubber deteriorates with age and valve stem replacement will never be as convenient as now.

b. If the rear tire has a directional arrow molded in the sidewall (**Figure 72**), make sure the arrow points the way the wheel turns.

c. After the tire is on the rim, bounce the wheel several times while turning the wheel. This helps seat the bead. If an initial air seal is hard to get, your motorcycle or auto repair shop may have a bead seater to make the job easy.

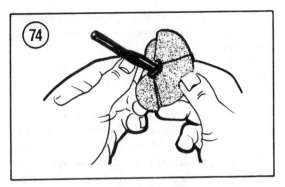

d. After inflating the tire, check to see that the beads are fully seated and that the tire rim lines next to the rim are parallel to the rim (**Figure 73**). If the beads won't seat, deflate the tire, re-lubricate the rim and beads with soapy water and re-inflate the tire.

Tubeless Tire Repair

Do not rely on a plug or cord patch applied from outside the tire. Use a combination plug/patch applied from inside the tire. See **Figure 74**.

1. Remove the tire from the rim.

2. Inspect the rim inner flange. Smooth any scratches on the sealing surface with emery cloth. If a scratch is deeper than 0.5 mm (0.020 in.), the wheel should be replaced.

3. Inspect the tire inside and out. Replace a tire if any of the following is found:

    a. A puncture larger than 3 mm (1/8 in.)

    b. A punctured or damaged sidewall

    c. More than 2 punctures in the tire

4. Apply the plug/patch, following the instructions supplied with the patch.

WHEEL BEARINGS

Replace the wheel bearings if there is noticeable play in the hub or if the wheel does not turn smoothly. To service or replace the bearing, proceed as follows:

1. Remove the wheel (refer to *Front Wheel* or *Rear Wheel* sections, this supplement).

2. Clean the outside of the wheel hub.

3. Remove the disc retaining bolts, then the brake disc (**Figure 75**).

4. Remove the cap, grease seal and snap ring (**Figure 76**).

10

5. Bleed the rear brake system (**Figure 80**). Refer to *Brake Bleeding* section in this supplement.

6. Pry out the grease seal, then tap out the remaining bearing. The spacer will come out at the same time.

7. Clean bearings in solvent. Inspect for galling, pitting, signs of overheating or any other defects. Then oil lightly and spin by hand. The bearing should spin easily, with no noise or binding. Replace any defective bearing immediately.

8. Pack the bearing with medium weight waterproof wheel bearing grease.

CAUTION
Do not overpack bearing with grease.

9. Carefully tap the wheel bearing squarely into place. (If no bearing driver is available, a socket wrench of the appropriate diameter may be substituted.)

10. Install a new grease seal, then the snap ring and cap.

11. Install the disc and tighten bolts securely. Be sure to bend the tabs on the lockwashers over (**Figure 75**).

REAR DISC
BRAKE CALIPER

Removal/Installation

1. Unscrew the bolt that connects the brake line banjo fitting to the caliper (**Figure 78**). Plug the brake line to prevent dirt from entering.

2. Remove the cotter pin from the brake anchor bolt on the caliper and unscrew the nut and bolt (**Figure 79**).

3. Unscrew the caliper mounting bolts and lift the caliper off the disc.

4. Reverse the preceding steps to install the caliper. Tighten the caliper mounting bolts to 28.9-36.2 ft.-lb. (4.5-5.0 mkg). Then install and tighten the brake anchor nut and bolt securely.

5. Bleed the rear brake system (**Figure 61**). Refer to *Brake Bleeding* section in this supplement.

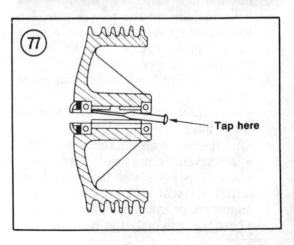

Tap here

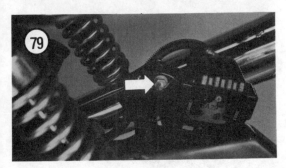

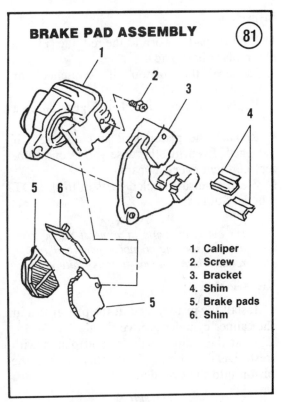

BRAKE PAD ASSEMBLY

1. Caliper
2. Screw
3. Bracket
4. Shim
5. Brake pads
6. Shim

10

CALIPER

Front and rear calipers are disassembled and assembled the same way.

Disassembly

1. Remove the pad screw (**Figure 81**).
2. Remove the brake pads (**Figure 81**).
3. Remove the support bolt and the pad spring (**Figure 82**).
4. Remove the retaining ring and dust seal.

WARNING
When removing the caliper piston in Step 5, pad the caliper with shop rags so the piston does not cause injury or become damaged as it is forced out. Keep your fingers out of the way.

5. Force the piston out by blowing compressed air into the brake fluid inlet (**Figure 83**).
6. Remove the piston seal and dust seal (**Figure 84**).

Inspection

1. If either pad is worn to the red line (**Figure 85**), replace both pads.
2. Replace the piston if scratched or otherwise damaged.
3. Replace all items listed in **Figure 86** as a set.
4. Replace the piston seal and dust seal if damaged. Even in otherwise good condition, replace them every 2 years.
5. Clean all disassembled parts in fresh DOT 3 brake fluid.

> *WARNING*
> *Do not clean parts in mineral oil or alcohol; swelling of rubber parts could result, which can lead to brake failure.*

Reassembly

1. Install the piston, then fit the piston seal in the caliper cylinder groove.
2. Coat the caliper cylinder and piston with fresh DOT 3 brake fluid, then insert the piston into the cylinder.

> *CAUTION*
> *Do not twist the piston when inserting it into the cylinder.*

3. Fit the piston boot in the groove around the piston and caliper. Install the retaining ring.
4. Assemble the caliper and support bracket with the support bolt. Install the brake pads and screw. Tighten the screw securely.
5. Tighten the support bolt to 10.8-14.5 ft.-lb. (15-20 N•m).

REAR MASTER CYLINDER

Removal/Installation

1. Disconnect the brake pedal linkage from the master cylinder (**Figure 87**).
2. Unscrew the bolt that holds the brake line banjo to the top of the master cylinder. Plug the line. Take care not to drip brake fluid on painted surfaces.
3. Unscrew the bolts that connect the master cylinder to the frame and remove the master cylinder.
4. Reverse the preceding steps to install the rear master cylinder. Tighten the brake line connections to 16.6-20.3 ft.-lb. (2.3-2.8 mkg).

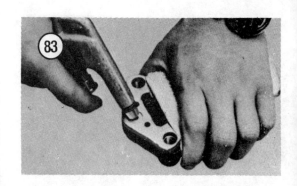

5. Bleed the hydraulic brake (refer to *Brake Bleeding* section, this supplement).

MASTER CYLINDER OVERHAUL

The front and rear master cylinders have similar service procedures.

> *WARNING*
> *Use the utmost care in cleanliness when working on any part of the hydraulic brake system. Even the smallest bits of foreign matter in the brake system can cause brake failure. It is highly recommended that you leave the job of rebuilding the master cylinder to your Yamaha dealer.*

Disassembly

1. Remove the master cylinder as outlined in this supplement.

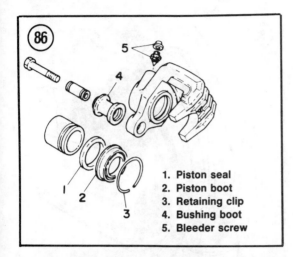

1. Piston seal
2. Piston boot
3. Retaining clip
4. Bushing boot
5. Bleeder screw

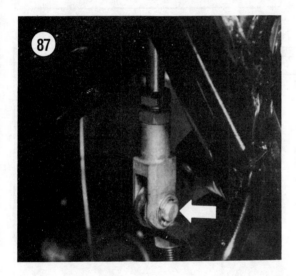

2. Remove the master cylinder reservoir cap and the diaphragm. Pour out the old brake fluid and discard it.

3. Remove the boot, snap ring and piston.

NOTE
The spring remains in the master cylinder.

4. Remove the return spring, valve and stopper plate.

5. Remove the cup.

Inspection

1. Wash the master cylinder and reservoir in clean brake fluid and dry with compressed air.

2. Examine the master cylinder bore for scratches or corrosion. Replace the master cylinder if there is the slightest doubt about its condition.

3. Be sure that the port is not clogged.

4. Discard all old parts and replace with a new Yamaha master cylinder repair kit.

Assembly

1. To assemble the master cylinder, perform the following:

    a. Coat the master cylinder bore with fresh brake fluid. Place all of the internal parts in a shallow container of fresh brake fluid.

    b. Reverse Steps 1-5 under *Disassembly* to assemble the master cylinder.

2. Install the master cylinder. Bleed the brake system (refer to *Brake Bleeding* section, following).

BRAKE BLEEDING

The brake system must be bled to remove air from the cylinder and hydraulic lines each time a line or hose is disconnected; a cylinder or caliper is removed and disassembled; or when the lever or pedal feel is spongy, indicating that there is air in the systems.

The procedure is similar for both front and rear systems:

1. Remove the reservoir cap and add sufficient brake fluid to fill the reservoir. Use only brake fluid conforming to DOT 3 specifications, and only add fluid from a sealed container.

2. Connect one end of a 12-inch clear plastic tube to a bleeder valve (**Figure 88**). Submerge the other end of the tube in a container holding a small quantity of brake fluid.

3. Operate the brake lever or pedal several times until resistance is felt; it may feel spongy at this time. Hold the lever or brake pedal in the brake-applied position.

4. Open the bleed valve slightly, then continue to squeeze the hand lever or depress the rear brake pedal until it goes all of the way down. Hold the lever or pedal in this position, then tighten the bleed valve.

10

5. Repeat the preceding steps until the fluid leaving the system is free of air bubbles and the hand lever or rear brake pedal "feel" is firm.

NOTE
Do not allow the master cylinder reservoir to empty during bleeding or more air will be drawn into the system, requiring it to be bled completely once again.

6. When the fluid is free of air, tighten the bleed valve to 2.9-5.1 ft.-lb. (0.4-0.7 mkg), remove the hose and install the dust cap. Hold the lever or pedal down tightly and check the connections for leaks. Correct any that are found. Fill the reservoir to the "FULL" mark and install the diaphragm and cap tightly.

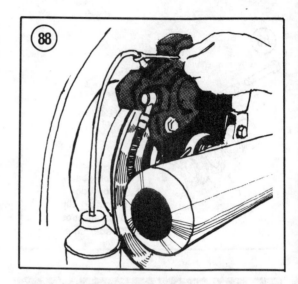

Table 5 BRAKE AND CHASSIS TIGHTENING TORQUES (1982 XS650SJ)

	ft.-lb.	N·m
Front axle nut	77.5	105
Front fork and axle holder clamp	10	13.7
Steering stem bolt	39	53
Handlebar clamps	13	17.7
Front fork pinch bolts		
Upper	7.23	9.8
Lower	14.5	19.6
Brake disc and hub	14.5	19.6
Caliper and support bracket	13	17.7
Front caliper @ front fork	25.5	34.3
Pivot shaft	47	63.7
Rear axle nut	108.5	147
Rear brake caliper plate	13	17.7
Tension bar @ swing arm	23	31.4
Rear shock absorber		
Upper	21.5	29.4
Lower	28	38.2

INDEX

11

XS1 & XS1B

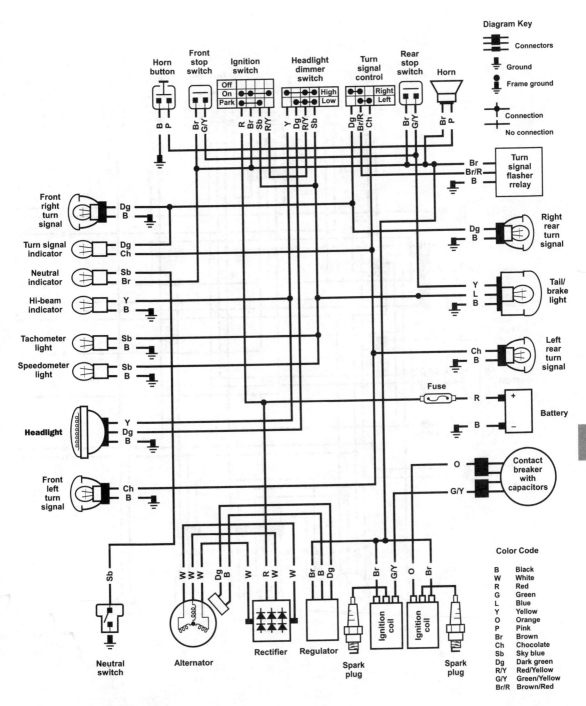

XS2 & TX650

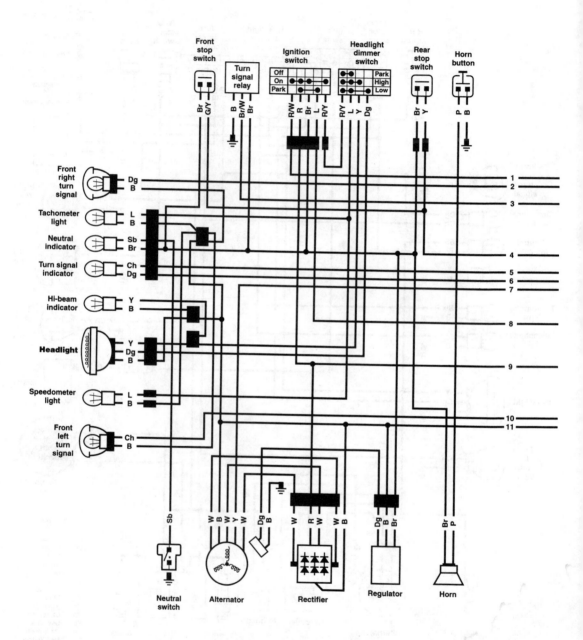

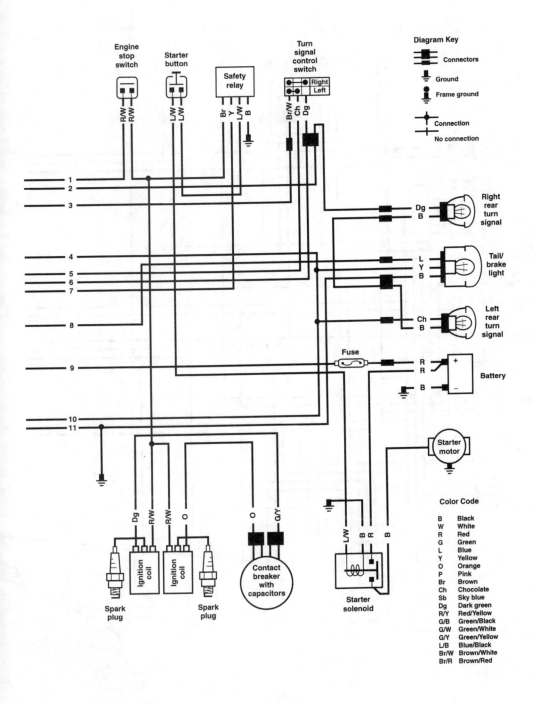

Diagram Key

Connectors
Ground
Frame ground
Connection
No connection

Color Code

B	Black
W	White
R	Red
G	Green
L	Blue
Y	Yellow
O	Orange
P	Pink
Br	Brown
Ch	Chocolate
Sb	Sky blue
Dg	Dark green
R/Y	Red/Yellow
G/B	Green/Black
G/W	Green/White
G/Y	Green/Yellow
L/B	Blue/Black
Br/W	Brown/White
Br/R	Brown/Red

11

TX650A

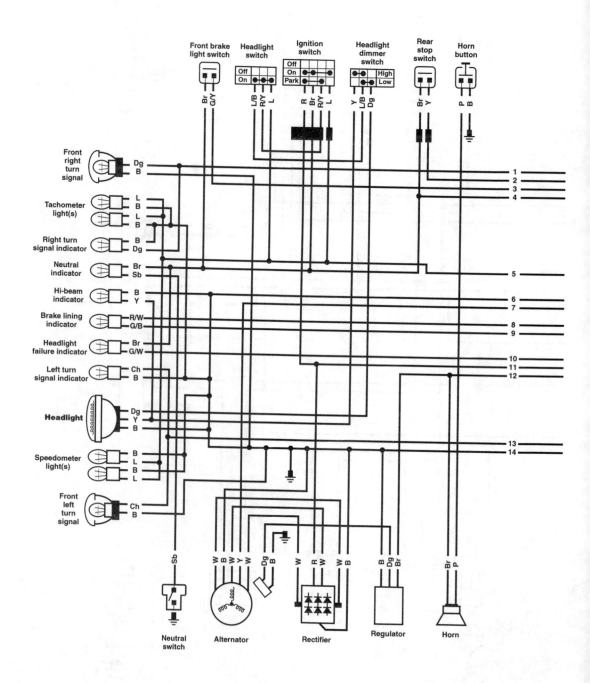

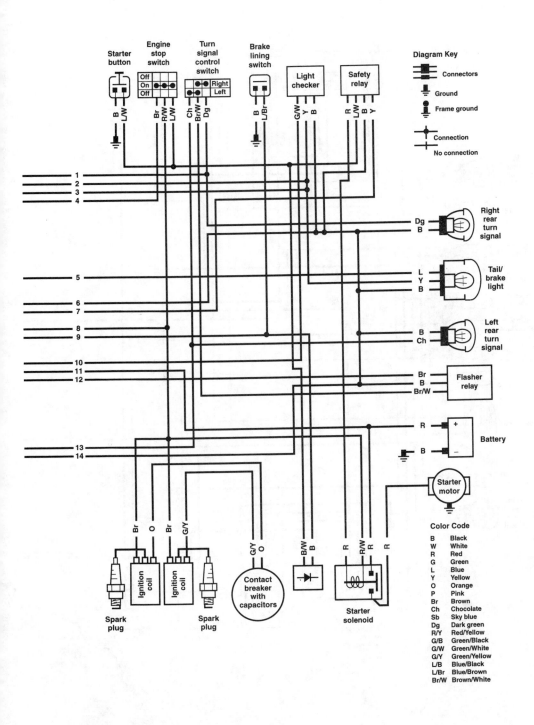

Color Code

B	Black
W	White
R	Red
G	Green
L	Blue
Y	Yellow
O	Orange
P	Pink
Br	Brown
Ch	Chocolate
Sb	Sky blue
Dg	Dark green
R/Y	Red/Yellow
G/B	Green/Black
G/W	Green/White
G/Y	Green/Yellow
L/B	Blue/Black
L/Br	Blue/Brown
Br/W	Brown/White

11

XS650B & C

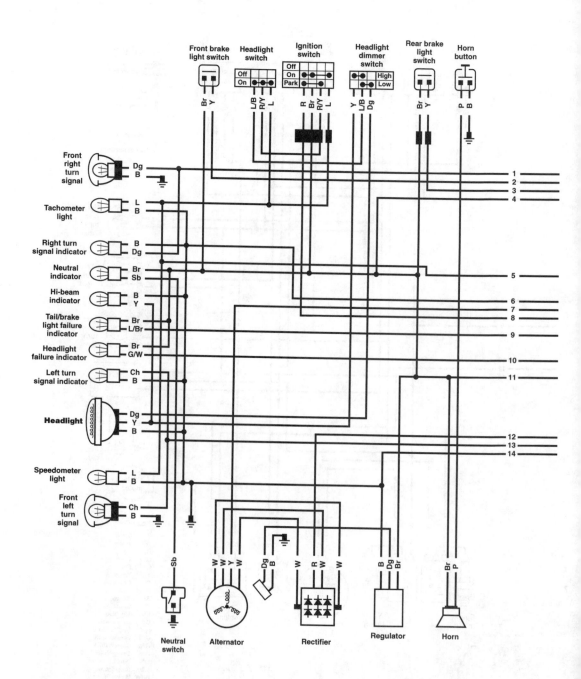

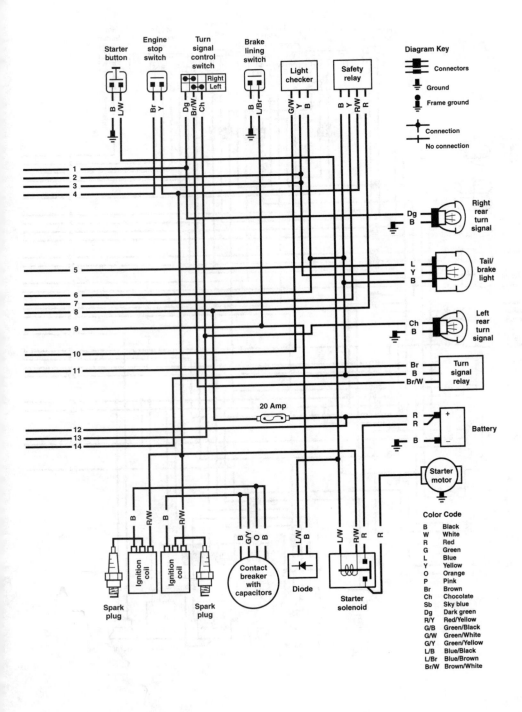

Diagram Key

	Connectors
	Ground
	Frame ground
	Connection
	No connection

Starter button
Engine stop switch
Turn signal control switch
Brake lining switch
Light checker
Safety relay

Right Left

B L/W
Br Y
Dg Br/W Ch
B L/Br
G/W Y B
B Y R/W R

Dg
B — Right rear turn signal

L
Y
B — Tail/brake light

Ch
B — Left rear turn signal

Br
B
Br/W — Turn signal relay

20 Amp

R
R
B — Battery

Starter motor

B R/W B R/W
Spark plug — Ignition coil — Ignition coil — Spark plug

B G/Y O B
Contact breaker with capacitors

L/W B
Diode

L/W R/W R
Starter solenoid

R

Color Code

B	Black
W	White
R	Red
G	Green
L	Blue
Y	Yellow
O	Orange
P	Pink
Br	Brown
Ch	Chocolate
Sb	Sky blue
Dg	Dark green
R/Y	Red/Yellow
G/B	Green/Black
G/W	Green/White
G/Y	Green/Yellow
L/B	Blue/Black
L/Br	Blue/Brown
Br/W	Brown/White

11

XS650D

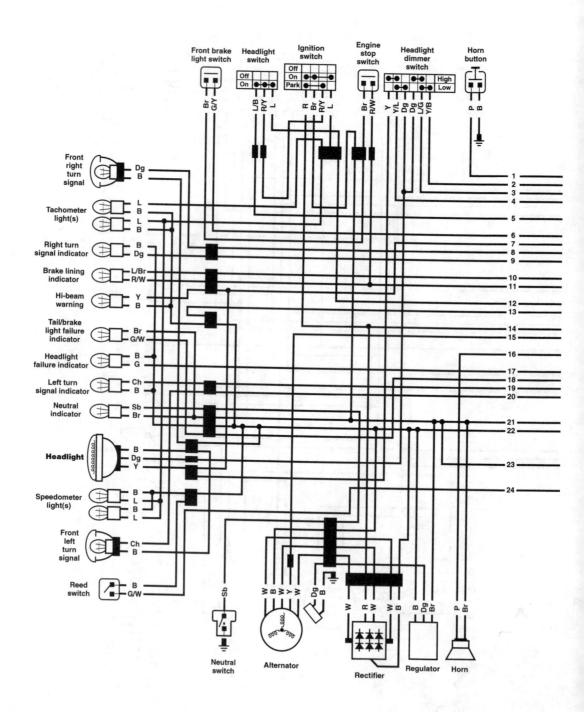

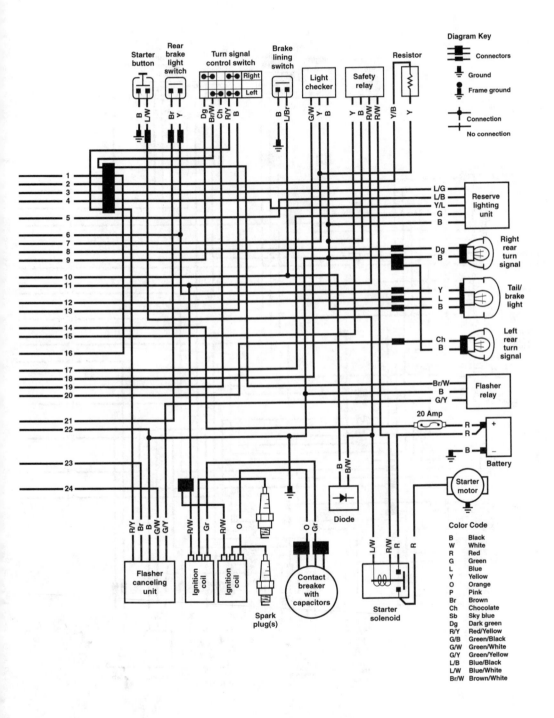

EARLY XS650E
(ENGINE SN: 2F0-000101—2F0-006501)

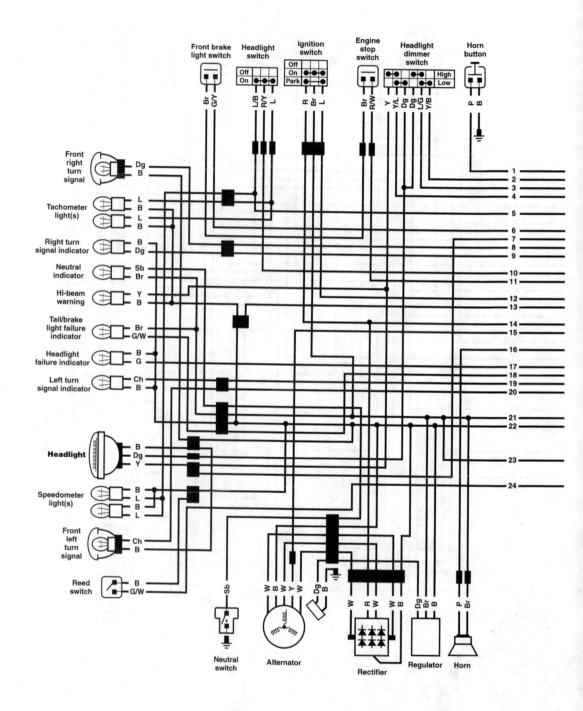

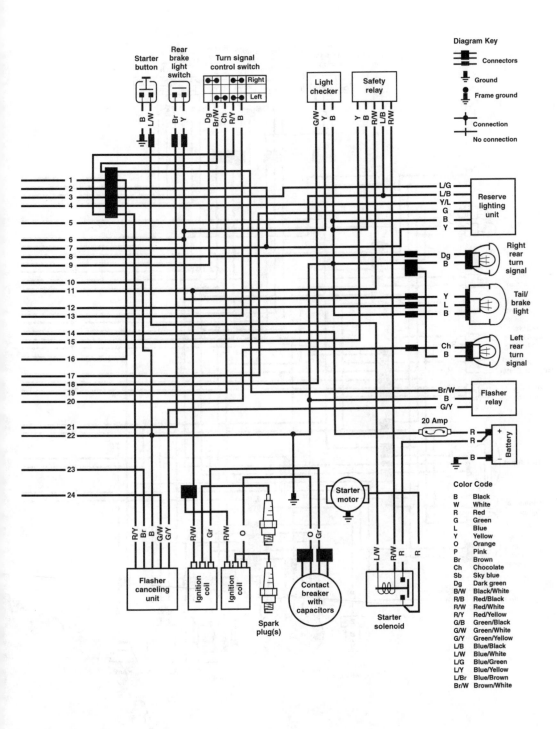

LATE XS650E (AFTER ENGINE SN: 2F0-006501) & ALL XS650SE, 2F & SF

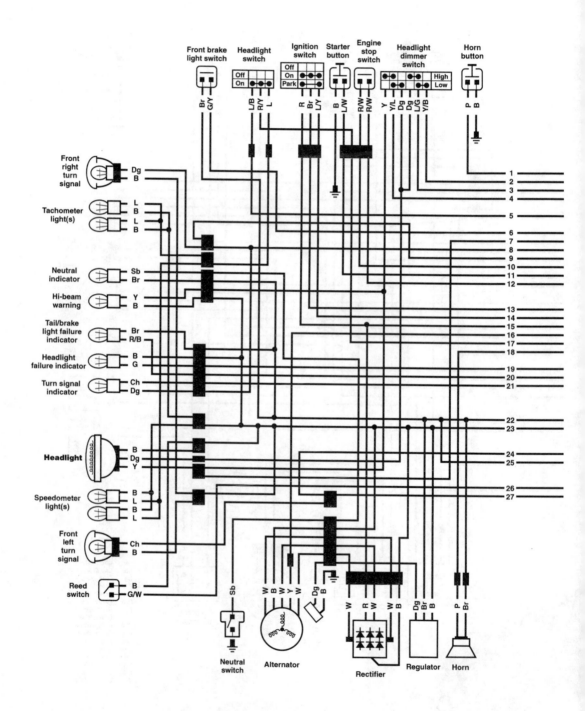

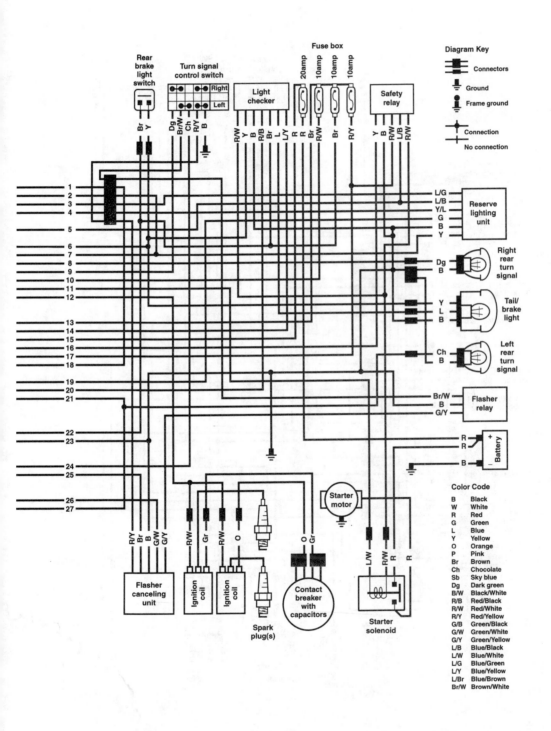

11

XS650G

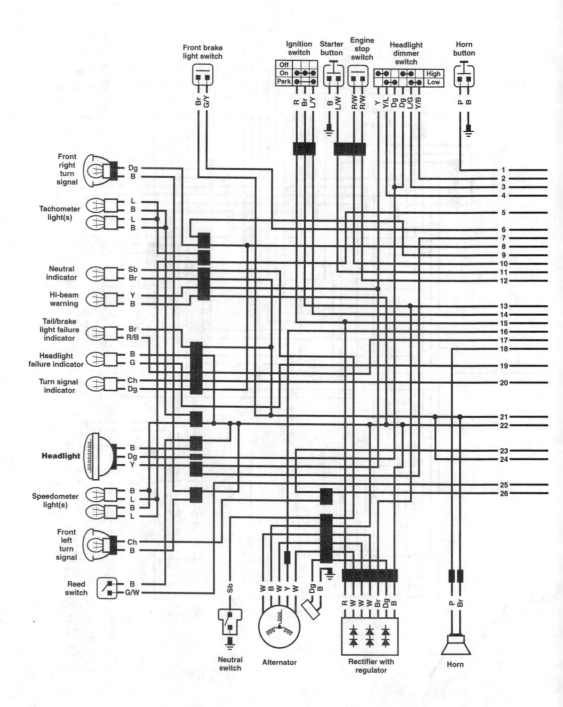

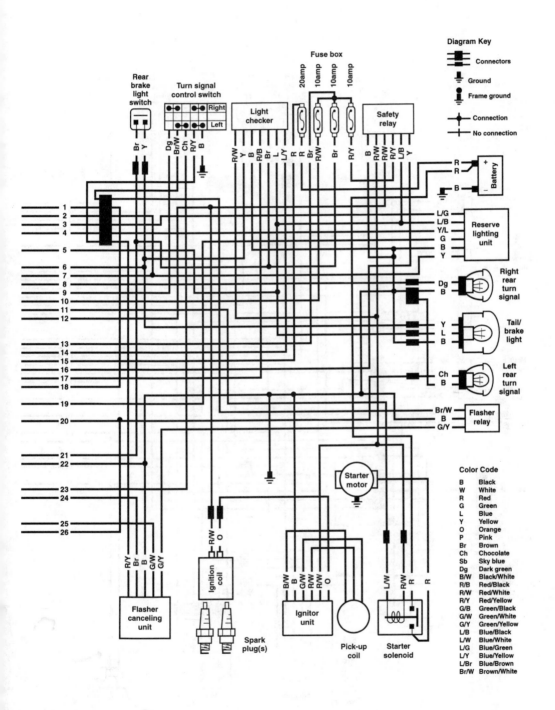

XS650SG, H & SH

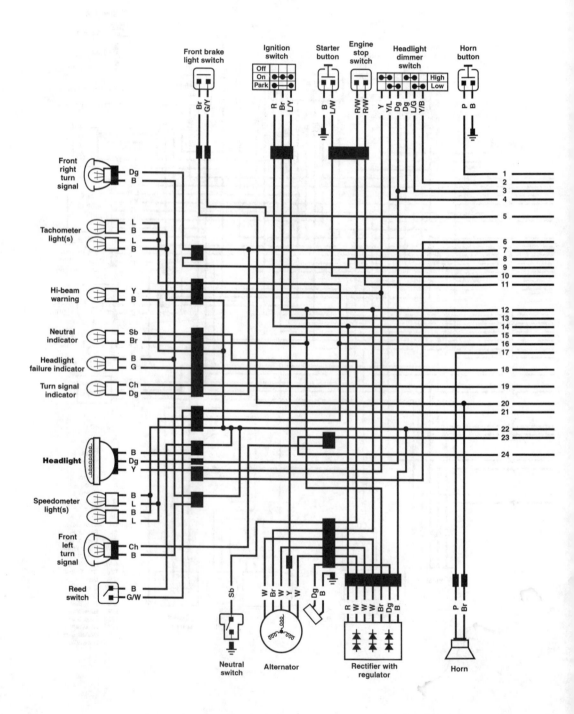

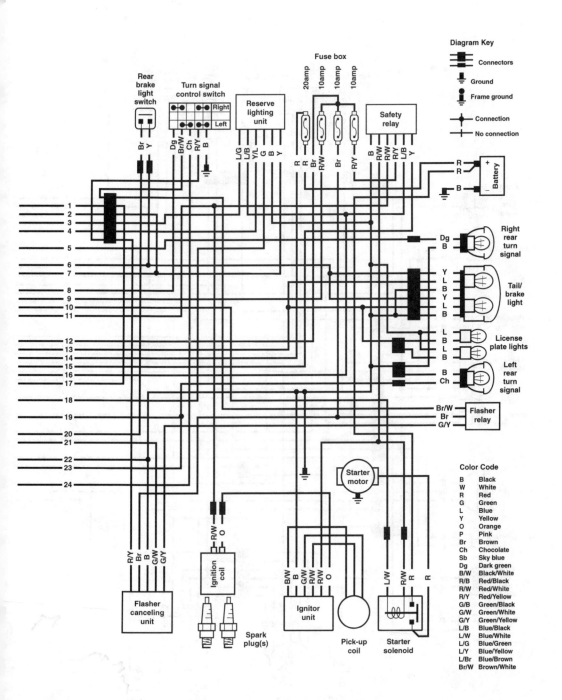

XS650SJ

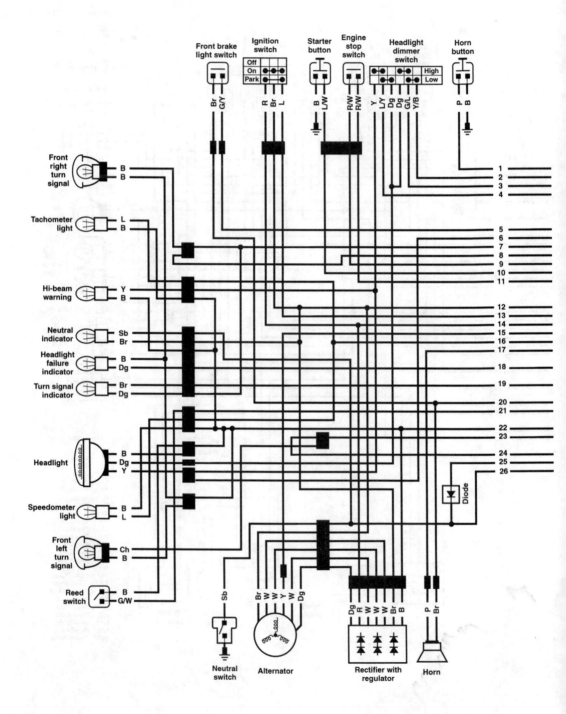

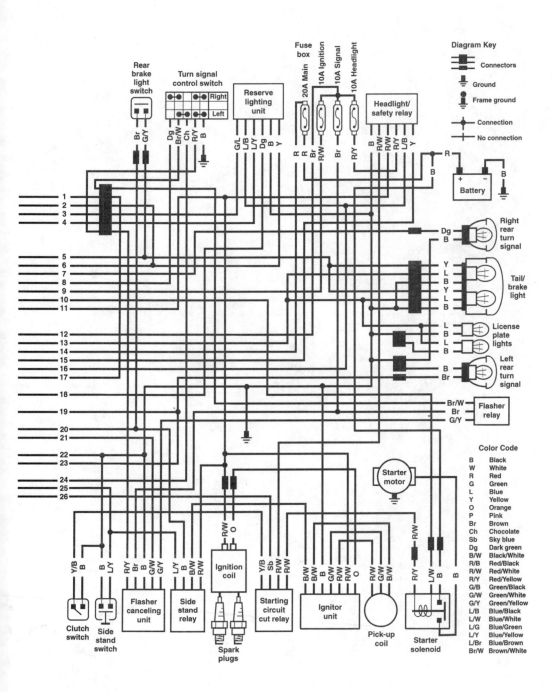

NOTES

NOTES

NOTES

MAINTENANCE LOG

Date	Miles	Type of Service

Check out *clymer.com* for our full line of powersport repair manuals.